A Saucy, Hilarious, Touching Memoir

OUT OF IOWA

INTO OKLAHOMA

You Can Take the Girl Out of Iowa, but
You Can't take the Iowa Out of the Girl

Nikki Hanna

OUT OF IOWA - INTO OKLAHOMA

Published by Patina Publishing
727 S. Norfolk Avenue
Tulsa, Oklahoma 74120
neqhanna@sbcglobal.net

IBSN 978-0-9828726-0-4 (pc)

ISBN 978-0-9828726-4-2 (ec)

Manufactured in the United States of America

Nikki Hanna
www.nikkihanna.com

Dedicated to:

Mom and Dad

Shuppy and Weezie

R E V I E W S

A sensitive, thought-provoking and often humorous exposé of the events and people that shaped a remarkable life perspective.

Wesley Lawrence Huntington, III
Founder, Dyslexic Writers Foundation

After I read it, I knowd tractors and chickens was important. It were more interestin than the zigzag pattern in my saddle blanket. I took a likin to the roadkill parts. If I was a bettin man, I'd bet the wooman writin it has nice child-bearin hips.

Jim Bob (Catfish) Hunt
The Oklahoma River Review

This book reminded me to consider events and people that shaped who I am today. It also inspired me to get rid of Ralph, redecorate the house, and get my name off the grandkids' student loans. I ain't co-signing no more for NOBODY.

Ms. Effie Mae Walter

This story made me laugh and cry. It was a captivating and stimulating read which raised many questions, some of them answered by the author and some not. She was often confused, wondering what just happened. I can relate to that. The author made me realize I was trying too hard, so I quit.

Cookie Stewart
Retired Homemaker

Read it.

Moose
Oklahoma Redneck Paroled
Bikers Association

Note from Author: There were no reviews, so I made some up. This is an integrity gap. Sometimes I do things I shouldn't.

TABLE OF CONTENTS

ACKNOWLEDGEMENTS

Every few weeks, sometimes more often, I take my laptop to the *Apple* store at a nearby mall and sit with young technical geniuses, who I politely and respectfully refer to as "the children." They facilitate the evolution of whatever befuddling technical encounter or ambitious project I am facing. In spite of the fact that we are at least two generations apart, we have connected. This book would not have happened without them.

To the *Apple* children, Brice Davis, Andrew DeClue, Lani Burns, and Joe Faber, I am immensely grateful. A special thanks to Brice who supplied invaluable graphic design advice. In this mix is Jim Misch, a man of my generation with a similar corporate background whose encouragement has been especially motivating, and Gioia Kerlin, who put me on to vital sources that brought me up to date on the modern nuances of producing a written product.

I call the *Apple* store my happy place. I can tell you there is nothing else like it. Before I discovered it, my technical frustrations were so frequent and intense that an email was barely possible, let alone a book. I did it! I wrote a book--my freshman effort. There are more to come. Now I know what to do with my next thirty years. Thank you, *Apple*.

Thanks to the amazing Annie Murrell for putting me on to the *Apple* experience, for counseling so many of my friends and loved ones over the years, and for saving me from despair at one of my lowest moments. Annie gives away peace of mind like candy.

Considerable credit goes to Donna Parsons, Cheryl Briggs, Sam Harbour, and Damien Hartzell who have generously enhanced my work, turning it into a viable commodity. Additionally, Donna Garrett who, after polishing me up for twenty some years as my administrative assistant, once again added some shine.

The Un-Book Club Salon and Saloon, The Diva Consortium, The Friday Night Adventurers, my enlightened coffee buddies with whom I contemplate the world situation and the nature of the universe, my neighbor Penny Schell, and numerous other friends have been invaluable sources of encouragement. Much credit goes to John Harris for his intuitive and humorous contributions and to Toni Ellis for her keen eye and astute input on the cover. A special thanks to Toni, Terri Walker, and Donna Parsons for being my biggest champions.

My brother Kelly Walter (who always stands by me unconditionally) and especially my daughter Melanie Corbin (the most incredible woman I know), kept me going when I thought my story was not worth telling or when I felt too self-absorbed writing it to continue. This memoir would not have happened without "The Mel."

Just as important, thanks to my son Marty Hanna for allowing me to share some of his earlier escapades and to him and his buddies at Owasso's Fishbonz Pool Hall for noticing how joyful I look on a tractor. Finally, much credit goes to Damien Hartzell, my surprise child, who views everything with wonder, including my story.

INTRODUCTION

Just Trying to Matter

I was born and raised on a farm in Iowa, a place steeped in midwestern traditions and rural values. Over time I shed the rural inclinations and eventually evolved into a fiercely independent metropolitan career woman, although those Iowa beginnings fortunately continue to this day to shape my experiences. In a sense I have realized the best of both worlds. Although the contrast of rural and city cultures has occasionally generated internal conflict and significant adaptation, it has also produced a robust and varied life.

With the encouragement of my daughter I decided to write this book. She said, "Do it for my kids. I want them to know where they came from and what it was like for you. I want them to know what you know." That was a compelling call to action and just the nudge I needed to retrace my early years, reflect on how they influenced the rest of my life, and record those recollections for future generations. I do so in spite of serious reservations--Aunt Nik (myself) is not always a good role model.

I am *Out of Iowa,* and in a sense, so are my grandchildren and any future descendants. They may never see Iowa, but they will know it because I told my story. It is a good thing to know. Iowa is a wonderful place to grow up and a great place to be from. It is a part of me and of them.

My developmental years were colored by a playful and irreverent father and a mother whose valiant efforts at propriety were often exercises in futility. Rounding out the primary players in those early years were an ornery,

13

rambunctious, and diverse band of brothers, a playful grandmother described lovingly, and I do mean lovingly, as a delightful terror, and two devoted aunts. Once I grew up, these influences directed and sustained me as I went through several divergent phases:

- **MY TWENTIES** were spent being married, having babies, and homemaking, which is what every woman in my world did in the 1960's. I didn't always do what everyone else did, though. I worked. At that time, a wife and mother having a job was rather unconventional.

- **MY THIRTIES** involved getting divorced, degreed and obtaining every credential I could get my hands on. This was not what most women did in the 1970's, and I did it while raising children and having more fun than I probably should have.

- **IN MY FORTIES** I broke the glass ceiling and built a career exceeding any expectations I could have imagined in the early Iowa years. I also found love--or so I thought.

- **IN MY FIFTIES** my career skyrocketed, and I reaped countless rewards from the earlier years of sacrifice and effort. On a personal level, I became an empty nester, endured grueling heartbreak, and then blossomed.

- **TODAY AT SIXTY-SOMETHING** I have a vibrant, purposeful plan for my next thirty years. Although at times I feel that the older I get, the better I was, in reality I am more vigorous than ever. Life has never been better. That is, except for the people living in my attic who sneak down at night to steal slippers, hide reading glasses, and disable the TV remote.

After leaving rural Iowa in 1962, I embraced metropolitan living in Omaha and Chicago, ultimately transitioning into an urban Tulsa lifestyle while tiptoeing occasionally into the orbit of rural Oklahoma. Furthermore, I have California connections--a room in my daughter's house where I go for long visits to be terrorized by Thing I and Thing II (my grandchildren). These geographical influences and the adventures surrounding them added dimension to my life, as did the characters who crossed my path.

I hesitate to disappoint, but this is not a comprehensive life story, and not all dimensions and players are represented here. Some experiences are beyond the scope of this book, but touching on them in this introduction sets the framework for this biography. (I may write about them later, after a number of ex-boyfriends, a few outrageous friends, a bad boy boss, and a couple of cowboys have died.) Following is a brief summary of those topics that are excluded:

Career-wise I had quite a ride starting in the early sixties as an executive secretary, one of the few options available to women at that time. My career ended forty some years later as a corporate executive for a multi-billion dollar company out of Chicago. It was in this environment that I learned a lot about sports. Now I know that *March Madness* is not a sale at Macy's, and I have the answer to the question: How many quarters are there in a football game? I also know that some men in corporate America view everything as a game, and if something good happened to a woman, their team lost. This career component of my life, which I will write about someday, is about progress and plateaus, pioneering, aspiration, survival, determination, surrender and redemption, loneliness, mooning (really), wonderful men, mad men, and a lot of wondering about: *Who died and left them in charge?*

Experiencing the Oklahoma cowboy culture first-hand, I learned how many bales of hay fit in the trunk of my car and that when leaving a redneck it is a good idea to run in a zigzag pattern. Mess with a cowboy and you feel like a dog chasing a race car. It's a hopeless proposition because you can never love a cowboy as much as his dog and his horse do. This portion of my life was about deer meat chili, adorable reckless men, and the allure of simultaneously existing in two drastically diverse cultures--the business world and cowboy country. Although at times disconcerting, it was never, ever boring and often left me wondering: *What the hell just happened?*

Over the span of thirty-five years of being single, I have had the good fortune, and on occasion the misfortune, of experiencing several romantic interludes, some of which might be described as an experience similar to hazing. Participating in more involvements than I'd like to admit, in retrospect I have to question my judgment, as evidenced by the fact that I was once engaged to a Marine bomb squad robot, and that is not the worst of it. A couple of dalliances left me feeling like a butterfly in a hail storm and asking: *How done with that do you have to be before you stop the madness?*

These romances occasionally caused me to take a right turn down crazy street, and I didn't always signal. Still, I would not have missed any of them for the world (well, maybe a couple--you can't get that time back). The wonderfully engaging men around whom I built fantasies have inspired many of life's most exhilarating moments, blissful emotional highs, and constructive lessons learned. This is an abundant, sad, sorrowful, exhilarating, poignant, captivating, and comedic untold story of love found and hope lost that has left me thinking: *You are kidding, right?*

I've been blessed with an array of interesting and hugely diverse friends who have counseled and consoled each other through a multitude of personal crises, some self-inflicted and others the random occurrences of life happening. Often the advice and counsel are not taken, which yields richly entertaining outcomes. Nothing is more intriguing than someone making bad decisions. We have all done it. In troubled times, these friendships--some fleeting and others enduring--have been the answer to the question: *Who do I see about that?*

If these things are not included, what is the focus of this book? What is left? The Iowa connections; beginnings, endings, and family matters; the developmental years from my earliest memories in the 1940's up through my thirties when I became independent and found my stride; and the family I came from and the one I created. This life story characterizes the wrenching experiences of saving babies, the gleeful ones of watching children and grandchildren thrive, and the challenging realities of aging. Revealing geographical and social shifts, it reflects adjustments over space and time as I moved *Into Oklahoma,* a fascinating world rich in character and contradictions. Finally, it portrays the love and loss of intensely devoted and loving parents and the hope and meaning of my own inevitable end-of-life "encore years."

These musings also encompass my views on generation gaps, ironing (really), recliners (really), and relationships. They describe family connections and values, portray entertaining human idiosyncrasies, and demonstrate the ebb and flow of a life fully lived. Additionally, they reflect on a clan of siblings, a safe and nurturing community, and the value of wonderful nests. In total, these reflections cover the basics, the core things that provide sustenance, the fortitude to face the world, and a soft place to land when the world is not kind. Sometimes the world is not kind. Occasionally my impressions cross over into philosophical meanderings. I apologize for those up front. I like to think, and unfortunately for the reader, I now have time to do so.

Finally, there are the lessons learned, which are summarized at the end of the book. The early years in Iowa provided a solid foundation. Many wonderful things about my life have happened because I grew up there, and I am exceedingly grateful for them. On the other hand, these beginnings also left me ill-prepared for some of the paths I took. As a consequence, I learned many lessons the hard way. This has made me wiser but hard enough to roller skate on. For this reason, I have included at the end of this book a summary of *lessons learned,* which I hope will provide some measure of wisdom to the reader, particularly future generations.

Perhaps my conclusions from these lessons will mitigate for someone else the naiveté-induced heartache and trauma I experienced. (Everyone needs to know to stay away from people with guns looking for their anti-depressants.) Although I don't pretend to have all the answers and acknowledge that my conclusions may not always resonate with others, I suggest that they are at least worthy of thought. These lessons are valid for me, and I would be remiss in not sharing them here.

People are flawed and sometimes they behave badly. Certainly I have done so--once in 1977. It is not my intent or desire to embarrass anyone, other than myself, or to even any scores while telling my story. I have tried to be gentle with people. In some cases, I changed the names of characters and tweaked a few minor facts and circumstances to achieve that objective.

It is not unusual for me to tell a story by starting in the middle and working out in both directions at the same time. It takes only one frozen strawberry drink with an umbrella in it to induce me to do so. Additionally, in pursuit of entertainment, I have been known to embellish. Since the chronicling of a life is too important to take such liberties, I endeavored to stick to the facts, while recognizing that my feelings and interpretations around those facts are subjective and may be different from others who were there. Admittedly, though, I did embellished in a few instances, primarily in the interest of entertainment. There are limits to my impulse control.

Where I have failed to paint a true picture and perhaps lacked the discipline to research extensively, please understand that I'm not painting a Monet here. It's just a book from the heart of an Iowa farm girl who has not quieted her obsessions and, if she were a child, would have been put in time out.

Memories are interpretive realities. Science has proven that when we recall things we often reconstruct them. These are my interpretations, which may occasionally stray from reality in spite of any best intentions to stay true to the facts. In reality, universal truth is elusive. This book reflects my personal truth as I see it.

Life is a mosaic blend of things you can control and things you cannot. From the first time you say "No!" as a two-year-old child you are seeking some kind of control, and the futile struggle for it begins. It is futile because life happens.

> My friend's little boy went to kindergarten in the mornings. When he started first grade he began packing up his backpack at noon. The teacher asked him what he was doing, and he told her he was getting ready to go home. She explained that in first grade you go to school all day. The little fellow, quite shocked at the news, thought a minute and said, "Well, who signed me up for this?"

Throughout my life I have often asked myself that question. I know it is how I felt when I unexpectedly became pregnant, and it is certainly how I felt when the contractions started. It is also how I felt each time I found myself attached to a redneck, and it is definitely how I felt when a foam rubber shoulder pad fell out of my blouse onto the floor in front of my date. It is how I feel today when faced with the consequences of aging. Who signed me up for this?

Life is full of surprises. Some are scary, like when your gynecologist says "Interesting," your doctor says "Oops," or your computer geek says "Shit." Other surprises are fun, like when you learn your grandchild will be a boy, or a girl, or you discover that El Niño makes you shop. Then there are the surprises that are not good on any level. The baby is not okay. Then you are not okay. Nothing is okay. Nothing. Nobody signs up for that.

Although it makes me feel self-indulgent to actually do it, I signed up for capturing my life story. Why? Because my daughter asked me to, but also because living can perhaps be defined as just trying to matter. I see my life that way. Even here in the journaling of it, I suggest that I am just trying to matter. We touch and influence others with every encounter. Every contact is significant beyond our imagination. Everything matters. Everyone matters.

How we live, how we age, and how we die matter. In my encore years I have come to understand the importance of the role we play when we show those following us how to do those things. When we don't do them well, we put a burden on the people we care about most by painting a gloomy picture of their future. Living from a place of gratefulness for still being here to experience life happening allows us to inspire others. Whether we realize it or not, we are always leading. The slightest interaction makes a difference in that moment and beyond. Everything matters. Everything you do and are matters, and everyone's history matters.

Along this line, there is magic in discovering during the course of one's life something for which you have a passion and getting to do it. That is a rewarding and joyful way to matter. I ultimately realized that joy, although I had to leave my roots to find it, and find it I did--*Out of Iowa.*

1

MY LIFE HAS COME TO THIS

The Anti-Bucket List

I sat cross-legged on the floor in the closet, now a hastily established hide-out, putting stickers of ice cream cones, brightly colored cupcakes, and candied apples in a notebook with scribbles all over it. Thing I and Thing II, ages two and four, have darted away, having the attention span of mosquitoes. Their mother enters the room, spots me on the closet floor, and looks at me strangely. I say simply, "My life has come to this."

On another day, I sat in a car with high school girlfriends as we glided up the coast of California, wine coolers in the trunk and Monterey Bay in our sights. We were in our late-fifties and one might think we were working our bucket lists, but I don't have one. I have an anti-bucket list--a long bulleted account of things I never want to do again. Lessons learned. We were on a mission. We were girls again, and girls just want to have fun. My life has also come to this.

My high school girlfriends and I reconnected around the time of our forty-year class reunion, after experiencing the loss of a classmate and a husband. This was after many years of hardly any contact. Since then we've taken vacations together every other year or so. I call it running amuck, perhaps a strange description for women of our age, but it is reflective of the potential for unrestrained but harmless activity born from the seed of sisterhood.

I would suggest that we are better friends now than we were in high school, having outgrown the immaturities that complicate teenage relationships. As a bellman was escorting us to our hotel rooms on the ocean front of Monterey, our dialogue went something like this, which provides a flavor of our more mature interaction:

Nikki: "Shut up!"

Annabelle: "You shut up!"

Nikki: "No, You shut up!"

Donna Mae: "You both shut up!"

Nikki: "Donna Mae, you shut up!

Russ, Donna Mae and Annabelle: "You SHUT UP! "

Bellman: "Are you guys sisters?"

Nikki: "No...You guys just SHUT UP!"

Annabelle: "You shut up!"

Bellman: "You **are** sisters, right?"

RUNNING AMUCK

On the way up the coast in the vicinity of the Hearst Mansion, we found ourselves at a roadside store late at night in a quest for food. It was there that we encountered law enforcement. A patrolman and sheriff's deputy were in for coffee. They were so cute in their uniforms, badges, hats and all those weapons, holsters, handcuffs, stun guns, flashlights, and radio gear.

We were enchantingly festive, or so we thought, and struck up a conversation. After educating them on the fact that Iowa stood for Idiots Out Wandering Around, we asked if they would like to hear one of our high school cheers. They agreed, somewhat hesitantly, so we did our cheer. We had been practicing cheers on the plane to California. Really, we did.

> A bottle of Coke, a big banana,
> We're from southern Indiana.
> That's a lie, that's a bluff,
> We're from Prescott, that's the stuff!

Everyone was fascinated, especially since when we did the last line we stuck our thumbs in our arm pits and our elbows out for emphasis, just like we did in high school. (You can't make this stuff up.) Indications are that they particularly enjoyed the hand action on the big banana part. We ended with a maneuver somewhat reminiscent of a jump with splits, at least as close to it as women in their fifties can get and within the constraints of the grocery racks, lotto machine, coin changer, and ATM.

Although the officers appeared to be in somewhat of a state of shock, along with the store clerk and several patrons, we asked if they would like to hear our school song. Someone said, "No," but the officers seemed up for it, so we did it anyway. There was no holding us back now. We belted out *Beer, Beer for Old Prescott High* with gusto. This might have been pressing our fun because one of the officers asked if we had been drinking. I responded with, "We don't got no-o-o-o wine coolers."

Having some experience with law enforcement while on patrol with deputies in Oklahoma, I intuitively knew we needed a distraction, kind of like when I ask patrolmen to take Mom to jail when we are being *Thelma and Louise* and get stopped for speeding. Rather than sacrifice one of my friends to the slammer, I simply asked, "If I laid down on the sidewalk outside, would you draw around me with that there chalk you guys carry around with you?" Someone told me to SHUT UP and we hurried away quickly before the officers realized the lie-down-on-the-sidewalk thing could be construed as solicitation.

I was never worried that they would take us seriously. I had been on patrol many times with night shift sheriff's deputies in Oklahoma. I knew they were delighted to have some excitement to break up the night, although I doubt they expected to be entertained by a group of graying, fifty-something women from

Iowa singing about beer, cheering about bananas, and attempting the splits.

At any rate, it is certain the dispatch staff, jailers, and fellow officers heard about the encounter soon after. Our entertainment would be a refreshing break from drunks full of liquid courage who pee and puke in patrol cars and jail cells, not to mention the tattooed, pierced folks with warrants who claim they ain't done nothin', spit, and call the deputy's momma names. Those perpetrators have no sense of humor, and we were refreshingly on the other end of the lawlessness spectrum. Still, there was some risk the deputy would haul us in just so everyone at the county jail could get a look at us, kind of like: You are not going to believe this. Because of this and the fact that we did have wine coolers, a quick getaway seemed prudent, so we left and went to Monterey to run amuck there.

We decided to take glamour shots of ourselves on Monterey beach, although we had enough sense and dignity to know we were not candidates for bikinis. Since photo-shopping had not been invented yet and a successful quest for long-line swimsuits with sleeves was unlikely, we accosted a frogman on the beach, offering him money to borrow his wet suit for photos.

Although we were intimidating and he was outnumbered, he refused, primarily he said because he wasn't wearing anything under it. One of the girls, I won't say who, said she wasn't wearing any underwear either. Someone told her to SHUT UP! She said, "You SHUT UP!" Someone else said, "You all SHUT UP!" You get the picture.

While we were arguing, he took off hurriedly down the beach, his little frog feet flopping in the sand, and we headed off in the other direction speculating about whether accosting a frogman on a sandy Monterey beach was a felony or a misdemeanor. At any rate, our vacation agenda didn't include getting arrested, although we contemplated the fact that cute guys in uniforms with weapons and handcuffs would be involved. Resigned to the end of our adventure, we stepped up our pace back to the spa where soft bathrobes and room service awaited us along with a waiter in the dining room who was still trying to figure out just who we were. The night before at dinner we said to him, "You don't know who we are, do you?" This was after we asked the people at the table next to us with wonderful food, "Are you

24

going to eat all that?" Later we alluded to a menage a trois between the three aluminum foil animals encasing our leftovers.

My most recent running amuck experience occurred when I took a road trip to California with Donna Mae, who was moving there. We had a dog and a U-Haul both of which added interest to the trip, the U-Haul because we could not ever, ever back up. Donna Mae drove from Cincinnati to California, five days of driving and four nights at motels, and she never backed up once. Her dog, Toby, made the trip interesting because it was too hot to leave him in the car, so we had to eat all our meals at drive-throughs and because he had to pee.

I placed him down among the cacti to do his business in the Mojave Desert. There was no grass to be found. He started dancing around pretty good on the hot sand, so I picked him up and held him a few inches above the ground, shaking him gently to induce him to pee, which he had not done since Prescott, Arizona. He was way overdue. Toby looked back at me like, "What the hell are you doing?" I finally gave up and tossed him in the car, telling Donna Mae we needed to get out of there pronto. "We must find grass," I said in a tone of severe desperation, which caused her to give me a strange look until I explained Toby's dilemma.

Toby can be temperamental. Perhaps that is an understatement. When I'm unable to reach Donna Mae by phone, I worry that Toby has eaten her. She walked him late every night before we went to sleep, which concerned me somewhat but not enough to miss my favorite television show, so I didn't accompany her one evening. As she was leaving the hotel room with an overenthusiastic Toby in tow, I asked her, "If you don't come back, can I have your car?"

I am in California every other month, and I spend time with Donna Mae. We run amuck and get in the way of other drivers, which is more fun in California than anywhere else on the planet. Our escapades give me a break from Thing I and Thing II as well as Yo Gabba Gabba and The Disney Channel, but they introduce their own set of challenges. Donna May has unpleasant conversations with the bitch on her GPS while I white knuckle. Also, in spite of the GPS and our daily doses of the memory enhancing herbs of Ginkgo Biloba, DHA, Hawthorn, Gotu Kola, Bacopin, Rosemary, and Omega 3, we get lost a lot, and not just on the roads. We wandered out of the door of one furniture store and back in another door of the same store and thought we were in a different one. We marveled at the fact that this store had the same furniture as the last one. We had pretty much shopped the whole store when reality hit, which had me considering adding prescription drugs to my daily memory-inducing herbal medications. No doubt they would clear up the mind, but I am afraid they would cause me to remember Hank, and I don't want to do that.

A few years ago, I sat with these girlfriends in my living room in Tulsa, Oklahoma. They rallied around in my time of loss and turmoil. Then another loss brought another sisterhood connection. Our losses escalate--another classmate, husband, neighbor, and friend--some generating *what ifs* and *if only's*. Moms and dads are now gone. Losses, constant and exponential, leaving us unanchored. I ask myself: My life has come to this?

Not really. You see, I am now well-seasoned, which smooths life out a bit. I have my anti-bucket list and an astute awareness of the things not to do again. This prevents distractions and allows me to relish the ones that count. And then there are Thing I, Thing II, Thing III, and another on the way. They imply a paradigm shift that shuffles the deck and makes everything matter. They don't know it yet, but to them, my life is a legacy. For them I am still creating it, and legacies are forever.

My life has come to this--just trying to matter, the path to creating a legacy that serves those who follow. My parents and grandparents did that, probably unconsciously, but they did it. Next I share their legacy. For certain, they mattered.

2

THE LEGACY

Somewhat Lucky

Iowa is a great place to be from. I was fortunate to be raised on a farm in southwestern Iowa with a father who had a propensity to amuse and entertain, a devoted and self-sacrificing mother, a lively and diverse band of brothers, free-range chickens, and puppies. I also had the good fortune to leave that environment for a metropolitan life and a business career, which was a more comfortable fit for me. Although I thrived as a result, I was ill-prepared for life outside of Iowa in some respects.

The gap between the rural culture where I began and the urban and corporate one where I ended up was huge. This contrast generated interesting and captivating life scenarios, but it also presented challenges which required serious adjustments. Fortunately, the core values and solid foundation instilled by my family and the small rural community where I grew up gave me the fortitude to prevail through those challenges. With the exception of a few traumatic episodes, which unfortunately left a mark and colored my world forever, I generally managed the adjustments well. Certainly I realized some magnificent outcomes as a result.

In addition to living in divergent environments, it has been my choice to embrace many diverse and, at first blush, conflicting interests along with a somewhat non-conventional life style. I can hang with almost any group, ranging from the social set, corporations, boards, churches, book clubs, professionals, academics, dancers, law enforcement officers, military men (including my fiancé, a Marine bomb squad robot, Suicide Sam-- I'm attracted to reckless men), farmers, Oklahoma cowboys, politicians, gays, and bikers. They all hold a fascination for me, especially cowboys and robots--and pirates, although I never got engaged to one. Pirates don't get engaged.

I am uncertain if this attribute of embracing diversity is a strength or a weakness, but it has made me multi-faceted. I can behave myself in uppity social situations, on the surface at least (you might be shocked at what was going on in my mind). Conversely, I can swear like a sailor in others (where you might also be shocked at what was going through my mind). At a biker bar I might feel like I was asked to join a band and was the only musician in it, but with a bit of tequila I can hang with guys like Mole, Dog and Dirt and, against all odds, still manage to stay off a motorcycle.

I have also managed to stay off a horse. An affinity for cowboys is clearly a sickness, and I've learned there is a huge difference between an Iowa farm boy and an Oklahoma cowboy in spite of their rural commonality. Cowboys are like country boys on speed. Still, I navigated the western world pretty well and learned that cowboys aren't easy to love, you can never have too much fun, there is a fine line between hunting and looking stupid, herding dogs are amazing, and deer meat jerky can be produced in your very own kitchen. My strategy for staying off a horse, in spite of how "purdy" some cowboy might say I would look on his appaloosa, was high heels. I would say: "In these shoes, I don't think so."

I have further learned that dancing is an addiction, and that the dance world is occupied by a broad range of characters spanning the gamut from traditional conservative types to wild and crazy colorful ones. Either end of this spectrum is not a good fit for me. Gravitating pretty much to the middle, I occasionally stumbled across the outliers in doses intense enough to know I didn't want to go there, but just enough to be royally entertained in the moment and, in some cases, enlightened forever.

Corporate America, wherein I operated so successfully, is a blatant contradiction to all these worlds, and breaking the glass ceiling in the seventies was a pioneer experience I would not want to repeat. Although the end result made the trauma and grueling determination worthwhile, I can't imagine having the fortitude and audacity to go through all that again today. I had to be hugely but discreetly pissed and innately persevering to survive it. Although a certain amount of finesse was involved in achieving what I did, I never embraced the good-old-boy network. Accomplishments were the result of putting my nose to the grindstone, doing the job, and delivering outcomes. It is hard to argue with outcomes in any circumstance except politics.

In spite of significant success in the business arena, I was never comfortable there. For me it was incredibly lonely at the top. In the male dominated executive suite and board of directors forum, I often felt like a lizard in a sand storm. I consciously and precariously walked the line between being effective and not being threatening, all the while enduring the pack mentality of wolves. The wave of change over the course of my career in this regard is both heartening and disappointing. I still observe contentious gender conflicts which cause me to ask: Are we not past that nonsense already? (Perhaps I should not call my co-workers wolves; however, a few were wolves by any definition.)

I was divorced in 1975 and never remarried. A thirty-five-year span of being single is unusual, I know. During this time I had several meaningful relationships. One of them lasted seventeen years and involved raising a child. A few relationships were intense; most were not, and I avoided marriage. I never found anyone I could imagine forever with, and my choices in men further complicated any prospect of a permanent connection. My independent nature and need to rescue further muddled affairs of the heart. I suspect that at this point I'm too emotionally exhausted to ever couple up again, and I'm okay with that. It is comforting to be done with romance and to never again experience the desperate emotions of someone drowning when love is lost. Life is spirited, purposeful, rich, and full. I'm happy and contented, and I don't want to mess that up.

This almost overwhelming blend of interests and lifestyle decisions, some of them not particularly compatible, have made my life colorful yet complex. The resulting conglomeration of experiences did not just simply turn up in my life. I chose them. Understanding why I did that and how I navigated through them requires some interpretation of the developing years.

Viewing those early years with the wisdom of a wiser, older person, I can see what shaped me. I understand what led to the overpowering need to rescue, the aversion to the ordinary, the enthusiastic pursuit of amusement, the driving ambition, the courage to take risks, and the fierce independence. No doubt, the midwestern core values my mother devotedly embraced are reflected in my more conventional chosen paths, but more importantly, the influences of my father's willful nature, rational convictions, sense of humor, and fascination with novelty reflect the unusual choices. Both of their legacies delighted me in the good times and saved my soul in the bad ones.

DAD'S LEGACY

While retrospectively contemplating my life, I searched for an overall theme and found myself reflecting on a significant childhood incident. It is one of my earliest memories, and I've come to understand that this somewhat obscure event, which was subsequently reinforced throughout my childhood, had a profound influence on shaping my life's journey. It produced struggles and rewards, hurts and joys, and it defined who I am.

Until this realization, I would not have subscribed to the prospect that a singular "defining event" in a small child's life could manifest itself profoundly throughout life. However, through the introspection of the biographical process, it became clear that this event did in fact influence *my view of the world*. Subsequent circumstances reinforced that perception, and as a result, it defined the context in which my life unfolded.

I have no idea how old I was when this incident occurred. I was a small child. The memory is somewhat fuzzy, but the thoughts running through my mind in this brief moment in time, sixty some years ago on a farm in Iowa, are vivid to this day.

> Dad, who was not known for his patience, was angry, steaming mad, and swearing. He stomped out to the car and sped off, probably to the local tavern. Mom, standing at the window among four anxious children and fighting back tears, watched him drive away on the dirt road, dust billowing from the tires. Feeling so sorry for him, she made a remark that has stuck in my mind forever: "Your poor dad. He can never get a break."

I revered my dad, and although the language in my child's mind in reaction to this incident was simple, its impact was powerful. I said to myself: "It's not fair." I have repeated that simple, concise thought over and over in my mind throughout my life, and it set the theme for how I lived it--rescue.

I didn't know what had happened to Dad, but I knew unequivocally that it was not fair. I wanted desperately to fix it, to make it right, to rescue him from the grips of despair. I yearned to right the wrong, to make it better. I wanted him to come back so Mom would stop crying. I wanted Dad to be okay-- to get a break.

My interpretation of this experience explains many of my choices, unraveling the mystery of what drives me. Mom asked me: "Why do you have such a fire in your belly?" I didn't know how to answer that then, but I know now that it is my need to *save the day*. Dad said more than once: "You should have been a boy." Now I understand that it was my driving ambition and independent nature that made him say that. I've asked myself: "Why do I not have a life partner?" Now I understand how my choices made an enduring relationship a long shot and that a woman's fierce independence and tendency to rescue are incompatible with a man's self-image.

An awakening of sorts, these revelations are healing, and they have sparked a broader sense of self-acceptance and contentment. Before that awareness, I was often confused about what just happened, another prevailing theme in my life. Now I know who I am, and I understand the genesis of my choices. I'm Ray Walter's daughter, and how I related to him framed my life.

Although Dad embraced life with exuberance and good humor and worked hard, he struggled with the weight of a large family, an uncertain farming occupation, and the burdens of a heartland culture where he never quite fit in. These issues and his lack of patience made him prone to occasional outbursts of temper.

I don't recall him lashing out at us kids, nor was he ever violent. We felt loved and protected. He and Mom rarely argued. His frustrations seemed mostly the result of circumstances. When frustrated he occasionally had a fit. This might involve whacking a car or tractor part with a tool while spewing cuss words with some stomping, pacing, and leaving thrown in. Leaving is defined as a trip to the local tavern. This usually involved modest consumption, but enough to come home all jolly. He sang about having the wings of an angel and flying over prison walls, or, more intriguing to us kids, he crooned about a dead skunk in the middle of the road, you know, roadkill.

Being notorious for my lack of patience, I'm without a doubt my father's child. I don't stomp off and get drunk, well, not usually. I mean, I have done it, but normally I just throw myself into a housecleaning frenzy, eat sunflower seeds, down some lemon cake, and chew bubble gum--not necessarily in that order.

Although I never sang about roadkill--well, maybe I did, but I didn't make a habit of it--I have been known to throw a fit. For me, a more feminine interpretation of a fit involves a controlled, well-articulated verbal rant, sprinkled with refined cadence swearing, and a well-manicured finger in someone's face. If a child was involved, it might include a thump on the head--child abuse by today's standards, but a custom of the day. I guess I've mellowed. I can't remember the last time I had a fit, and I'm not allowed to thump my grandchildren on the head, although there are times I would like to and have no doubt they would benefit from the experience.

How did this incident of Dad storming off and Mom remarking that he can't get a break shape me? I became a rescuer, gravitating to the underdog and unfortunate so I could make it better. In some respects this is a good thing. I mean, worse things could happen, but rescuing has produced agonizing consequences in some circumstances.

And so, with considerable introspection, I discovered the theme, the primary context in which I lived my life: *rescue*. My history is rich with situations where I concluded *it's not fair* and stepped up to save the day, spending much of my life's energy relentlessly trying to fix something or someone. I did it in relationships, seeking out poor wronged souls who deserved better--the guys who couldn't get a break or got a bad one. I gravitated to friends who made bad decisions. I sponsored counseling to save relationships and to encourage peace of mind, and I put my heart and soul into saving babies who were born with a burden they didn't deserve. There is even an element of rescue in this book by virtue of the sharing of lessons learned.

I did it in my career by taking over disastrous projects or crippled departments and making them sing and by mentoring talented employees. I did it by creating beautiful nests for people who otherwise would not have one. Postured to strike instantly at anyone or anything that threatened my children, I did it with them. Distracted as I was at times by career, ambition, education, and life's pleasures, when the chips were down, when the need arose, I was there for the rescue. It was what I did best. It was who I was. It is who I am to this day.

Dad's influence has affected me in another profound way. I have an aversion to being boring, to doing the usual, and to some extent to conforming. He saw the novelty in things and had a knack for turning simple situations into the quaint and bizarre, and it was just an absolute hoot to witness him in action. I identified with that. Not only did this enhance my natural aversion to the ordinary, it inspired ambition, a novel attribute for a woman in my era. It was not ordinary to do some of the things I did, and that is exactly why I did them.

I pretty much conformed in my formative years, but as I began to control my life as an adult and express myself freely, my decisions were driven by a basic inclination to avoid the norm. Fortunately, this was tempered by an intense sense of responsibility and a desire for achievement without which I might have become a nude hang glider or, worse yet, taken a job in customer service in the insurance industry. Oh wait, I did that--the customer service thing, not the hang gliding one. Anyway, an attraction to excitement can cause a person to create crises just to keep up the excitement level. I learned early on to control this impulse. Fortunately, Iowans are not much into drama, and I am grateful for this Iowa grounding influence.

Dad was all about fun. He had a zest for life and a joyous, somewhat oddball sense of humor. He found amusement in things that most would miss, and he loved a good joke. This is, in my mind, his greatest legacy. In times of depression and desperation, I clung stubbornly to my sense of humor, knowing intuitively it would be my salvation. The few times I lost it, I knew I was really in trouble. Humor was a lifeline.

Dad's irreverence modeled maverick behavior. I can behave myself if I choose to do so, but sometimes I don't. If there is a conga line in a restaurant, I'm in it. If I sit down at a banquet table and the dessert is already there, I consider it an appetizer and eat it. If it is tasty, I ask the person next to me if they are

33

going to eat theirs. I may recommend the appetizer to others. The more formal the event, the more snobby the crowd, the more enticing the action. If I have a date and he can't deal with that, he needs to get a new girlfriend.

Dad complained to waiters that he added up the tab twice and got the same thing both times, implying that this was a pressing problem requiring immediate resolution. He'd ask for the manager. I suggest to waiters that I don't know the men I am with, and they are bothering me. I ask for the restaurant security officer. When being seated in one of those restaurants where the tables are too close together, I tell people at nearby tables: "We will be dining with you tonight. Are you going to eat all that?"

I did a bad and irreverent thing just the other day, and although I knew in my heart it should just be a thought that would provide a chuckle limited to myself, I just had to do it. A girlfriend asked me for directions to a high-end furniture store. She and a friend from out of town were going shopping. I gave them directions to an adult book warehouse. Dad would have been proud. Mom would have shook her finger in disdain, and Grandma Bray would have had a downright conniption fit. Dad's influences usually win out. I wonder if they bought anything. I bet they did.

Considerable irreverent behavior on my part is driven by my admiration of Dad's appreciation for absurd humor. I loved that mischievous twinkle in his eye that prompted those of us who knew him well to pay attention, knowing something entertaining was about to happen. I gravitate to people like that, avoiding those who are quick to judge offbeat amusements. In my younger years, I often chastised myself for quirky behavior. Now, I roll with it. At my age it matters less what someone else thinks than that people are having fun. You can never have too much fun. Although it is probably not age appropriate for women in their sixties to have a food fight in a sushi bar, I am up for it as long as no children are harmed, the perpetrators help clean up, and someone leaves a ridiculous tip.

In addition to the influence of his humor, Dad's way in the world also inspired courage. He didn't necessarily follow the social norms of his time or meet the requirements of his community. In his environment, this required courage. It was quiet courage. He didn't say much; he just did his thing. This influenced me to not be afraid to take risks and to step out beyond the parameters of normalcy. Like him, I did that pretty much without drama. In my career I blazed many trails. In my romantic life, I defied the customs of the day and was rarely driven by what was required by society. Had I embraced tradition, I'd have married every man I fell in love with, which means I would have had way more husbands than Elizabeth Taylor.

PHILOSOPHICAL MEANDERINGS
(In a Loop)

I promised in the Introduction, or threatened, depending on how you look at it, some philosophical meanderings. I can't help myself. It comes from not being gainfully employed and adequately distracted. Before I start, let me say that I know that just because I think something, that doesn't make it true. This applies to everybody, although when most people think something in their head, they believe it is then true. I have a friend who thinks his gambling gains exceed his losses. I don't think that's true. If by some long shot it is true at the point he said it, it will not be true after another trip or two to the casino. That's what I think, but just because I think what he thinks is not true does not mean that what I think is true either although I'm sure it is, but maybe not........I'm in a loop.

I often think of Dad when I am in the mode of philosophical thought. He was somewhat of a thinking man, a rational, down-to-earth, common sense kind of guy, although he certainly had his idiosyncrasies. He obviously thought it was okay to lie if the lie was outrageous enough that only a fool would believe it. On second thought, he probably didn't actually have any honorable criteria for fibbing, and it was simply okay to lie if it was in some manner funny. On third thought, I doubt he thought about it at all. He just made stuff up.

I've been proffering a preposterous lie when people ask me what I am doing now that I'm retired. I tell them I'm training for the Olympics. If this were true, I would be preoccupied with meaningful physical activities and concentrating on getting *in the zone*. Philosophical ramblings would not happen. Bottom line, the Olympics thing is an outright fabrication, I have no distractions, so I think about things. I like to think.

Being realistic and pragmatic to a fault, I've adopted Dad's propensity for rational, logical thought. It doesn't take me long to get to the heart of a matter, and I am not easily swayed by rhetoric or irrational thinking. If something doesn't make sense, I'm not going to buy it. If I get into a state of denial, it doesn't last long. I pretty much face reality head on.

Like Dad, I am an independent thinker, and I'm not going to buy all of the opinions of any group or any single source. I'm constantly amazed at people's willingness to ignore all sense of logic and to buy into ridiculous, often hateful, messages someone created to serve their own purposes. At the same time I support their right to irrational thought. Some people pursue it like a moth to light. It fulfills a need. Good for them. I just don't want to be a part of it, and therein lies the challenge.

My conservative friends, who have all the answers, think I'm a liberal. My liberal friends, who have all the answers, think I'm a conservative. Neither have any concept of going both ways and drawing conclusions issue by issue. I don't believe any political party is right all the time. How anyone can believe that is a mystery to me. I doubt that anyone has all the answers, and I have to wonder what makes anybody think they do. Are they so special that they get to know and the rest of us don't? I suspect they need to know, but they don't really know, although they believe they know. Nevertheless, I could be wrong about that since I don't really know if they know or not, although I'm relatively certain they don't know, but they don't know that. However, I suppose I could be wrong and they know everything. That makes no sense, though.........another loop.

When we believe we have all the answers and everyone who doesn't agree with us is wrong, we become judgmental and waste our energy endeavoring to make everything right by our definition. We only seek out information that supports what we already believe, ignoring all the rest. This is a wonderful way to assure that you are always right and to avoid doing the work required for rational thought. It also sets people up to be manipulated by those who profess to know--and who hate.

I try not to be too preoccupied with being right, especially since my right might not be someone else's. I don't have all the answers. I am not that special. I find it easier to tell what isn't true than what is, especially since untruth and distortion are so rampant. The real challenge, though, is keeping a peaceful heart in the midst of those who profess to have answers, who are hateful, use negative words and labels to distort and manipulate, and who defy common sense interpretations. They provoke a challenge which makes me defensive and places me squarely in the loop of being right in my own mind. This makes me more like them and robs me of a peaceful heart. (This is the meandering part of the philosophical meanderings.) I don't know how to solve this problem. I'm certain someone with all the answers does, but if he has all of them, I'm not going to buy it because I won't believe it...another loop, which makes me just want to have coffee and get smoked off. I should explain.

I was in an American Indian home recently where a medicine woman was ceremoniously spreading smoke from cedar and sweet grass throughout the home, fanning it with a sacred eagle's wing. There was no doubt in my mind but that she was in a spiritual state. After she smoked the house, she did it to the home owners themselves and then, by golly, she smoked me. This was undoubtedly an incredibly generous gesture on her part, especially since I am not an Indian. I felt exceedingly honored, deeply touched, and I stood very still while being smoked. I have a feeling she doesn't do that for just anybody.

The next day I was thinking about the significance of this act and became curious about the ceremony and what it meant. So I called my friend whose house was being smoked and asked, "What happened to me yesterday? Was I smoked *up* or smoked *down*?" She laughed and told me I had been smoked *off*.

Now that I knew what it was called, I thought about the meaning, and something occurred to me. I have never known an American Indian to endeavor to convince anyone to believe what they believe. Taking their beliefs as seriously as anyone, they insist that they be respected with tenacity, but they don't advocate them for others. They simply own them. I rather like that.

Anyway, I am focused on practical theory, if there is such a thing, and my theory is simple. As long as anyone's personal truth doesn't lead them to spew hate and distortion, kill, maim or otherwise harm anyone, I'm pretty much up for whatever they want to believe. That level of tolerance is vital to my diverse coffee groups. When I'm not training for the Olympics, I'm having coffee. That's what you do for recreation when you live in the city. No one I have coffee with is into killing and maiming. Most are rational thinkers, and we engage in civil discourse even when we disagree. If someone gets unhinged, we switch them to decaf and ask if they forgot to take their medication that day.

I doubt Dad thought deeply enough about any of these things to hypothesize about them. He was a simple man. If something didn't make sense, he simply wasn't buying it, but he was for sure going to get a kick out of it. I like to imagine Dad listening to someone who is suggesting that their religion requires them to kill all non-believers. Dad would say something like: "You sold me on that bull shit. Hang tight while I get my gun."

Memories of Dad weave their way through my mind now as I anticipate that early defining *it's not fair* moment which so profoundly influenced my life. It is the enigma of him, the man, that made the interpretation of unfairness so powerfully relevant. As a child, I felt his strong, reassuring presence as a "coat from the cold" contrasted with his essence as a worthy, vulnerable man who could not get a break. As a result, I've been attracted to that kind of man all my life. The unfortunate reality is that this kind of man does not deal well with a fiercely independent woman ready for the rescue. Rescuing is his job.

You will see that defining moment of Dad storming off, his aversion to conformity, and his legacy of humor surfacing throughout these musings about my life. They influenced my decisions and sustained me through challenges. Although there are times they inspired me to do things I shouldn't, I hope that overall they resulted in my making positive contributions to others. For those times when they drove me to cross the lines of appropriate boundaries in an overenthusiastic attempt to rescue, or to obsessively endeavor to solve a problem that was not mine, I hope I am forgiven.

MOM'S LEGACY

In contrast to Dad, Mom was compliant and dutiful about following the rules and norms of the world in which she lived.

She was steady, sure, rock solid, and responsible. Except when the mother tiger came out when she felt the need to defend one of her offspring, she stuck to convention. Her deep sense of responsibility role modeled important qualities which have fortunately tempered my sense of the outrageous. This left its mark, and I am, without a question, Virlee Walter's daughter.

Mom's devotion and intense, unconditional love for Dad was reflected in her pain over his misfortune and her comment about him "not getting a break" as he sped down that dirt road. Her sensitivity was reflected in her tears. Don't interpret those tears as weakness. She was a tower of strength. She had his back.

After all this dialogue about Dad, this short account of Mom's legacy seems strange in comparison. I loved my mom. She literally saved me at one point in my life, and her unconditional love and devotion for me and my siblings was without question. The twinkle in her eyes every time any of her children walked into a room spoke for itself. Her steady, sure nature provided a level of security conducive to children blossoming, and blossom we did. You absolutely without fail could count on her, both in regard to the daily activities of life and when the chips were down. She was a rock. There were things about Mom and how she lived her life that I did not want to emulate, but I always wanted to be a rock.

The combination of this and Dad's influence on my psyche have contributed to my preoccupation with rescue, and both served to provide a composite of life experiences which were unique enough to be exhilarating and centered enough to keep me out of serious trouble. Those are the contributions of my parents to shaping my life as I see it--their legacy.

Human behavior is complicated. Legacy doesn't explain life's experiences in their entirety, but clearly my parents gave me a solid base of character which has allowed me to live a fulfilling and productive life. Furthermore, their diverse personalities inspired a robust and interesting one--a life played out as Ray and Virlee Walter's daughter.

I raised an amazing young man from the age of two who lost his mother when he was a baby. I was told by a child psychologist that as a teen he was likely to feel anger about that and act out as a result. He didn't do that. Instead he described himself as *somewhat lucky* because he had no mother but he had people who loved him, and life was good. His view of the world is inspiring, and I use it when looking back on my life.

> I was lucky to have the family I was born into and to benefit from the solid base my early years provided. On the other hand, along with this legacy came handicaps and limitations which left me ill-prepared for many of life's episodes. As a result, I experienced some bruising interludes.

> I am also lucky to possess several innate qualities that have contributed to my successes, but on the other hand, I had to invest a tremendous amount of hard work and sacrifice in order to realize those accomplishments. Nothing just fell into my lap. No one ever gave me anything. I paid my dues and earned everything I got.

Considering this composition of pros and cons in my life, I guess you could say that I am *somewhat lucky*. I'll take that.

3

FREE-RANGE CHILDREN

Iowa = Idiots Out Wandering Around

I learned early in life that you can say bad things about your family members, but it is generally not a good idea for anyone else to do so. This applies to other people's families as well. They may talk about skeletons in their closets, family feuds, faults, and black sheep, but you best not join in. The same is true of where you are from. I was born and raised in Iowa, and I can make a joke suggesting that Iowa stands for "idiots out wandering around," but if you are not also from Iowa, you probably shouldn't do so.

There were large, closely-connected families on both my father's and mother's sides and most lived near each other on farms outside of the small rural community of Prescott, Iowa. This provided constant opportunities for interaction with grandparents, aunts, uncles, and cousins while growing up.

We were at a family dinner on my Dad's side. Uncle Fred had a pet raccoon who sat at his feet as we stood in a circle hand-in-hand in the expansive front yard, heads bowed while cousin Mary said the blessing. Mary had recently moved to Arkansas and converted to the Southern Baptist religion. This inspired her to take on the mission of converting her Methodist relatives in the interest of saving our souls from eternal damnation. The probability of actually turning Iowa Methodists into Baptists was an unlikely proposition; however, the reality of this was lost on Mary, who remained hopeful against all odds. Consequently, her prayers were long and passionate.

A cat joined the prayer group and was moving around the circle brushing up against people's legs as cats do. When she got near the raccoon, he reached out, grabbed her and started hunching her. (You can't make this stuff up.) A terrible racket ensued, the kids' eyes got really big, and adults looked on in horror. Cousin Mary, being totally vested in her determination to save us heathens, didn't miss a beat in her prayer but abandoned bowing her head and began praying to the heavens. Uncle Fred finally kicked the raccoon who rolled out into the middle of the circle and ran off as the cat slunk away in the opposite direction.

The raccoon was a radical nuisance by any definition, but a comical genius as well. In addition to prayer-induced cat abuse, he terrorized anyone going into one of the outbuildings on the farm. It was his home base, and when he saw someone headed that way he ran quickly to a back entrance. When the person entered, he jumped down on them from the rafters.

This was an unfathomable shock to anyone experiencing it. Uncle Fred thought it was hilarious and connived to get unsuspecting souls to go into the building for some enticing reason, then waited anxiously to observe the attack. You would think you were going to retrieve a basket of peaches and end up being punked from above by a wild masked bandit. It was unsettling, to say the least, and if cousin Mary had been there at that instant she might have been able to wring a successful conversion out of a determined Methodist.

Families back then were large by today's standards. It has been suggested that farmers had large families because they needed children to work the farm. This is not true. It was because there was no reliable birth control. Mom confirmed this saying: "After you got married, children just happened." It is not like she set out to create a bunch of farm hands.

Mom and Dad had eight babies, most right after they got married. In fact, they had four babies in four years, after which there was a bit more spacing between children. Three of the eight were so premature that they died within days. The technology was not there to save babies born early, and people often talked in terms of surviving children, something we rarely think about today. The depth of Dad's pain resulting from these losses was reflected in an unnerving comment he made to one of my brothers.

> When Dad was a boy, an older brother whom he idolized died. Penicillin had not been discovered yet, and when his brother was kicked in the leg by a horse, an infection developed in the wound, and it overtook him. Enduring the torturous death of this young boy was traumatic for the entire family and wounded Dad deeply. That combined with the loss of the three babies left scars that became vividly clear when Dad said to my brother, who was playing with his toddler, "You shouldn't get too attached to her. You could lose her."

The scars ran deep and the fear of loss festered, driving Mom into constant worrying frenzies and Dad into a remoteness he did a good job of hiding most of the time. However, when my brother was in a precarious situation in Vietnam for some time, both the mental and physical toll on both of them was obvious. It is a blessing that neither of them outlived any of their five remaining children.

All of Mom and Dad's surviving babies were boys, except me. I was the third born and the second surviving. My older brother and three younger ones have been one of the biggest blessings of my life. We are an incredibly diverse bunch, each choosing different paths in life, but always connected by the common bond of growing up together.

THE SUPPORTING PLAYERS

My earliest memories of Iowa are of a chamber pot under the bed, a flash camera that made my little brother cry, a brown plaid wool blanket and massive quilts in which we snuggled, Dad in overalls, and Mom and Grandma in aprons. Also in the mix were Aunts Shuppy and Weezie, my Mom's sisters, who played key roles throughout our lives. We kids couldn't pronounce Shirley or Mary Louise, thus the nicknames, more appropriate for puppies than people, that these poor women bore the rest of their lives. They were exuberant teenagers when Mom had three children and took quite a fancy to the babies, continuing to nurture us throughout our lives. The profound influence they had on me has been a legacy.

Aunt Shuppy started to college at the age of forty, a highly unusual thing to do in those days. I was old enough to be impressed, and because I idolized her so much, this no doubt sparked my ambition. She was fun, extremely smart and often a source of encouragement and inspiration. Shuppy once said to me: "You can be anything you want to be." Who says such a thing to a young girl in Iowa in the 1950's? It was unheard of, and I recall being quite amazed by it. She put ideas in my head that may not have occurred to me otherwise.

In an environment of large families you can feel somewhat lost in the shuffle. Shuppy made me feel special. She embraced all of us kids and was the instigator of many of our fun family adventures. Her connection with me, though, was especially tight. As I got older, our relationship became woman-to-woman, and it was powerful.

I remember vividly her last hug a few months before she died. I was a grown woman with babies of my own. We were at Grandpa and Grandma Bray's anniversary celebration. She held me longer and harder than usual, like she didn't want to let go. Shortly thereafter we learned she had terminal liver cancer. I always wondered if she had an inkling of the future when she gave me that extra-long hug.

Shuppy

Aunt Weezie rescued me from bad childhood perms, advised me on make-up, reinforced in me the budding concept of solid work ethic, guided and directed me with common sense advice, and was an amazing cook. To this day I pester her to bake me pies. After Dad died, she was comforting me and saying how sorry she was. I responded with a whiny, weepy request: "Weezie, would you bake me a pie?"

Weezie

There is something innately sweet about Weezie. I don't recall her ever saying a bad word about anyone, an unusual quality in a small gossipy community where everyone knows everyone else. My daughter is that way and she reminds me a lot of Weezie. That is about as good a compliment as you will ever get--to be like Weezie.

There was always a clear sense that Weezie's love and caring was unconditional. As a small child, no matter how naughty you were, you knew she loved you anyway. Throughout my growing up years, anytime I felt sorry for myself because I thought no one cared, I always knew that Weezie did. She was just so solid, like Mom, except Mom was a rock. Weezie was like a soft mattress topped off with a fluffy feather comforter.

If I were to describe my aunts in one word, it would be "nice." Occasionally, when I need to make a tough decision I ask myself: "What would Weezie do?" or "What would Shuppy think?" The answer would be a savvy, insightful conclusion.

One of the best compliments I ever received was from a young man I raised from the age of two. He remarked that as he gained exposure to the world he came to realize that my two children and I are the nicest people he has ever known. I describe all four of my brothers and their children as nice as well. Shuppy and Weezie apparently did their job well. Their love and devotion shaped five little people, probably in more ways than they can imagine, and that influence created a legacy that is descending through generations.

Grandpa and Grandma Bray, Mom's parents, were exceptional people. They were also nice. We were taught to revere them, and for good reason. Not only were they hard-working reputable farmers and pillars of the community, they were just the most wonderful, kind, generous and upbeat people, the kind of Christians who have a glow about them--a spirit of love. They did have that edge of judgment common to the midwestern culture, but they were kind, playful and full of charity. Both were community minded and church focused. I don't think they would have liked the hateful political climate propagated on the radio and internet today. It would have hurt them deeply to see how mean people in this country have become.

Grandma Bray was a good-natured, somewhat silly character, as reflected in this incident. She was playing with a little tot who picked up a ball and said, "Mine." She picked up another ball and said, "Mine, and it is bigger than yours." Then she smiled and handed it to him.

If we pouted about anything she shamed us by sticking out her lower lip, upping us with her own dramatic pouting routine. She sang sadly about how nobody liked her and she was going to the garden to eat worms. Next she went into considerable detail describing the worms, wrinkling up her nose and scrunching up her face. Of course this snapped us out of our own little "woe is me" episode, and we ended up laughing. What kid wouldn't break into a giggle over that scenario? When she tucked us in at night she told us not to let the bed bugs bite. I never actually worried about bed bugs. Grandma made things up.

Grandma and Grandpa Bray had mulberry trees. We climbed them and gorged ourselves. Our bare feet were purple from stepping on those that fell out of the trees. It was impossible to wash it off. Grandma had a fit when we came in the house. She was a delightful terror.

As with Dad, I feel the need to define the term fit in respect to Grandma lest anyone conclude she was provoked into profoundly irrational temper tantrums. Fit is a term of the era. Mom threatened us with the prospect saying things like: "Wash your ears or Grandma will have a fit." "Grandma would have a fit if she saw this banana peel under the sofa cushion." "If you pee in anything but the toilet, Grandma will have a fit." This last threat was necessary because of my four brothers. It was not directed at me. Mom was not aware that I peed on the roof of the sheep shed (that was a sporting event--details later). Other than that, I never peed anywhere but in the toilet--that I recall.

As a child I saw Grandma have a fit on numerous occasions, and although it was actually more of a good-natured drama than a punishment, it had just enough edge to it that I didn't want to deal with her having another one.

Grandma could also have a "conniption" we were told, something I assumed was similar to a fit. The distinction was not clear to me as I was never sure I ever actually saw a conniption, but I was relatively certain I did not want her to have one of those either. Then there was the frightening prospect of a "conniption fit," some kind of compound reaction which took Grandma's response to a whole new level, something I suspect on the scale of a fit on speed. No one I know of ever saw one of those, but the threat was always there, omnipresent and foreboding.

You could also get a "jawing," which is something similar to a rant with flair. Grandma had attitude when she was jawing, the rhythm of which would put a rapper to shame. That's not all. Grandma had a plethora of attack strategies in her arsenal. She sometimes threatened to "box our ears." I don't recall ever getting my ears boxed. I have threatened my grandchildren with the prospect, but if I had to execute it, I'd have no idea what to do. Between fits, conniptions, jawings, and threats to box our ears, Grandma kept us in line. She was a force to be reckoned with and Mom used intimidating threats of her reactions often, even into my adulthood, and they had their intended effect.

We got baths only on Saturday nights, so sometimes we were crusty dirty when we went to visit Grandma Bray. She'd have a fit, drag us into the bathroom, and scrub us up. We came out smelling of Jergen's lotion with red blotches all over us from the scrubbing. Grandma hated dirt.

For little people, we were pretty good at destruction. For some reason, probably the rainy day desperation of an exasperated parent, Mom let us ride our tricycles in the dining room. We scraped the buffet with the handles, scarring it beyond repair. It was a family heirloom and Grandma Bray had a really big fit over our mutilating it. In fact, she had repeated fits, jawing us every time she came to our house.

Once Mom turned us loose upstairs unsupervised with glue and construction paper for Halloween. She spent some time showing us what to do with it, but I remember being quite confused. We were pre-school age and had never seen glue or construction paper before. We figured it out, though, and stuck torn pieces of orange and black construction paper all over the newly wallpapered blue and pink floral walls in Mom and Dad's bedroom. When Grandma found out, she had a fit and chastised us royally. We kept Grandma busy.

Grandpa was injured in a car accident in California on vacation. He and Grandma were hit by a drunk driver. After that he walked with a cane and used it to poke kids and to flip Grandma's skirt. Grandpa didn't hear well. Grandma's voice box was damaged during thyroid surgery and she talked in a raspy whisper. (To everyone's surprise, this did not hamper her ability to jaw us. In fact, it enhanced the impact. In a peculiar way, it was downright scary.) We laughed at Grandpa and Grandma arguing playfully when he couldn't hear and she couldn't talk.

When I was three years old, Grandpa was shingling the wash house and left the shingle cutter out. My brother and I played with it, and the blade cut my fingers pretty bad. Someone carried me into the house with me crying so hard I couldn't catch my breath. I heard Grandpa say it was his fault, and he shouldn't have let us play with it. I'm sure he felt really bad about it.

Everyone was fussing over me, and someone held me in the car all the way to the doctor, my hand wrapped in a towel. I look at my three-year-old grandson's wee fingers and wonder how awful it must have been for my folks to see my little fingers all cut up like that. Visualizing a shingle cutter today, I'm amazed that my tiny fingers were not completely cut off.

The fingers were saved, although one never healed right. I had surgery on it when I was in high school. After the procedure, it throbbed when I held it down to my side. Holding it up allowed me to innocently give everyone with whom I came into contact a resounding finger. I took great delight in going around school with a bandaged third finger, somewhat reminiscent of a miniature mummy, and the humor in this entertained me thoroughly. I had to have surgery again thirty years later and joyfully gave everyone at the office and in the board room the finger. It gives me trouble still today, sixty-some years later, and I may give a whole new audience the finger soon.

In contrast to Grandpa and Grandma Bray, my Dad's father, Grandpa Walter, was widowed, smoked a pipe, didn't go to church, and was crotchety. When he came to Sunday dinner, he wore a felt hat and black lace-up dress shoes with his overalls. A man I knew in Chicago showed up for a date in a hat, black lace-up shoes like Grandpa Walter's, and substantial tweed. I was already traumatized by his appearance when he took out his pipe after dinner. It didn't help that his first name was Gephart. Perhaps I could have gotten past the name, but there was no way I could get into a man who reminded me of Grandpa Walter, although the guy did have a sense of humor. When I waved pipe smoke away from my face, he said "Hi" and waved back. When food dropped off his fork, he looked up at the ceiling like it had come from above. I laughed, but humor could not overcome the grandpa image spinning in my head--and the tweed.

We kids were sure Grandpa Walter didn't like us. When we were quite young, we were jumping on a metal tank turned upside down in the back yard, pretending to be Indians dancing around a camp fire. This made a tremendous noise. Grandpa watched us from the house looking grouchy. For some reason we decided to take our clothes off, I guess to shock him, and we danced around naked. (You can't make this stuff up.) Mom saw us and stopped the madness. I expect she was mortified. Certainly she must have had considerable concern about the brood of perverts she was raising. As a parent you take what you get.

I don't remember much about Grandma Walter except our being at their house when she died of heart disease, I am guessing in her early fifties. We kids were very young, but we knew something was up. Mom took coloring books and paper dolls to keep us occupied. Everyone was whispering. The hush in the house made quite an impression since we were not accustomed to being quiet, except when staring at Dale, the teenage farm hand Dad hired. I was in love with Dale.

We moved to a white farm house on a dirt road when I was four. I always remembered it as large, but I visited it a few years back, just before it was to be demolished, and was surprised to find it quite small. It had a porch and a huge yard all around.

The facilities on Iowa farms were just moving into the era of indoor plumbing and hot water heaters. Dad installed a bathroom before we moved in, so the chamber pot was no longer needed and all three of us kids took baths in the tub together. Before that we took baths in large pans in the yard or in the kitchen sink. Water from the well was limited, so we bathed only on Saturdays so we would be clean for church. Dad installed a tank on the top of the wash house to catch rain water for his showers.

I and brother Dallas getting a bath

Midwestern farms in those years were typically composed of a white farm house and many wooden outbuildings, often painted red. Typical structures included a barn, chicken house, wash house, tool shed, corn crib, hog shed, garage, and possibly even a silo--all wonderful places for a child to explore. Today, most of those structures are gone. Many white houses remain, surrounded by one or two steel buildings with metal siding.

Our farm was 160 acres, a quarter of a square mile, located a mile outside of Prescott, a very small town of about 300. White farm houses like ours dotted the landscape. This was a normal sized farm for the 1940's and typically supported a family. By the sixties this was no longer true. The economy changed and more land was required to survive financially. In the forties and fifties, boys got out of high school and began farming. By the sixties they could no longer make it unless they had family land. Not only was more land required to be successful, the price per acre was up from a few hundred dollars an acre to thousands. Small scale farms could never earn enough from crops to pay for the land and equipment. Corporations and large, established farmers bought out the smaller farms, and they faded away.

As a result, the small Iowa towns that were so vibrant have become almost ghost towns today. Prescott is one of those communities. There is no gas station, feed store, general store, drug store, restaurant, hardware store, bank, or barber shop anymore. Only a post office, a tavern and some vacant buildings are left. The junior high and high school are no more. Houses are getting old and run down. There was once a movie theater in which you could see a show for ten cents. The American Legion no longer has dances, and the telephone building in which an operator routed calls stands vacant. It is sad to see Prescott as it is today compared to the vibrancy I remember.

FREE-RANGE CHILDREN

We were free-range children, allowed to explore the farm freely and expansively. This is illustrated by the fact that at a relatively young age two of my brothers wheeled their toddler sibling to a pond in the pasture in an old worn out stroller. It wasn't working well, so they threw it into the pond. This left them with a toddler to haul back to the house, if they didn't throw him in as well. The toddler was, no doubt, delighted to be included on a high-trek adventure with the big kids--completely unaware of the precariousness of his situation. Common sense prevailed, and all three made it back to the homestead, probably with cockleburs stuck to pants and pond mud on shoes. This exploit is not that unusual. It was how free-range farm kids grew up, but you have to ask yourself: Where was Mom that this was possible?

That question is relatively easy to answer. She had a brood to manage and all the required farm work, gardening, laundry, cooking, canning, and housework. In the early years when she went shopping, three of us held on to her coattails as she went from store to store. She was carrying the fourth. One time in the dime store, I got hold of another woman's coattail by mistake and began tagging her around the store, which I am sure was quite a shock to her. When I realized it, I was a wreck. Where was Mom? I remember the fear as I wandered the store searching for her. As we got older, we each got a dime to spend. I often spent mine on office supplies. Really, I did.

Mom bribed us to be good by promising Dairy Queen treats at the end of a shopping excursion. Four of us were piled in the back seat of the car on the way home with our ice cream cones. Initially we competed to see who could eat their ice cream first. Then someone said to the winners, "Your ice cream is gone, and I still have mine." This introduced a paradigm shift that reshuffled the deck big time. We each wanted to be the one with ice cream left when everyone else's was gone. The result was drippy, sticky messes in the back seat as we struggled to muster enough self-discipline to delay the last few bites.

Along with the warm, fuzzy times, there were worrisome ones as well. There were a lot of people crippled from polio in the forties and I recall rather vividly Mom and Dad worrying about us kids getting it. They fretted about polio season and people in iron lungs. It was a very scary thing. My first grade teacher got it, which brought the prospect of one of us getting it even closer to home and increased the daunting tone of those times.

We didn't go to the doctor for much, but when the polio vaccine came out, the folks hauled us down to Doctor Brunk's office pronto. The early vaccine was in injection form. Since there were no immunizations back then, we had never had shots before and had no clue what was about to befall us. Mom and Dad displayed considerable excitement over the vaccine. Consequently, we were anticipating our polio shots with great delight. That is, until the first one of us got one. It was not pretty. Later, though, we bragged about the shots. In our own minds, we had been very brave. Smallpox shots came out next, a wicked vaccine that left big scars on our arms that are visible to this day. We got them at school where you desperately did not want to cry, but they really hurt. There was child chatter about who cried getting their shot.

Polio was a seasonal illness, hitting in the summer months. From that perspective, winter was a welcome relief, but Iowa winters were bitterly cold. Dad got up early and fired up the wood stove so there was some warmth when we kids got up. We awakened to Mom yelling "everybody up" and the smell of bacon frying. Often we brought our clothes downstairs to dress by the fire, hovering around the stove with our fronts hot and our backs cold or vice versa, turning like chickens on rotisseries.

We were still fairly little when Dad hired a teenage farm hand named Dale. We kids worshipped Dale and followed him around making a general nuisance of ourselves while he tried to work. We were obsessed with this new distraction and chanted "Dale, Dale, Dale, Dale, Dale" while chewing gum. I was in love with Dale. Mom prepared a big farmers' meal at lunch every day, and he sat at the kitchen table eating fried chicken, mashed potatoes and gravy, and corn on the cob with all of us staring at him. One day he winked at me. I will never forget it. Be still my heart. Is it possible I've been attracted to country boys all these years looking for Dale?

Another farm hand bragged to us kids that he could jump over the barn if he wanted to. We got all excited about the prospect and were severely disappointed when he said he didn't want to. We tried to hang with him, but he hid from us.

When the rains didn't happen, crops failed, and Dad had to sell the hogs. Mom struggled to feed her brood. Because we had laying hens and she raised brooder chickens, we had eggs and chicken over and over when money was tight. It is hard to imagine getting tired of home fried chicken and eggs prepared any way you want, but we were sick of them, so Dad cooked eggs over a fire outside, even for supper, and we thought they were delicious. Mom opened cans of baked beans and spread them on toast with mayonnaise. We loved our bean sandwiches. When times weren't so lean, I still wanted them.

Dad raised hogs and cattle off and on throughout the years and had a milk cow for awhile. We kids drank well over a gallon a day. In the refrigerator the cream separated from the milk and floated to the top of the container. Mom skimmed it off to use in cooking. Cream or bacon grease were generously added to almost every dish.

We had sheep at one point. The old, dilapidated sheep shed had a corrugated metal roof. We kids climbed to the top of the building, peed at the top of the slanted roof and watched excitedly to see whose pee got to the bottom first. We had pee races, yes we did. (You can't make this stuff up.) For obvious anatomical reasons, I never won any pee races, but I was happy for whichever brother did.

When we raised hogs, we had plenty of bacon. Mom poured the bacon grease into a jar on the stove so it was handy to add flavor to almost everything we ate. Chicken was fried in bacon grease or lard rendered from the hogs we butchered. Lard was also used to make pie crusts until Crisco was invented. Iowa women fried everything in a cast iron skillet. (I was married and poring over a Betty Crocker cook book when I discovered broiling.) Even a T-bone steak was dipped in flour and fried. Mom never broiled, and no one had ever heard of a charcoaler in those early years, although Dad developed a fascination with them later.

One day a bad storm came in so fast that Dad got caught in the field. By the time he headed to the house large hail was beating down. Mom and we kids were standing on the front porch worrying when we saw him running for the house with a bucket over his head. The hail made loud clanking noises as it hit the metal bucket. He was whooping and hollering. We kids found this tremendously exciting, and we wanted to run around in the hail with buckets on our heads. Mom was having none of it. However, one stormy day she was distracted, and we got our chance. When she discovered us running around in the yard, squealing delightedly, occasionally crashing into each other, hail clanking loudly on the buckets on our heads, she yelled from the porch for us to get in the house before we got struck by lightening. We rarely did anything Mom asked on the first request and made an additional round or so in the yard before giving it up. No one got struck by lightening, but the ear damage was likely equivalent to a shotgun blast or a front row seat at a rock concert. Years later, I was able to top the boyhood BB gun stories of a bunch of businessmen by telling about running around in a hail storm with a bucket on my head.

Dad's antics were always entertaining. He sang silly songs to us kids, some of them rather adult. Mom disapproved, but he did it anyway. He was ornery and irreverent. One of his favorite songs was about having a drink, it all going to his head, and him wanting to go home and go to bed. He also sang about getting out of prison and, our favorite, dead skunks. He even came up with a song about a monkey getting drunk, which I sing to my grandchildren at bath time, when their parents aren't present. It is important to pass on family traditions.

We kids loved his songs and sang them ourselves much to Mom's chagrin. Being the upstanding Christian woman she was, she didn't deal well with her children singing songs about being drunk or getting out of prison. Roadkill songs were a bit more tolerable, but not much. I don't believe we ever sang Dad's songs in public or in front of Grandma Bray, who would have surely had a fit. Mom's disapproval registered just enough to cause us to be civilized in public.

Mom and Dad lay in bed at night and talked, mostly about us kids. We were the center of their world--all they really cared about. We all slept upstairs in pretty cramped conditions, two of us in the same room as the folks. Their conversations kept us awake. One of us would yell: "Shut up!" They would stop briefly only to start up again shortly thereafter. Soon someone else from another room would yell: "Shut up!" It might take several more shut ups from several different sources to get them to be quiet. If necessary, we stretched it out for emphasis: "S-h-u-u-t U-u-p!" This brings to mind a television show wherein family members lovingly called out "Goodnight" from various rooms throughout the house. In contrast, our family was yelling, "Shut up!"

Some people find the phrase shut up offensive. Our family did not. If you wanted someone to be quiet, you said "Shut up." If we cried for no good reason Mom said, "Shut up, or I will give you something to cry about." Occasionally she delivered on that threat. She was generally a pushover, though. I remember her chasing us around with a yardstick and us running and laughing. Soon she was laughing as well.

One day she was mad at me about something and commanded me to "Come here." I refused. "You come here right now!" she demanded, which took her instruction to a whole new level. Still, I maintained my position and said, "I don't have to, and you can't make me because you can't run," and I took off. She caught me in short order, dragging me by the arm toward the house. I'd never seen her run before and didn't know she could do that, so this was quite a shock. Years later I learned she was the fastest runner in her high school.

We kids were constantly messing up the house and Mom, busy with farm work, canning, laundry and meals, struggled to keep up. She resorted to drastic means and swept our toys into a pile in the middle of a room and commanded with great authority that we get our stuff or she would throw it away. This caused quite a scramble as we retrieved our items, only to place them in other rooms and mess them up.

After lunch we sometimes hid in the corn field to avoid naps. Mom yelled threats from the front porch with growing intensity until we finally gave up our hiding spot, or we may have given it up because we saw a huge, creepy spider among the corn. When she did corral us, there was a lot of bed jumping. She napped us all in the same room, an invitation to mutiny. I can imagine her in the kitchen listening to all the racket in the bedroom, probably just grateful to have us out of her hair for awhile.

Mom was skilled at crochet and made volumes of doilies, which were starched and spread on most every surface in the house. Even the toilet tank was adorned with a doily. Sofa throws, called afghans, made of colorful crocheted squares were thrown over couches. Women made colorful intricate quilts. Every woman had a sewing machine. Feed sacks were made out of printed fabric, and after the farmers used up the feed, women laundered the fabric and sewed clothes out of it. I had feed sack dresses when I was small. Women wore homemade calico dresses and printed aprons. The farmers wore overalls, work shirts, lace-up work boots and caps, often made out of the same striped fabric as their overalls. Their arms and faces were tan, but their foreheads were white from wearing the caps.

On hot summer days, Dad frequently drove his brood to the lake or to a pool in a neighboring town to swim after he got in from the field. We usually piled in a few neighbor kids as well. Since we didn't have seat belts, the only limit to how many kids you could haul around was how deep you could stack them.

My brothers built tree houses, huge multi-room, multi-level tree houses. Perhaps I am exaggerating, but in my child's mind they were wonderful tree houses. Older brother Dallas and a cousin made a ladder so they could pull it up and keep the rest of us out. They sat up there in their exclusive club and taunted us while we begged and groused around below, members of the lower caste. We made play houses in any vacant place we could find--feed bins, out-buildings, corncribs. Wonderful play houses. Using clothes lines, sheets, and blankets we made huge, long multi-compartment tents in the yard. In the house we made tents so big they filled a room. Wonderful tents. It was wonderful.

When I was a small child, Dad killed a bull snake and left it in the yard. I was fascinated with it and pulled it around by the tail with a pair of pliers. He got the outrageous idea to make me a necklace out of the bones. I remember every detail of the process: Dad boiling the snake in an iron pot over a fire outside, sorting out the bones and arranging them by size, me excitedly obtaining food coloring from the kitchen to dye them pink (which aroused Mom's curiosity), searching for string just the right size, and Dad tying the knot after we strung them up. When he put the string of bones carefully over my head, he was my hero, and I was his very special little girl. I worshiped him. I wore the necklace to school one day. The guys thought it was cool. The girls, not so much. I doubt they envied me, but nothing could change my mind about the beauty and wonder of my necklace. I still have it, and I wear it occasionally as an alternative to getting a nose ring or a snake tattoo.

We were blessed with lots of puppies growing up. Happiness is a litter of squirmy, panting puppies jumping around and licking you as you lie on the ground. There is nothing else like it, short of holding a baby while he sleeps. Farm dogs Queeny and Teeny produced a continuous supply of mutts, and each kid picked and named his own pup from each litter. As the pups were weaned, we had to give them up, but on the farm a child becomes accustomed to animals coming and going.

> I wanted my kids to have the puppy experience, so we raised fluffy little white bichon frises for awhile. We always named the smallest male dog in the litter Killer. The little runt's name entertained potential buyers, and he was often the first to go. There is something magical about a tiny white fluffy thing frolicking around happily with the name Killer.

We were a pretty excitable bunch. On Christmas Day, the first kid up woke everyone else up. Mom and Dad wouldn't let us come downstairs until he started a fire to warm the house and we were all up and gathered at the top of the stairs together. Barefoot and in our flannel pajamas, we wiggled and juggled for position, hardly able to contain ourselves, but assuring that the smaller siblings were postured to safely negotiate the steps. I think the folks were as excited as we were.

The anticipation was almost more than we could stand, and we all had to pee. When the folks finally gave the word, we flew down the stairs and into the living room where each of us had a chair with a stocking hung on it which was filled with an orange, some nuts, and maybe a small toy. We surveyed the jackpot of toys on our chairs and pretended to be excited about the orange and nuts. We were crossing our legs, holding our crotches, and dancing a jig. When we couldn't hold it anymore, we paraded to the bathroom. It was chaos. Mom and Dad had a glow about them on Christmas mornings, delighting in the joyfulness.

Our main toy was on our chair with a few other things placed around and below it. Each one of us got one nice thing, which was something we requested after seeing it in a store in town or in the Sears catalogue, and we got a number of little things. Mom collected Green Stamps at the grocery store. We kids happily licked pages and pages of them, sticking them in little books so she could redeem them for gifts. When I was older I got a Monopoly game, one of my more memorable presents. I played for many hours with friends and brothers over the years. We played with abandon, making up our own rules.

We didn't exchange gifts as much as people do today. Sometimes we drew names, but mostly we just got together and ate with Grandpa and Grandma Bray, Shuppy, and Weezie, and their families. Brother Dally gave Weezie monkey gifts--all kinds of monkeys. Mom made him stop after a few years. Weezie didn't know what to do with all those monkeys. I was disappointed. Weezie was too nice to throw a fit when she got a monkey gift, but it was still fun to watch her reaction.

Next to Christmas, May Day was our favorite holiday. Every year on May 1st we made and decorated little baskets, usually out of construction paper, filling them with candy. Mom had a knack for making exceptionally elaborate baskets. We deposited them on the doorsteps of friends and neighbors, yelled "May Basket" and then ran like crazy while kids flew out of houses or appeared from hiding spots and lookout posts to chase us down and kiss us. Of course we got to reciprocate when baskets were left on our porch. A lot of strategic planning went into surprising friends and neighbors with May Baskets so you could get away without getting caught and kissed.

We spent every May 1st anticipating the deliveries, setting up lookouts, and curiously observing any car coming down the road. A friendly May basket competition developed with a large family living nearby. It was quite a fiasco with all us kids running around screaming and chasing each other. The feuding family was composed of girls older than we were, and I took great delight in them catching my older brother and kissing him. It was impossible for me to ever get the better of him, so I vicariously enjoyed other girls doing so. We continued to do May Baskets into our early teens when most kids had outgrown it, mostly because the feud with the neighbor girls was so enticing.

I sent an early copy of this book to one of these girls, and on the next May 1st, fifty-some years after our neighborhood fiascos, a UPS man delivered a May Basket to my front porch. It came all the way to Oklahoma from Florida. Had I realized soon enough what it was, I would have surely chased down the delivery man and given him a big kiss.

FREE-RANGE CHICKENS

We were free-range children, running all over the place unrestricted. Chickens ran free on the farm as well. In modern terms you could say they were free-range chickens. Everyone was constantly tiptoeing around chicken poop which was all over the place. We went barefoot all summer. When we stepped in chicken poop it squished up between our toes which sent us scampering for the water pump.

Of all the animals on the farm, chickens were what captivated us kids the most. They were accessible. With a little effort you could catch one and carry it around or whatever. There was a lot of whatever going on. To small children, chickens were at the lowest end of the pecking order with us just one rung up. This was not true of the other animals. They could get the better of us, but chickens, well, they were fair game, except for a couple of roosters who periodically made it clear where we really stood in the farmyard order of things.

The roosters were mean and intimidating. They chased us when we were small, wings spread to make them appear larger, necks outstretched, beaks forward. Once my brother and I declared war on them. We put on layers and layers of clothes so they couldn't peck us, took up a garden hoe and rake and went rooster fighting. We may have believed we won, but we did high-tail it for the front porch a couple of times with a raging rooster on our heels, garden tools abandoned in the dust. I can imagine Mom observing this from the kitchen window and wondering if her children were going to turn out all right. We envisioned ourselves as such warriors, while she was probably resigning herself to the much repeated thought that with children you take what you get. At any rate, as we got older and bigger the pecking order shifted, and we could look at a threatening, mean-spirited rooster with considerable arrogance and say: "Really?"

Our hometown had a pet parade as a community event. We had a couple of dogs and barn cats. With four brothers, all the real pets were spoken for, and I had to decide between a chicken and a baby pig. I chose the chicken, which was significantly quieter and somewhat easier to control than a squealing, twisting boar, at least so I thought.

Mom and I went out to the chicken house to pick out the hen to be my pet for the day. We selected an old one, thinking she would be mellow, overlooking the fact that she was excessively grumpy. Mom rigged up a basket for me to carry her in, dressed me in a bonnet and calico dress, and I carried "the little red hen" in the pet parade. Not being a real pet, the hen was not fond of the idea. Additionally, she was hungry. Chickens are always hungry. As I was struggling to load her into the basket, she spotted a mole on my neck, decided it was something to eat and pecked it off. (You can't make this stuff up.) I bled briefly, but was determined to be in the parade with my brothers, so I somehow wrangled her into the basket and kept her there long enough to get down the street in spite of her obvious and legitimate concerns about the proximity of several hyped-up bird dogs straining on their leashes.

After the parade, Mom was wrestling with limited success to transfer the angry "little red hen" into the trunk of the car. This was a good time, I thought, to suggest that we eat her for supper. Since she was an egg-laying hen and we kids had already murdered two of her compadres (one because of a wanton brother with grand hunting delusions and a BB gun and another because of her inability to fly when thrown off a tall building), Mom made it clear that having her for supper was not an option.

One of my brothers was randomly shooting chickens with a BB gun. With their thick feathers, this simply startled them, a generally harmless but entertaining outcome, at least for the perpetrator. Eventually, though, his luck ran out and he killed one, which shocked the pahoot out of him. He confessed to Mom who simply dressed her out and served her for supper.

Another brother and I injured a hen by tossing her off the roof of an outbuilding which meant another fried chicken dinner and Mom noting that with children you take what you get. When we fed the chickens and gathered eggs, the setting hens often pecked at us as we reached into the nest for eggs, so we had to grab them quickly by the necks and pull them out. The one we threw off the roof just happened to be an enthusiastic serial pecker. I reckon we showed her. It was group think--a dangerous thing. Neither of us would have done that on our own.

We hypnotized chickens. Really, we did. (You can't make this stuff up.) We put their heads under their wings and moved them around and around in a circle. They went into a coma-like state and remained dazed for some time afterwards. We left hypnotized chickens here and there all over the place.

At a young age I started dressing (butchering) chickens. Mom and Aunt Weezie raised them in brooder houses. Hundreds arrived from the feed store in card board boxes dotted with round holes for air. They were cute fuzzy little yellow chicks. I loved them. Some weeks later when they were mature enough, I killed them and cut them up with a butcher knife.

There were hundreds to dress out at one time. Mom and Weezie convinced me that dressing chickens was fun and bragged on me when I did it. Of course, that got me going, and each day I tried to beat my own record of how many I could dress in a day.

Dressing them involved holding them upside down by their feet, putting their heads on the ground under a broom stick, stepping on both sides of the stick, putting your whole weight on it, pulling till the chickens' heads separate from their bodies and throwing them into the yard to flop around a bit. Then we cut them up with huge butcher knives. We didn't have freezers so the ones Mom didn't sell were stored in a rented freezer compartment at a meat locker in town. There is nothing pretty about killing an animal, but on the farm it was done as a matter of course, and we thought nothing of it. If a dog killed a chicken, he was going to kill more and the farmer shot him. If dogs took down a small calf, they were out of here. When an animal broke a leg, he was gone. My favorite dog was lost that way. Today I couldn't kill a chicken. I wish I didn't eat them, but I do.

Animal relations were complicated on the farm, but another factor, religion, generated its share of awkward moments, as well. My Sunday school class was studying Ruth and Esther and their endless journey through the desert. The teacher prepared a skit about it to present to the congregation. A classmate and I portrayed Ruth and Esther as they settled in for the night after a long day of wandering. We were to bring fruit from home to eat for our supper. I innocently brought a banana. When we spread a blanket on the stage, sat down, and began eating our supper, teenage boys in the front row were overcome. Giggling outrageously to the point of disrupting the program, they simply could not contain themselves. A few chuckles rumbled throughout the congregation as well. Although I was too young to grasp the innuendo, I was astute enough to interpret the boy's hysteria as a sign that I should be embarrassed, and I was.

HARD LABOR - AN OBSESSION

Dressing chickens was not the only work to be done on the farm. We had many chores, but there were five of us kids to do them, and with four brothers I was spared much of it. Interestingly, I viewed this as being left out. I really wanted to milk the cow and drive the tractor but was relegated to chicken chores.

Finally, I was able to encroach on the task of hauling wood from the woodpile to the back porch, which my brothers happily relinquished to their sister. I interpreted this as meaning that I was somebody. I was all over it. In my mind this was serious chore work, a considerable step up from gathering eggs. It was my first experience with the feeling you get from doing more than you were asked. When I overheard Mom bragging to Grandma Bray about how much wood I hauled, it fired me up. I was a wood hauling fool, cramming the back porch with as much wood as I could get in there. This accomplishment reinforced an already developing work ethic. Both Mom and Dad set a good example, and this work ethic was ingrained in my brothers as well. When old enough, the Walter boys earned reputations as good workers and were much in demand as farm hands.

Iowa farm kids were known for being hard workers. Years later when I worked in the employment office for an airline in Chicago, we liked to hire the farm boys to load luggage onto airplanes because they were steady and such good workers. The unions had to teach them the proper pace and to take breaks.

In addition to convincing me that dressing chickens and hauling wood was a fun time, Mom was equally persuasive in the category of washing windows. She even shipped me off to Aunt Weezie's to wash her windows, where I got paid for doing so.

Actually, it was fun, and I was a window washing fool. To me work was fun and is to this day. Going to bed at night bone tired after physical labor has always been a high for me.

No one had to con me into gardening. I cheerfully took over Mom's garden as soon as I was able. It was huge, I'm guessing close to half an acre. I loved hoeing and pulling weeds and delighted in the feeling of looking back at the neat, clean rows after I'd worked them. Everyone had a garden and the ladies were always canning with steaming pressure cookers, storing jars of fruits, vegetables, and pickles in caves and basements with the potatoes and onions until freezers came into favor and changed everything.

Hauling buckets of water from a pump in the back yard, I watered plants, pretending they were speaking to me gratefully saying: "Thank you, thank you, thank you." I say that in my squeaky little plant voice to this day when I water plants, much to the delight of my grandson. I picked strawberries, cucumbers, peas, and beans; harvested sweet corn, lettuce, and tomatoes; and dug up potatoes and onions. I used to take care of my little brother Kelly, putting him in a stroller and hauling him to the garden while I worked. He ate strawberries and dirt.

As a teen, I still thought work was fun, and I wanted to make money. Mom and I got a job cleaning a laundromat daily. We split the money, giving me steady income for the first time. I'm not certain of this, but I think I earned twenty dollars a month. I do know that for the first time I had a $20 bill. I also cleaned house for an elderly lady in town. Then, the fact that I was a farm girl took on renewed significance when I finally moved into the big leagues. I got to work with the boys in the fields.

Farmers rotated corn and soy bean crops each year because corn took nitrogen out of the soil and beans put it back in. They didn't have the fertilizers we have today, relying mostly on manure and crop rotation. Corn from the previous crop grew up into the beans, decreasing the value of the crop. We were hired to walk the bean fields with machetes and cut out corn and weeds. This was primarily man's work, but a neighbor gave me a break and tried me out. After that, I was in. It is important to note that there were huge, I mean, HUGE spiders in the bean fields. This is relevant because my walking among them demonstrates the degree of my determination to work and earn money.

Most of my adult life I've spent my Saturdays and Sundays working diligently in a yard, garden, or flower bed, and I have done considerable landscaping. I've probably planted more trees than most men. I bought trees so large one time that I couldn't get them out of the truck I had borrowed. I told the guy if he wanted his truck back, he had to help. All this gardening was after working a job all week and taking care of a family, but although it was hard work, it was a relaxing diversion. I always had flower beds on all four sides of all of my homes. People rang my doorbell to ask how I grew such lush flowering plants in the Oklahoma sun. The secret is Osmocote fertilizer and water.

Gardening was always joyful work until a few years back when I realized I could no longer lug around bags of dirt, manure, and mulch and still stand up straight or get out of a chair without engaging in a three-step process. No one wants to roll off a couch onto your knees and walk with your body at a right angle for several minutes in front of a boyfriend, or roll around on your back in the yard like a turtle. Now all I have is a six-foot-by-six-foot front yard and two balcony patios. I don't have amazing flowers anymore; however, I have a view of the Tulsa skyline which lights up at night, blooms in all four seasons, and doesn't require watering. I'm so over gardening.

I recently spotted poison ivy in my small yard. I stood there going "eeeeek" along with a neighbor man who did the same thing. He was no good to me at all. I hired someone to get it out. As I said, I am so over gardening.

The early years on the farm were sweet. Then we had to go to school. There was no kindergarten in the forties and we were thrown into first grade all day where I learned to eat glue, sharpen pencils, and deal with the shame of bad perms, bangs cut too short, and being in the slow reader group. Overall, I was pretty much confused about the whole school thing.

SCHOOL AND ALL THAT IT IMPLIES

When my brothers and I started elementary school we became aware that there were city kids and country kids, at least that is how we saw it in our little minds. We talked tough about how country kids were better, and we were very snooty about it. This was a reaction to the fact that the city kids all knew each other, and we were more like members of a remote Samoan tribe.

Older brother Dally with his fun loving personality assimilated quickly. Denny and I were a bit shy. He took considerable teasing because he wore suspenders up through third grade. I suspect this was because he inherited his pants from his older brother. I don't remember my early elementary school years fondly, although I wasn't really traumatized by them either. I was simply happier when I was at home with my tribe.

We were shown a film in third or fourth grade that I remember to this day, although the topic of it is so outrageous that I have to wonder if it was a dream. I'm certain it was not, but I can't imagine why anyone with good sense would show such a movie to small children. It was about children orphaned when their parents were killed in a car crash. My parents being killed in a car wreck had never occurred to me before I saw it. Now it did. I will never forget the gloomy scene where some severe looking people came to the home to take the children away. It was awful.

The film most likely was related to the temperance movement. This was the post-prohibition era and there was still considerable Temperance League activity going on. We children were asked to join the Loyal Temperance League that met at the home of an older church woman in town. We were induced to sign pledges to never drink liquor. I signed and kept my pledge for ten years. Now, many Margaritas, Kendall Jacksons, and some peach schnapps later, I don't honor that pledge. I was under age and under duress from that awful movie. It is hard to think of anything more emotionally disturbing than some of the cartoons today, but that film topped them. Orphaned children hauled off by a stern lady in a long black coat after their parents die, come on now, what ne'er-do-well shows that to small children? It was worse than the movie *Old Yeller*, which had Mom consoling a hysterical, sobbing brood.

I think many of the cartoons and movies today scare children. Shoot, they scare me. The most frightening thing my generation watched was cowboys shooting it up in westerns. Cowboys didn't explode back then as they do today, and the horses never got hurt. They did tricks. The worst horror movie was *The Blob,* which we saw at a drive-in movie theater with Aunt Shuppy who had so many cousins in the car she could smuggle some of us in without paying. (No one would believe there were that many of us in there.) We scared ourselves a hundred times over for months afterwards. All anyone had to do was yell "the blob" and everyone screamed and ran in aimless configurations throughout the house or yard. With the gore and violence in action movies today, I doubt that anyone, even a child, would be too intimidated by a black and white jello-like glob of gunk rolling around slowly seeking victims.

I digress. Back to school stuff. I had trouble learning to read and didn't really get it until fourth grade at which time I experienced a breakthrough. Every day we were required to stand up and read a paragraph in class. I was always embarrassed at how bad I did. One day the teacher, for whatever reason, assigned paragraphs ahead of time. I read mine over and over the night before. A rhythm kicked in, and the next day, not only could I read my paragraph well, I could read everything better.

I didn't make good grades in early elementary school. In fifth grade my teacher, Mrs. Brandt, told me if I tried real hard I could make the honor roll. I was shocked. I had no concept that such a thing was achievable. I thought good grades were for other kids. Her confidence inspired me. I tried harder, and two report cards later, I made it. She saw something in me that no one else did. I just needed someone to tell me what I could do. I had no idea. Mrs. Brandt changed my life, and I made good grades from then on.

I was not popular in grade school, and my perspective was that certain things such as being smart and popular were not possible for me. In general I was not bothered by this. I just accepted it as my place in the world. There was little aspiration to accomplish anything, and I was primarily concerned with avoiding embarrassment. One of the girls in third or fourth grade began calling me "Old Walters," her derivative of my maiden name. She was mean and a bully by today's standards. I wore a new bracelet to school one day and was probably acting quite proud of it. She made fun of it and was so menacing on the playground that I took it off, hid it in my desk, and never wore it again. I just wanted to get back to my safe place--home.

Mrs. Brandt brought me out of the dark academically, but I was never popular until seventh grade. The bully moved to another town. I grew a long pony tail and began running around with cool girlfriends. Most importantly, I got boobs. By my teen years, I was rocking it pretty good.

During the junior high years we were sent to church camp every summer. The first night I cried myself to sleep. Everyone in the cabin heard me. The counselor sweetly talked to me and patted my back which made me feel better, but the incident did not get me off to a good start with the other girls. I was never a part of the group, but rather on the fringe of things. The little Christian girls were not particularly inclusive.

Years later, teenage campers were hashing over old experiences. One of the girls said, "If you think that was bad, listen to this. I had to share a cabin with Nequita Walter." Her face expressed the eeeew factor as I sat there in shock and wonderment thinking: "Hey, that's me." I was going by the name Nikki by that time and was quite a different girl from the one crying in her bed. The snobby gal apparently didn't realize that girl and I were one and the same. A couple of people glanced at me awkwardly, and the girl suddenly realized what she had done. She seemed embarrassed at her unfortunate comment, and I rather enjoyed her discomfort. It was no big deal to me, though. I was smart and shaping up nicely. She was born on third base and thought she'd hit a triple, and I knew it.

Many people harbor hurtful memories of their early years. Writing this book allowed me to experience myself as a child and to do so with an enlightened, grown up perspective. I felt overwhelming compassion and love for her—that child who was me back then. I sensed her vulnerability, acknowledged her pain, and felt her joy. This shines a fresh light on the person I am now, the product of that child. I realize now the preciousness of that evolving little girl and of the woman I have become through her. Separated by time and experience, she and I are still one and the same, both loved by me with a renewed intensity.

Other than normal sibling rivalry, a few arm twistings and knuckle punches from my exuberant, fun-loving older brother, and what I perceived as an undeserved spanking when I thought I was too old to get one, life was good. There were the difficult elementary school adjustments, Mom telling embarrassing stories of our escapades to Grandma, and a multitude of other minor traumas. It was not all good, but it was mostly good. Moving into the difficult teenage years I hit a few bumps, but overall they were positive times as well.

TEENAGE TROUBLE

As my brothers and I entered our teens, we started getting into trouble. Nothing significant really, but we were feeling our oats. The community was small and gossip was a common pastime. After a couple of humiliating experiences of finding out about her children's antics through the rumor mill, Mom had a little talk with us. She was *mortified*, as she put it, from hearing about our mischievous incidents from some busybody and made it clear that in the future when we did something wrong we were to tell her immediately. Occasionally we complied.

The worst thing I ever did, other than drink vodka (once), was to break Coke bottles on the sidewalk outside of the American Legion dance hall with a couple of friends. We wanted so badly to be bad, but we were really candy-ass wimps, certainly by today's standards. Nevertheless, we did what we could with our so-o-o-o bad rock and roll mentality and without drugs, tattoos, body piercing, rap idols, and slutty role models. Anyway, the doorman saw us, so I confessed when I got home, knowing it would be all over town, and Mom would hear about it. I felt bad and wanted to protect her from being mortified.

I didn't get caught with the vodka and didn't drink enough to have to make swamp noises in the bathroom, so I made no confession over that misfortune. My brothers were into sports, and I don't believe they drank much either, although I do recall Dad joking that one of them had the flu as he was worshiping the porcelain god late one night in the bathroom--an isolated incident, I'm certain.

With four teenagers around the house, there were many youthful misfortunes. One of my brothers caught an upstairs bed on fire playing with lighter fluid. Unbeknown to the folks, we learned of this flaming fire activity from a cousin (you know who you are), and we all had played with it before. We poured a streak of fluid along the linoleum floor, lit it at one end, and watched in fascination as the flame flowed along the path. This time the bedding caught fire.

When my brother realized he was in over his head and could not put it out he began yelling "Fire! Fire!" with enough fervor that it was clear to everyone it was not a joke. We all came running. Mom yelled for us kids to bring water. I ran into my room and came back with a glass of water that was on my bedside stand-- not what she had in mind. Finally, out of desperation she opened the window and threw flaming bedding out of it, saving our old farm house from disaster. When Grandma Bray heard about it, she had a fit.

WATERMELON STEALING

There were not many entertainment opportunities in small Iowa towns in the sixties. Watermelon stealing was a pastime for teenagers. Farmers planted melons knowing teens would steal them. Certainly Dad did so. One year no one came to steal his melons, so he conspired with one of the town's teenage boys to bring some friends out after dark. Dad was waiting for them with a shotgun. When he shot it into the air, kids in the melon patch started screaming and scattering. He heard one of them say, "The old lady thinks we're stealing her chickens."

I got caught stealing watermelons once. A farmer pulled in the driveway, his car lights skimming his patch while a bunch of us were in it. I hit the ditch with some guy. The farmer stopped his car and asked what we were doing. We said we were taking a walk, got up, and strolled nonchalantly to the car parked down the road as he hustled off to confront other scattering perpetrators. Undoubtedly, when he saw cars along the road as he drove up, he knew what was happening in his watermelon patch and was anticipating the thrill of ambush.

When I went to business school in Omaha after high school, I told my new city friends in the dorm about watermelon stealing. A roommate, Marlene, came home with me one weekend and wanted to experience melon theft firsthand. Dad confided to me that it was too late in the season and there were no patches left that he knew of, but he did have a few melons remaining in ours. My brother and I drove Marlene around the countryside a bit to get her lost and then came up to our house from the back side and stole watermelons from our own patch. No shotguns were fired, but still a good time was had by all. Marlene got to be a criminal, and we got to pull off a cunning con.

TEENAGE ADVENTURE

Since there was little to do in the small town of Prescott, we were creative about diversions. For Halloween, boys prowled the streets upsetting outhouses, much to the dismay of the residents. Unfortunately, one of my brothers fell into a hole one night while in the act of "tipping," providing Mom and Dad with a significant clue when he got home as to what mischief he had been up to. Fortunately, he was successful at convincing a pal to pull him out, or he could have easily pulled an all-nighter.

For more proper entertainment, we went to a neighboring town to roller skate in the upstairs of a store. Skating to recorded organ music in rented skates on waffly wooden floors, we had to strategically dodge support poles grasped by novice skaters in the middle of the cramped rink in order to make our rounds. I was driving home from skating in a terrible ice storm with brother Denny and a couple of our friends. It was treacherous and very scary. The kids in the car were not attuned to the magnitude of the situation and were laughing and having a high old time. It was incredibly slick, and it took everything I had to keep the car on the road. I recall telling myself to focus, be strong, hold on, and get these partying fools home safely. I felt a huge sense of responsibility in the midst of all that silliness. I got everyone home. Mom was peering out the farm house window when I drove in the driveway with Denny safely in tow. She was a wreck worrying about us. I felt good. I delivered.

Summer fun was focused on swimming. As a teenager, I swam every day. My girlfriends and I used to get as tan as we could get. We used baby oil with iodine in it for tanning lotion. We believed the iodine attracted the sun. It's more likely it stained the skin. We were very tan.

I was a good swimmer and earned a Red Cross lifeguard badge. We wore them on the lower right side of our bathing suits. I was really proud of it. Although not that good at racing, I had amazing endurance. One day at lessons the instructor told us to swim laps until we couldn't swim anymore. Everyone eventually quit but me. I had to ultimately stop so they could close the pool. I don't recall how many miles I swam this day, but once I got my second wind, I felt like I could swim forever.

As teenagers, my husband and I were at a lake in Omaha and two girls who tried to swim across the lake got cramps and yelled for help. He, another man, and I swam out and pulled them in. As it turned out, I wasn't that much help. I almost didn't make it back myself. When we hit the shore I was so exhausted I couldn't even climb up the bank. I just lay there like a beached whale. People pulled us up. An ambulance took the girls off. They wrote us a thank you note, and our names were in the paper. I'm embarrassed we didn't take something that floated with us out into the lake, one of the first rules of rescue.

Farming is risky business and sometimes the crops failed. Dad supplemented our income by driving a school bus, which generated a small but steady income for nine months of the year. He drove the bus to our basketball games, much to our delight. He got to hear us sing *Beer, Beer for Old Prescott High* and other innovative beer drinking songs, not that we ever drank any to speak of.

Dad never really took to farming much. I think he did it because that is what all young men in rural Iowa did back then. There simply were no other options. Once the babies started coming, he was locked in. So he farmed. At any rate, it never really lit his fire. He seemed to enjoy the jobs he picked up more. If he got a good one, he'd let the farming slide. One year, when fertilizer became available, he had someone fertilize a field but never got around to planting anything in it. He grew the biggest crop of weeds you ever saw. Mom was embarrassed, and Grandpa Bray, a diligent farmer, was most likely appalled. Dad, on the other hand, was a happy man, working hard at his job and having a cool beer afterward at the tavern.

In later years, Dad worked road construction throughout Iowa. My teenage brothers worked with him in the summers. He and brother Denny were coming home for a break from the road crew. Denny was sleeping in the back seat. Dad stopped for gas, and not realizing Denny had gotten out to go to the restroom, left him there. Miles later he looked back to an empty back seat. He found Denny waiting patiently at the station. Dad was such a prankster that Denny wasn't worried. He thought Dad was playing a joke on him.

Dad and my brothers used to capture pigeons from barns in the area and sell them. This was done at night when the birds were roosting in the rafters. They trapped them in the barn by sneaking up and quickly closing doors to the farmer's hay loft, which Dad had carefully scouted out in daylight. I went with them a couple of times to hold the sacks in which they put the captured birds. I must have been in the way, or perhaps all the dust and hay in my hair and clothes was a problem for Mom. At any rate, I was deeply hurt when she said I couldn't go anymore.

It was quite a sight to see the boys scaling the rafters and jumping hay bales in pursuit of pigeons, beams from flashlights darting over the hay and rafters. Occasionally, one of them would be running along and disappear into a hole in the hay. It is a wonder no one was hurt. To them it was high adventure, and they gleefully hashed over tales of pigeon captures when the evening was done, too keyed up to go to bed. Mom enjoyed the frivolity of the stories, but she was a worry wart. I imagine she endured considerable angst on pigeon hunting nights, something equivalent to her anxiety when Dad headed out with a chain saw to get firewood. You could sense her torment.

We had pens full of pigeons, which was quite a novelty. Neighbors and people from town dropped by to see them. Dad tucked one in his shirt and turned it loose in the tavern. He put one in a buddy's truck. Pigeons were turning up everywhere.

DRIVING IOWA ROADS

Dad was a good mechanic, and he always had several junkers sitting around the farm. When a car broke down, he fixed the one that was easiest to fix. As a result, we never knew for certain from one day to the next which car we would be driving. It might be an old '34 Chevy, whose brakes sometimes worked and sometimes didn't (we all knew how to downshift if the brakes failed), or a blue '42 Plymouth named Bessie, or whatever. Most cars had names, and all had standard shifts since automatic transmissions were not available yet.

When I was preparing to get my driver's license, Dad parked two junk cars in the expansive driveway and fired up another. I practiced parallel parking without any worry about hooking a bumper or denting a fender. I bragged to my girlfriend: "You've got to see this." She had a horse. I had three junk cars. Dad taught me how to position the car and to count so I knew exactly when to turn the wheel each direction to parallel park perfectly every time. I drove on the tractor paths in the fields, and even developed considerable skill at driving backwards. I had no trouble passing the driving test. I whipped right into the parallel parking spot and was disappointed I didn't get to back up more. I could drive around town backwards.

The mud roads in rural Iowa were often a challenge in the early years. Dad was always putting chains on vehicles so we could get around. I remember a snow storm so bad that when we drove to town the piles of snow left on the side of the road by the snow grader were higher than the car windows in some places. My brothers and I were peering out the windows in awe. It was like driving in a tunnel.

We lived on a mud road for years. After a rain, the soft black Iowa soil allowed car tires to sink in deep--quite different from the clay soil of Oklahoma. Even walking in mud was a challenge as it stuck to boots in big clumps. Tires left deep ruts in the road, and cars often got stuck in the muck. Dad bought an old school bus which he transformed into a flatbed truck. It was handy to drive us and the neighbor kids to school when the roads were too muddy or snowy to get cars out. A few of us could fit in the cab but the rest sat precariously on the truck bed. Mom's worry was reflected in her face as she waved goodbye, but to the boys, at least, getting bounced off would have been interpreted as an adventure. When the roads dried up, the deep ruts became hard, and it was a rough ride in a car until the road grader came and smoothed it all out.

Later most of the roads were gravel. (Today many are paved.) People drive down the middle of gravel roads wearing a tire path in the gravel. Masses of white dust billows from behind the cars, sometimes blinding oncoming traffic. Everyone drives in that path because you can go faster. The gravel along the sides of the road is loose. You must slow down to drive on it. Otherwise, you can lose control. When cresting a hill you need to get out of the path into the loose gravel in case you met someone. Sometimes people do not get over soon enough resulting in fatal head-on accidents. I remember a story about a farmer who was on a tractor in his field when he observed his teenage son going down the road from one direction and his daughter from the other. They had a head-on collision at the top of the hill.

Brother Dallas and I popped over a hill one day and ran head on into a herd of hogs that had escaped a neighbor's pen. We mowed several of them down, but Dal was able to maintain control of the car. A number of hogs were squealing and flopping around in the ditches--not a pretty sight. The neighbor was grateful no one was hurt and set about butchering hogs, and Dad was never much worried about any damage to his old cars.

When I was in high school, three friends and I were going to swimming lessons. Pam, the driver, was inexperienced and had just gotten her license. She got into loose gravel on the side of the road and lost control. We did a slow roll into a deep ditch and ended up in a pasture right side up.

I was in the passenger seat. Pam fell on top of me as we rolled (we didn't have seat belts). Strangely, I thought she should be driving. A fence post came through a window. When the car rolled, it pulled it out of the ground, flinging dirt all over us. My door was gone when the car started to go over again. I saw my sunglasses on the ground and thought about reaching out to get them, but the car fell back the other way landing right side up. The ceiling was mashed in, and we had to crawl out. Four girls came out of that car unhurt. Pam ran around the pasture screaming. She had just mangled her brother's brand new super-sharp red and white Buick. We chased her down while the radio continued playing loud music in spite of the damage to the car. We were lucky to be alive, and we knew it. Pam's brother was not very lucky that day.

CHURCH AND POLITICS

It was at church camp during my senior year of high school that a handsome, popular, and charismatic aspiring minister chased my ass big time. This frightened me beyond measure. I could not imagine living up to the requirements of being a minister's wife. It would be a fiasco of mammoth proportions, at best. I was having none of it, but he was persistent. When he showed up and continued the pursuit a year later in Omaha where I was attending business school, I ran like a car jacker on COPS.

Religion was inevitable in the midwest. Consequently, churches were the hub of community life in rural Iowa towns, and there were two in Prescott: Methodist and Christian. They were competitive, and this competition bled over into the schools. Everyone clearly knew which teachers, staff and students were affiliated with which church, resulting in a somewhat adversarial political environment. This conflict was not lost on me because most of the administration, school board, and teachers were Methodist, and I was Christian. To my amazement, some years later, long after I left home, the two churches in Prescott combined. It happened only because there was no alternative. The congregations became so small that they could no longer afford two buildings and two preachers.

Local politics were not the only influence. The international climate of the fifties and sixties presented political implications as well. It was threatening. A dark, looming cloud hung over us in the form of The Cold War. The threat of nuclear attack by the Russians put fear in the hearts of all Americans. This reminds me of the terrorist concerns today. There was an enemy out there who wanted to annihilate us.

This foreboding prospect generated a preoccupation with fall-out shelters, and at school we were shown black and white films on reel-to-reel projectors of nuclear blasts with frightening consequences. We were told to get under our desks if a flash of light occurred, like that was going to do any good. It was clear from the film that if there was a nuclear blast, you were screwed. It was incredibly disturbing. Many years later I made a trip to Russia where I discovered that the people there were just as fearful. They were told by their leaders that we wanted to annihilate them. Just like us, they didn't care about the international politics. They just wanted their families to be safe.

My folks were staunch Republicans, as were most people in our hometown. Everyone had "I Like Ike" campaign buttons. In school, I only knew of one girl who was not for Ike. The rest of us thought there was something wrong with her, and we made sure she knew it. Group think was as alive then as it is today.

75

HIGH SCHOOL

My older brother, Dallas, was quite the athlete, and since he was very popular in high school, I rode his coattails down the happy trail of popularity. High school kids pretty much coupled up in the fifties and sixties. Everyone wanted to "go steady." This meant wearing your boyfriend's class ring on a chain around your neck or on your finger with mounds of rolled up tape to make it fit, painted with colorful nail polish. It was the ultimate status symbol. There wasn't much playing the field, and kids didn't run in packs as they do today. We only went out on dates about once a week, if that much.

When we weren't wearing a pony tail, we girls curled our hair by forming little curls and pinning them tight to our heads with criss crossed bobby pins. We tied scarves around them to go to school, taking our hair down for ballgames and other activities. The pin curls produced blossoming curls. We wore rolled up jeans and bobby socks. Shoes were either penny loafers, white suede, or black and white saddle oxfords. Tennis shoes were high-tops and worn only for gym. Instead of blouses, we wore baggy men's shirts, usually plaid, which we considered trendy since they worked well with our rolled up jeans.

Most people got married right out of high school or shortly thereafter. I went steady with a sharp guy my freshman through junior year. He was a year ahead of me in school. For some reason, after he graduated I got restless and wanted to date other guys, so we broke up. I was an idiot. I dated a couple of out of town boys, which made them immensely unpopular with the Prescott guys. Then I started dating a boy in my class. After graduation we married, which was pretty much what everyone did. There were ten girls and five boys in my class. I got one.

My high school experiences were the launching pad for my career. When my older brother took typing his junior year, we got a typewriter, and I used his typing book to teach myself. I practiced for hours each day all summer, working my way through the entire book. In my first typing class I could type like nobody's business, quickly working up to 80 wpm on a manual typewriter. I was soon typing the school paper and tests, etc., and was a de facto secretary to the teachers.

I practiced shorthand like crazy as well, and by the time I got out of high school I was easily doing 120 words per minute. You had to be a good speller to transcribe shorthand into typed page, and I was not, so I spent a summer studying spelling from a list of the most commonly misspelled words and from old spelling workbooks. By the end of the summer I could transcribe shorthand without looking up words. Aunt Shuppy lived in Arizona, and we corresponded in shorthand. When I went to business school after high school, I passed out of the typing and shorthand classes within weeks. As I became an executive in the business world, my secretary and I wrote each other notes in shorthand, and I could make notes in meetings that no one around me could read, which was a real asset--one of the few advantages I had over the men.

After many years of being a secretary, I took a typing class in college because my degree was in business education, and I would be teaching it. I was shocked to type over 100 wpm and thought something was wrong with the formula. The professor explained that my speed many years ago was on a manual typewriter and on an electric one and with years of secretarial experience, 100+ wpm was possible. I was shocked. Today we keyboard. I can make a keyboard light up like an all-night liquor store, but so can an eight year old. In my era, it was a valued skill. Today it is a prerequisite to daily life for children.

I tried to drop out of high school my junior year. I had a huge argument with my folks about it. The prospect of my actually doing so in that environment was slim. In those small Iowa farm communities, it was scandalous to do so. (No one dropped out unless they were pregnant, in which case you were forced to do so.) Nevertheless, I was fed up and determined not to go back to school. The reasons were stupid and complicated, relating primarily to immaturity and typical teenage rebellion issues. I wanted out of that town. The straw that broke the camel's back was one of the boys picking on me. I was overly sensitive. My solution was to *take my marbles and go home*--to quit.

We didn't have school counselors, but Mr. Rosener, the English teacher, talked some sense into me. He told me things that happen in high school are not important in the whole scheme of life and that in future years I would realize that many incidents I thought were so significant will later seem silly in retrospect. This was news to me, but I could imagine it was true, and it was.

Years later, as an executive in the business community, I volunteered for Junior Achievement programs at disadvantaged schools and a school for dropouts. I shared Mr. Rosener's message with students by drawing a line across all the boards in the room to signify a student's life. Then I identified a small section representing junior high and high school, visually putting those years into perspective. I suggested that the idea that these are the best years of their life was a myth. It is a difficult time for many, but life can get better. There are many things teens cannot control, but for the whole rest of their lives they can call the shots, make good decisions, and do something with their lives.

When my daughter was in college, she spoke to them. To these kids college was a mystery, something they could not imagine aspiring to. Like Mrs. Brandt encouraging me to do something I never thought I could, she told them they were smarter than they think and that they could go to college if they wanted to, even if they had no money. They had no money.

To make non-college-bound kids feel good about their future, my son, a car guy, showed pictures of street rods and race cars, did a window tinting demo, and told them how he came to own his business, another hopeful message.

My senior year I rather came into my own. Things that were important to me before suddenly didn't matter. Being popular was no longer on the agenda. I was focused on getting out of town and on with my life. I dropped out of extracurricular activities, most of which I had participate in because I wanted to be "in." I remained only in marching band, the only activity I really enjoyed. During band practice, the band instructor marched us downtown, drums pounding and music blaring. People came out of stores to watch us. We entered contests and won many. We were exceptionally good for such a small school.

I went to ball games only if I felt like it. Mom and Dad thought I was out of my mind. School activities were the hub of the community, and everyone attended. On Tuesday nights I stayed home from basketball games to watch *The Gary Moore Show* with Carol Burnett. For fun, I went to dances at the *Chicken Inn* in a nearby town where I jitterbugged with girlfriends and, for the first time, saw college kids do a brand new sultry dance called the twist. We thought it was so-o-o bad.

COLLEGE BOUND--SOME DAY, BUT NOT YET

After high school I ended up in business school in Omaha, Nebraska, because I believed I could not afford to go to college. I had a burning desire to go but didn't understand that you could work your way through and get financial help. No teachers told me that, and at that time there was no such thing as a school counselor. So I gave up.

When I begged my folks to send me to college, Dad said he couldn't afford it, that he had boys to put through school. He advised me to go to Des Moines and get a job with an insurance company until I got married like all the other girls. I never resented this. We were all ignorant. I had no idea what college cost and neither did my folks. We just knew it was a lot of money. Our ignorance was the motivator for me in later years to get the message out to underprivileged kids that they can go to college if they want to, even if they don't have money.

It was a revelation to me years later when I began taking college courses to discover that business college tuition was actually more expensive per month than college would have been. I worked my way through a costly business school. I'm sure I could have worked my way through college.

My senior year I was on track to be valedictorian of my class. I made straight A's every semester. My two best friends were just a few tenths of a decimal point behind. It was close. The last semester the business teacher gave me B's in my classes which put me in third place. I was stunned. I missed two days because of surgery on my finger but made up all the work. Although I was handicapped in typing for a couple of weeks, I could still out-type anybody. There was no basis for the lower grades.

When I asked the teacher why he gave me B's, he said the faculty decided the other girls were going to college and they needed the honors and I didn't. Also, they took more math and science courses which were more difficult than my business courses, so they deserved it more. He had a rather sorrowful expression on his face when he told me that, knowing how disappointed I was.

There was logic behind what the teachers did, and I now have some understanding of their motives, but in the moment I resented it immensely and felt horribly betrayed. The faculty was trying to be fair, but fairness is in the eye of the beholder, and to me it was unfair. Mom and Dad were angry but didn't do anything about it, and I didn't expect them to. I didn't want to stir up any controversy with my best friends involved, but I sure was ready to get away from that school, that town, and the conspiring Methodist faculty.

I didn't want to go to graduation, but Mom made me, so I went and saw my best friends get valedictorian and salutatorian. I cut my hair as short as I could before the event and looked pretty strange in pictures taken that evening. This was the first time I self-mutilated by cutting my hair, a behavioral pattern I've repeated throughout the years. More sophisticated forms of mutilation and revolt such as tattoos, nose piercings, black nail polish, gothic hair, and vulgar t-shirts were not on the menu yet.

This whole episode festered in my mind for some years, eventually fading into immateriality. When I think back on it, though, I can see that it was a pivotal event. I perceived it as enormously unfair, and it fueled a fire in my belly that sparked smoldering ambition and resolve. I had something to prove, not so much to anyone else, but to myself, and I was soon to set about rescuing myself:

> Starting in my twenties, I spent ten years going to night school to get a B.S. degree while working and raising children. I graduated with a 4.0 GPA. I took plenty of math and science courses and aced every one of them. Then I spent six years getting an MBA while studying for and passing the Certified Public Accountant exam. I tested out of college courses and scored so high I was once accused of cheating to which I took great offense, demanded an apology, and got it. I was not that smart. I was a driven overachiever. I had something to prove to myself, and I did it. I even became a Methodist.

That was then, this is now. My aspirations these days are to be dressed by noon, work out if I feel like it, and consume thirty grams of fiber.

OUT OF THE NEST

Once I got to business school in Omaha to take an executive secretarial course, I worked evenings and Sundays as the secretary to a hospital administrator. I also washed dishes and bussed tables at a cafeteria at noon for a free meal and a dollar and fifty cents and cleaned a house on Saturdays. I walked two miles to school and to my jobs in good weather to save bus fare.

One day I was on a bridge over railroad tracks walking to the hospital when a toothless man asked me if I'd like to hop a freight train to Denver. (You can't make this stuff up.) It cracked me up, the thought of me and some old guy named Percy or Orlo sitting in a cattle car smoking stogies on our way to Colorado, me in my plaid pleated skirt, starched white cotton blouse, cutesy head band, and penny loafers with a penny in them.

I was a naive country girl, and Omaha was a big city. As I was standing on a corner one rainy day waiting for a bus, it didn't occur to me to beware of the mud puddle in front of me. A vehicle came along and splattered me, totally drenching me from head to toe. I had one of those little plastic hats on my head and the water blew it off. I had to decide whether to go back to the dorm and clean up or take my muddy, wet self on to school. I saw the bus coming a few blocks away, purposely shifted away from the puddle of water, and went to school.

Staying in a dorm, I was rooming with three girls and was bothered by them getting into my things. Needless to say, my brothers never messed with my makeup or clothes, and this was a new experience. I didn't like it. I was walking down the hall one day at school and was quite shocked to see a roommate wearing the plaid skirt I had planned to wear when Orlo and I ran off to Colorado. I was really mad. The dorm room was crowded. There was constant noise which made it a challenge to study, and the place was a mess. Finally, a small room the size of a closet became available, and I moved into it.

Coming to the city of Omaha from the farm in 1962 was exciting. I was living in a dorm with a bunch of girls, going to business school and working. On my own and engaged to my high school boyfriend, I felt all grown up. By 1963 I had finished a twelve-month secretarial course in nine months and landed a good job at Union Pacific Railroad, the premier company to work for in Omaha, Nebraska. I was debt free, making good money, and I had a brand new Singer sewing machine. On the threshold of life, I had big plans.

Birth control pills had just come out, and the girls in the dorm were all abuzz about them. They were to change the world as we knew it; however, they were not to change mine, at least not yet. I'll get into the details of that soon, but first, let me regale you with tales related to the interpersonal dynamics of a family my mother tried desperately to make upstanding and proper while Dad unintentionally but flagrantly influenced to be just a tad outside of the norm...well, perhaps a bit more than a tad.

4

FAMILY MATTERS

You Kids Take Care of Each Other

In 1940, my dad, Ray Walter, bought a wedding ring for $10 after working many hours for $1 a day hauling manure on an Iowa farm to save the money to pay for it. He gave it to his sweetheart, Virlee Bray, a neighbor girl down the road. He might have gone off to World War II but the country needed farmers, so that's what he did. Sixty-eight years later, twenty-seven descendants are spread throughout the country, every one a productive member of society--no one unemployed, on the dole, or in jail.

Every small town has its characters, those notorious, standout individuals who are just enough outside the norm to inspire anticipation about what they will do next. Dad was one of those characters. Living life his way he was a rambler, junk collector, jokester, mobile home philosopher, and a recycler long before anyone ever heard of the word.

My favorite Ray Walter story comes from his sister who described an incident when he was a teenager on the farm.

> Dad was working alongside the barn when an inquisitive neighbor kid came to visit. He told the boy he had a twin brother named Roy. Twins Ray and Roy they were. The kid wasn't buying it, but Dad insisted, informing him that the only way to tell them apart was that he wore his hat frontwards and Roy wore his backwards. The kid still wasn't buying it. Dad persisted, stating that Roy was working on the other side of the barn. He suggested the kid go see for himself, so the boy headed out to search for Roy, not really believing he would actually find him.
>
> Dad ran around to the other side of the barn, turned his hat around, picked up a pitchfork and began working. The kid was amazed to discover Roy, working diligently with his hat on backwards, and after a brief chat, ran back to tell Ray the news. Dad was soon winded as this running back and forth went on for some time. Finally, the kid went home to announce to his dumbfounded family at the dinner table that evening that Ray had a twin brother, Roy, and he steadfastly maintained his position against all protestations. The story of the frontwards and backwards hats undoubtedly brought knowing glances from parents who had had their own encounters with Ray Walter.

In addition to his propensity to tell tall tales, Dad had a restless nature and rambled around the county checking out dump sites for treasures to add to the heap at home. He acquired old cars which he hid in ditches behind clumps of trees so Mom couldn't see them, at least until winter when the leaves fell off. He got up around 5:00 every morning, as Iowa farmers often do, and took off to a neighboring town for coffee. I liked to go with him, and as much as I hated getting up that early, I occasionally would. It was worth it. We be rambling, you know.

In rural Iowa in those days, when you met someone on the road you always waved. Farmers waved by sticking their forefinger up as they held on to the upper part of the steering wheel. Old Ray Walter kept the roads hot, rambling around waving with his forefinger, perhaps with a stolen Christmas tree in the trunk if it was the holiday season.

I don't know why a stolen Christmas tree incident stands out in my mind when there are such a multitude of deadpan lies told by Dad. It just struck me, and I never forgot it. When someone asked him what kind of Christmas tree we had, he said, "Stolen." Without a doubt, rambling Ray Walter never paid for a Christmas tree. We had many different kinds of trees. Some of them were not particularly attractive, and most of them scratchy and not something you wanted to touch or lean up against, and you sure didn't want to back into one. Determining whether any of them were actually stolen or not would require going down the slippery slope of defining stolen. What I do know is that Dad aspired to be a rebel, and no doubt it warmed his heart to think that his Christmas tree was, in fact, stolen.

As a junk collector, Dad was a master recycler. A perfect example was when he brought a rotisserie rod home from the dump. Mom and I drove in the driveway and noted a peculiar sight as Dad was balancing himself on the deck railing, somewhat like a tight rope walker, to avoid the splattering of meat juices flying out of a roast mounted on the rotisserie rod attached to a Black and Decker drill and spinning over a charcoal fire. Supper was very dry.

I watched him charcoal once, and he had a bunch of tools handy. He had rigged up the charcoaler with parts from the dump and had to use tools to open and close the lid and turn the knobs. He explained simply: "It takes a lot of tools to charcoal."

At one point, Dad even used a tool to steer a car. He was quite the mechanic, something achievable before the complicated computerized cars of today. He rigged up a car so he could steer it with a wrench hooked up to the steering column. The steering wheel itself was dysfunctional. He could take it off and still drive down the road. When people rode with him, he told them he was tired of driving, handed them the steering wheel, and told them to take over. This induced shock beyond a raccoon pouncing on you from the rafters in Uncle Fred's outbuilding or Cousin Mary vividly portraying the wraths of hell.

Dad found an old basketball scoreboard buzzer. He asked people to plug it in and watched gleefully as they jumped when it made a horrific noise. It was so astonishing that one of the grandkids plugged it in and wet his pants. I can imagine Dad's reaction the first time he plugged it in after hauling it home from the dump, most likely having no idea what it was but intrigued with the prospect of finding out. I expect that, after he got over the initial shock of the auditory blast, he became devilishly excited about the potential of perpetrating an awesome prank on as many people as possible. I can envision him ambling from his shop to the trailer with it in hand contemplating Mom's reaction.

He hauled home a piece of an old furnace, a large steel thing that looked like a giant upside down funnel, and was raising baby pheasants he had rescued in it, probably to protect them from critters. One night while feeding them he fell in head first and couldn't get out. Fortunately, Mom spotted him out of the trailer window head first in the funnel, his feet flailing in the air. (You can't make this stuff up.) She couldn't get him out. He was stuck. She was embarrassed to call a neighbor in such a situation, so she called my brother who was accustomed to rescuing the folks from unusual and colorful circumstances, although it is unlikely he anticipated anything like this one.

Pampas grass grew in the ditch down by the road and produced large, white fluffy plumes in the fall. Dad spray painted the plumes iridescent pink creating much interest among people driving by. He sat on the porch and watched cars slow down as they passed. Someone was so fascinated that they backed up, pulled in the driveway, and asked for seeds only to be directed to the spray paint section of the local hardware store.

Dad was into gadgets. He mass produced one he called a Bull Shit Baler which he proudly distributed to anyone who would take one. It was a useless but fascinating little hand-held grinding contraption. He was quite proud of it. Clearly it tickled him to give it to people, and they were tickled to get it. It was just such a happy little thing, the way its parts moved, just barely missing each other as you grind away on it. A marvel it was.

I recently received a package from a cousin who discovered a "quarter pounder" device he believed Dad had given his folks. It was a block of wood with an inlaid spot for a quarter and a small mallet with which you could pound the quarter. Another marvel it was. I later discovered the creator was brother Denny who inherited Dad's quirky gadget gene.

A man came by the house around Christmas to collect on a debt, and Dad wrote him a check. Later Mom had to deal with a very ticked off fellow on the front porch. The bank refused the check. It was signed by Santa Claus, and Dad was nowhere to be found.

Dad worked his way up to foreman of a road construction crew, and my brother Denny was working with him. Dad asked a new guy to keep an eye on a prisoner for him while he took a break, pointing to Dennis. The guy diligently watched Dennis like a hawk until Dad got back to relieve him of his prison guard duty.

We kids used to accuse Dad of cheating at cards. Now I realize he just wanted us to think he was cheating. He'd get this look on his face--a smirky smile and shifty eyes. I can see his antics across the card table as though it were yesterday. He looked like the cat who ate the mouse which convinced players that something rotten was up. This distracted us from whatever card playing strategy he had in mind and royally entertained him in the process. Dad was good at faking people out.

A bunch of his buddies looked out the window of the tavern as he parked his pickup truck. He got out, went around to the back of the truck and beat vigorously on something in the bed with his hat before entering the bar. As each person left the tavern, they peered into the bed to find nothing there.

Dad was a character, no doubt about it, and although he was fascinating, to me he was just Dad. To this day I can visualize clearly his unique gait as he walked the path to the house from the array of outbuildings or in from the fields. The essence of him was reassuring, warm, and solid with an enticing air of unpredictability. He wasn't perfect but it is easy to see why Mom loved him so. We all loved him so.

Mom and Dad had their share of struggles raising a family of five in the unpredictable world of farming. The southwestern Iowa soil is not the quality of the rich northern Iowa dirt, and the ravages of weather and lack of modern day farming technologies made it a precarious business. In spite of these challenges, they did a good job of producing a great bunch of kids, their most successful crop. It was undeniably clear that both of them were totally and enthusiastically dedicated to raising their family and were likewise incredibly proud of the results. I am certain all of us would say we felt loved, cherished, admired, and supported by our parents, extended family, and the community.

BAND OF BROTHERS

I have four fun loving brothers and can see my dad in each of them, particularly in their sense of humor. Fortunately, Mom's influence balances that and is evident in their responsible, steady natures. Although they lack Dad's straight-faced knack for lying outright, they have perfected a talent for bouncing humor off of each other that would rival any impromptu comedy routine. It is a challenge to describe the sibling dynamics, but let me put it this way. Some of the best times of my life happened when I was with my brothers. With them I feel a sense of belonging that is unique to their presence, and I find them totally hilarious. They are also mischievous.

For a family reunion we rented cabins on a lake, and the boys had a giant sling shot with which to fire water balloons out into the water. After shooting volleys at the tin roof of a boat dock lost its charm, the rascals began shooting at boats of night fishermen. Hearing a balloon splat near his boat, a fisherman excitedly exclaimed to his buddy: "Did you hear that! It was a big one!" (He probably fished all night.) The brothers could not contain themselves, but the prospect of actually hitting a boat finally occurred to them, and they waited until daylight to resume the balloon barrage at which time they targeted a sister-in-law out for her morning swim. Fortunately, Mom intervened.

Dallas, a year older than me, is an ornery good-old-boy type with a twinkle in his eye and a good-humored disposition. He is known to grow a wooly beard in the fall for hunting season and motorcycle riding, and for years he cut a fine bad ass figure on his bike on the way to a motorcycle rally or on a road trip to the top of Pikes Peak. He is a big guy, and no doubt anyone encountering him imagines a *don't mess with me, buddy* mentality, and they would be partially right, although he is really a gentle soul.

Dal supervised a road crew for many years, painting the lines on Iowa highways and running snow plows in the winter. He saw his work as purposeful, an opportunity to keep families safe.

As a child, Dal was adventurous and a bit of a dare devil. He poked a stick at a skunk one morning and got on the school bus reeking. Mom tells it this way: "The bus stopped. The kids got on. The door closed. The door opened. Dallas got off."

When he was a grade school kid, the high school girls on the bus picked on him a lot. If I got picked on, it hurt my feelings, but Dal was playful and bantered back. One day he was late for the bus after school. The girls were yelling "Leave him! Leave him!" while I desperately peered out the bus window anxiously looking for my brother. The bus driver finally gave up and left just as Dal came running out of the school house chasing the bus down the road. He was slapping his red cap on the side of his leg as we saw cowboys do in the movies. The girls continued to yell "Leave him!" while I cried.

Dallas and I were the perfect example of siblings who continuously fought with each other, but when someone else picked on either one of us, there was no doubt where we stood. He was my defender, and I was his.

Mom was frequently exasperated with our constant bickering. For Dal it was pure entertainment to pick on his little sister. He was a pest. Often when he did something to aggravate me, I squealed or yelled, and then I got into trouble for making noise. He walked away with no consequences, feeling pretty proud of himself. That was just wrong, and I knew it.

Sometimes, though, I egged him on and usually regretted it as he was pretty good at getting the better of me. It really wasn't a fair fight. How do you get the better of someone who just laughs at everything you do? Mom said we fought because we were so much alike. He teased me unmercifully, often rallying my younger brothers to his side.

I felt betrayed by my youngest brother, Kelly, when for the first time he took Dally's side in a squabble. Kelly was the baby of the family, and I practically raised him. When he got older and became one of the boys, it hurt. Dal was a strong leader, and he had no trouble winning Kelly over to loyalty to the pack. Looking back over growing up, my career, and the men I've dated with strong bonds to their friends, I realize I've dealt with packs of men all my life and did so pretty well. My brothers trained me up. I don't always like it, but I "get" the pack behavior, and I have an exceptionally effective bullshit-o-meter.

In our teens, Dal and I became very close. I admired him immensely and he was a strong influence. He was always my champion, and I knew without a doubt he had my back.

Dal had Dad's zest for life and was outrageously fun. A basketball star in high school, he played center and often was the high scorer on an exceptionally good team, especially for such a small school. I was fortunate to cheerlead at his games, one of the highlights of those high school years.

Dallas was my idol. The girls thought he looked like Ricky Nelson, a teen idol at the time, and he did. (My daughter claims to know who Ricky Nelson is, but she is not familiar with my other teenage crushes: Audie Murphy, Spin and Marty, and Alan Ladd. (Shane! Shane! Shane!)

As an adult, Dallas had a habit of leaving Mom notes such as: "I was here and you was gone, now you is here and I is gone." She loved it. One day she found ten roses on the counter with a note that said, "I bought fifty roses, but I got attacked by cows so only ten are left." Dally had an experience of being chased by cows as a small boy when he was putting fish in a pond in the pasture. We all remember him running from the pond and jumping a

barbed wire fence like it wasn't even there with a herd of cows chasing him. Everything to Dal was an adventure and he took things in stride, but I think perhaps the cows scarred him for life.

In our town, freshmen were informally initiated into high school. One of the things the seniors did was de-pant the freshmen boys and run their pants up a flag pole. This prospect would strike terror into the hearts of most boys, but I remember Dally running around downtown Prescott through streets and alleys laughing gleefully while dodging would-be tormentors. Mom, always the planner, kept an extra pair of pants in the car.

As an adult, Dal lived in our hometown of Prescott, the only one of us kids to do so, and he looked after the folks over the years. With some of Dad's mishaps and Mom's interesting quirks, this was at times a challenge. Whether pulling Dad out of an upside down furnace funnel or killing a rabid raccoon that almost ran into the house chasing Mom's dog, he was there for the rescue.

Dallas was Mom's favorite. I think she admired him so because of his playful, fun-loving outlook on life and his way of being in the world. I mean, you had to admire that. Certainly I did and do. That does not mitigate the fact that as a child I frequently wondered who died and left him in charge.

Dennis, a year younger than me, is just plain silly, and his comedic style is looking stupid and puzzled, rather reminiscent of Tommy Smothers in my mind. Kids love it, and so does everyone else. He has a delightful chuckle and twinkly eyes. A retired postman and Vietnam vet, he is our family hero.

Exceptionally creative, as a kid Dennis nailed his shoes to long boards so he could lean forward and backward without falling down. He changed the words to a song about a rubber duck to one about a plastic goose. Once he found an old dress dummy, painted the stubs of the arms and legs with red paint, and threw it out of a car window while driving down the road, traumatizing an Iowa driver. Brother Kelly was a co-conspirator. I suspect Dad interpreted this as a proud moment.

As young children, Dallas was my pest. Denny was my buddy. We were close and announced to Mom one day that we were getting married when we grew up. We were severely disappointed to learn that was not going to happen. Two generations later, my grandson was so full of love for his new baby sister that he said, "I love her so much. I just want to marry her." He was too small to understand why that couldn't happen, and she was not old enough to get into his stuff, which would have inevitably changed his mind. We settled on a serious multi-faceted distraction as an alternative to the suggested engagement: "You want to bake cookies, make a tent, look for crickets, and jump on the bed?" My inclination is that this will come up again.

Denny back from Vietnam overlooking our Oklahoma land with Dad.

Denny was one of those in the thick of it in Vietnam. He dropped out of college which made him eligible for the draft. With the war in full swing, no one wanted to be drafted. By joining the Navy, he expected to be stationed on a ship. Surprisingly though, he ended up a communications specialist stationed at an out post along the river dividing North and South Vietnam. This was not good, and we all knew it. Mom and Dad were a wreck. He was wounded twice, and has mortar in his neck to this day, but we got him back home. Some boys coming back to the States were not treated well. Not true of boys from Iowa. We were glad to get our boys back. Some didn't come back.

Denny lived with my husband and me for awhile when he relocated to Oklahoma a year after he got back from Vietnam. He worked as a postman in Tulsa for many years. I always thought he was the most sensitive of my brothers. Denny was always Mom's favorite, although the way he tinkers in his workshop and his quirky imagination reflect the fact that he is his father's son.

Dennis and Mel

Publishing a family newsletter for many years, Dennis dreamed up a multitude of colorful fictional characters with wildly disparaging qualities which richly entertained us and deepened family connections. One of his most profound inspirations is consistent with our family chicken influences. He started a series of jokes and cartoons about free-range chickens which ultimately led to all kinds of chicken paraphernalia being passed around amongst us.

I bought the whole stock of chicken feet slippers I stumbled across in a store, and for a family video, Denny and I ran around in his back yard in chicken costumes with a weenie dog chasing us. (You can't make this stuff up.) It is amazing how many greeting cards are out there with a chicken theme. It was the chicken era, and although a chicken still pops up occasionally, it has pretty much run its course, which is probably a good thing.

Denny had a lifelong friend who lived down the road from us who was handicapped. Those boys were a pair. I recall Denny diligently getting him out of the building during school fire drills. He always took care of his friend, whose parents were exceedingly grateful. I learned an important lesson from observing this friendship and have passed it on to my children. Befriend someone whom others leave out, and you will have the best friend you ever had. At first blush, you might think Denny's friend was the beneficiary here, but Denny had a loyal friend second to none. It does not get any better than that.

Denny's wife took parts of an old windmill from the farm and painted pictures of the home place on each fan blade, one for each of us. These keepsakes are all that is left now of the place where we grew up.

Gary, five years younger than I, is somewhat of a straight man. His humor is subtle with that oddball edge to it, and he has Dad's way of putting things simply. Ask Gary if he has lived in Iowa all his life and he will say: "Not Yet." Gary and I were idiots out wandering around on a trip to Washington, D.C. We were looking at a picture of a lineup of fire fighters in an old photo in a museum. One of the men was exceptionally short. Gary says: "Guess which one they call Stubby."

When his neighbor put a brightly painted hot rod in the front yard decorated with Christmas lights for the holidays, Gary threatened to pull his motor home into his yard and light it up.

"SUPPLIES!" he would say when he meant SURPRISE!--typical of his oddball humor. I guess I appreciate it more than most. To this day I often find myself wanting to say supplies when I mean surprise. It makes no sense, and no one gets the joke when I do it. I just look stupid. Can you imagine someone coming into a surprise birthday party and everyone yelling SUPPLIES? I can, but I couldn't convince anyone else. I can't explain why I think it is so funny. Dad would think it was funny.

I rode in the cart one day while Gary played golf. When he did poorly, I encouraged him with "that's unfortunate" or "that sucks." When he did well, I made sure I told him so: "Hey, that didn't suck." He was teeing off near a busy street, and I asked if the street noise bothered him. He said, "It never has, but it does now." He told brother Kelly about my ride along. I know this because I don't get to go golfing anymore with either of them.

Gary was a city manager for a couple of fairly good-sized Iowa towns. He has left his mark on these communities and is very highly regarded. I know this because when he takes me to the sale barn to eat, everyone is happy to see him.

Gary was Mom's favorite. He became her primary caretaker in the later years and visited her every day. He and his wife do volunteer work and are very civic minded.

Strangely, many of my experiences with Gary are centered around dancing. His square dance group entertains at senior centers. They took me dancing with them once. I have done quite a bit of other kinds of dancing but was rather overwhelmed with the technicalities of what they were doing. When they invited me to join in, I refused at first, but after much insistence, I gave in. The dancers swept me around, passed me from one to the other, turned me around and turned me back, and shoved and pulled me through moves like I was *Pac Man*.

Gary convinced me to go to a prom at the nursing home where Aunt June, Dad's sister, was living. (You can't make this stuff up.) We took Mom along. I waltzed with a sweet old man all dressed up for the event in a suit and tie. When I complimented him on his tie, he told me his wife gave it to him, and it was his favorite. He said he missed dancing with her. When the dance was over I escorted him back to his oxygen tank. I'm glad I danced with him. As it turns out, it was his last dance.

I pushed a lady in a wheelchair around the dance floor to music performed by a couple of old fiddlers who jazzed it up pretty good. When dancing with someone in a wheelchair, you get to lead. I always wanted to lead. The prom was a step up from Bingo and a good time was had by all.

Aunt June took the opportunity at the prom to introduce me to my brother: "This is my nephew, Gary," she said. I told him it was nice to meet him. Aunt June was, well, she was confused. I figured that out when some of us got two Christmas Cards from her in July. The good news is she is two Christmases ahead if she has a lapse of memory come December. Mom didn't understand why they let all these really old people in here, and said we better not drag her around to proms when she is that old. Mom was eighty-seven and somewhat out of touch with reality.

Another dancing interlude occurred when my teenage daughter and I were at a street dance in my hometown. We were standing there with Gary, Uncle Stan, and a few farmers when a rather strange looking fellow in a cowboy hat, a bit of a novelty for Iowa, walked across the dance floor and asked me to dance.

Melanie and me
with Aunt June's nephew

Recognizing that it takes courage for a guy to ask a girl to dance, I usually dance at least once with anyone who does so--unless he has the sleeves cut out of his shirt. (A girl has to have her standards.) So I danced. Well, not really. I wouldn't call it dancing. He asked me if I could two-step, and of course I said yes. I am thinking, well he looks weird but at least he can dance. Actually, he couldn't. His idea of two-stepping was running around in a big circle on the dance floor, not necessarily to the beat of the music. I was having to run backwards, and the farmers were getting quite a chuckle out of it.

Then he asked me if I could spin. Well, of course I can spin, but his idea of spinning was me turning in place while he ran around me in circles, not necessarily to the beat of the music. He was quite into his spinning and he ran around me one way and then reversed himself and ran around me in the other direction before running me backwards again.

Finally it was over. Uncle Stan took great delight in telling me the guy was an ex-con. (Sometimes Uncle Stan pulls my leg.) Later the guy walked across the dance floor to ask my daughter to dance. She was wide-eyed as he approached, rather like a deer in the headlights of a locomotive or UFO. To my relief she declined. I was afraid he would hurt her. Running backwards is not her forte. Unfortunately, he had to walk back across the floor alone, which I felt bad about, even if he was an ex con, which he probably was not. I was thinking that if he had cut the sleeves out of his shirt, we would have known up front, and we could have avoided the whole fiasco.

Kelly, the baby of the family, has a delightful personality. He is scary smart. The pastor of a church in Kansas City which he started from scratch, he does missionary work in India and the Philippines. Kelly is an inspirational leader, and he is changing the world. I'm not exaggerating. He has trained hundreds of ministers to date in some very remote places of the world, and he provides vital support to an overseas orphanage and other organizations. I am exceedingly proud of him.

He leads an interesting life. His trips overseas involve thirteen flights. He sends us pictures from his cell phone of giant bugs in the Philippines. Later, when he invited me to go with him on one of his trips there, I said to myself: "Did he forget the pictures of atrocious monster bugs he sent me on his cell phone?" We received an email from him while he was in India saying he was stuck in a cafe. He didn't know for how long because dogs were attacking a cow on the sidewalk outside causing quite a disturbance. He was staying put, catching up on his communications, and praying the cow did not decide to enter the cafe. I thought: "Holy Cow."

Being the baby of a large family, Kelly got plenty of attention, and we reveled in our little brother. He was such a cute little guy with dark curly hair, big brown eyes and an exceptionally engaging personality receptive to razzing. Because he was the only one of us kids with brown eyes, Dad teased him that he was adopted, which was ridiculous. Dad had brown eyes. Kelly was a bit of a pest to his older siblings. Since we were pretty rough and tumble and took no prisoners, he paid a heavy price for that. He tells us he thought for a long time he had two names: Kelly Shut Up and Kelly Get Out.

He survived all the joshing with good humor. As a teenager, he mysteriously started limping, and as it turns out, had to have surgery which resulted in a pin in his hip. I was sorry he had to go through that but was glad at the same time because I knew it would keep him out of the war.

Vietnam colored the world of my generation as World War II colored Dad's and as the Middle East does today. The difference was that back then there was the draft. With four brothers, the constant threat that they would get drafted loomed. After Denny's experience we adamantly did not want any more boys to end up in Vietnam. Dally had a baby which made him ineligible. Gary joined the Air Force when he finished college and was a weather man at SAC Air Force Base in Omaha, so he was safe. (Standing in his front yard one day looking skyward, I asked him what kind of clouds those were. He said they were BFC's. I'll let you figure out what that means.) Depending on what happened with the Vietnam war, Kelly could be at risk. Consequently, I saw what would ordinarily be an unfortunate medical crisis as a good thing. In that climate, no doubt my parents did as well.

Kelly and his family are the kind of inspirational Christians that exemplify goodwill without judgement and self-righteousness, making them a joy to be around, even though I am certain they consider me a little edgy. Let's face it, Aunt Nik is not always the best role model. In this regard, a couple of incidents that I would like do overs on involve Kelly.

He was in California with three other pastors for a conference while I was there visiting my daughter, Mel. The pastors invited me to go along on a day of touring. Mel was concerned about my impulse control and said to me, "Mom, you are not going to swear, are you?" Of course I had no intention of swearing in front of four pastors. But I did. They were so good about it, though. They prayed for me. When Mel met up with us for dinner later, the first thing she said was: "Mom, you swore didn't you?" I said, "W-e-l-l...." Then one of those nice pastors spoke up in my defense and said, "Let's just put it this way, Mel. We have been praying a lot for your Mother."

I try to be careful not to swear in front of my brother Kelly or his family. I am working at adopting alternative expressions such as darn, crap, holy cow, shoot, heck, frigging, and oh my gosh. It is only right that I respect their beliefs, but I do slip up now and then. Once at lunch with Kelly and his family, I unfortunately said a bad word. I knew right off I had done a bad thing because the kids' eyes got really big. Aunt Nik said a bad word.

It was a nightmare. I was so horrified that I let loose with another swear word, and then another, "Oh, shit. Oh, damn." I mean I was on the slippery slope to hell. Finally I just put my hand over my mouth and shut the frig up. They will never let me around their children again, I thought. I'll be banished. Kelly leaned over the table, looked me straight in the eyes and said: "It's okay, Aunt Nik. We will all pray for you." And they did. And they still do. I'm certain of it.

Kelly has counseled me through many situations and has provided tremendous moral support to my children. He has often been the voice of reason when anyone in our family dealt with a difficult situation. From the time he was born, he has been a blessing to me and a key player in my life. Although he has not been successful to date at influencing me to completely stop swearing, progress is being made, perhaps because brother Kelly is praying for me.

I like to imagine what he says, whether it is a simple: "Dear God, help Aunt Nik to stop swearing," or if it is a more impassioned plea full of tattle-tale testimony and details where he tells all the bad words I said. He might say something like: "Please forgive Aunt Nik and help her see the error of her ways. Give her the strength to not swear like an biker, especially in front of innocent little children, particularly mine." More likely he says: "Send her a lesson. She needs to stop it."

Kelly and I are both workout buffs. He bikes all over Missouri, and his workout involves an hour of intense weight training and some treadmill work. I worked out with him once, and personally, I think he overdoes it. Certainly, the treadmill thing gets the heart all churned up. That can't be good.

In contrast, my workout is age appropriate. I don't ride a bike because I like my front teeth and riding across Oklahoma requires money for a helmet that is better spent on a new cowboy hat (I have my priorities straight). My exercise program includes one minute of weight training with low intensity multiple repetitions followed by a lap around the indoor track with one pound weights strapped to my ankles to increase the intensity. I finish with a minute or two of yoga stretches to keep everything flexible so I can reach my feet to put on my socks.

It wears me out just thinking about it. The good news is my workout center has mirrors that make me look thinner than I really am. Nutrition is important so I follow up with a chocolate malt and cashews at a nearby drug store to get some much needed fluid and post-workout protein. Ralph, a spry old fellow in his late seventies at the workout center who wears black socks with his tennis shoes, chastises me about my workout. "Is that all you can do?" he says as I puff away on a torture machine. When he walks the track I yell at him, "Is that all the faster you can go?" Ralph is wanting me. I'm a younger woman.

Because we are such workout buffs, Kelly and I occasionally take on the persona of *Hans and Franz*, the Saturday Night Live fitness characters, and not necessarily in a workout setting. When someone takes our picture, we are a vision of propriety until the count of three at which time we assume the roles. At a wedding reception, some of the new in-laws were admiring us standing there all sophisticated in our nice clothes getting our picture taken when we suddenly got

into character. It didn't matter what they thought, the wedding was already over.

Kelly held a special place in our family because he was the youngest. He was Mom's favorite.

I was the favorite daughter. As the only girl I was often the odd man out, but I felt special for the same reason. This was the story of my life, as I was frequently the un-conventional member of a group, which I embraced, considering myself *somewhat lucky.*

As I gained independence in my thirties, it became obvious I was not the typical Iowa girl, and I've occasionally been a puzzlement to both Mom and Dad. I know this because they told me so. Dad failed to recognize in me the female embodiment of himself, and my ambition and independence mystified him. He couldn't grasp what I was up to and said more than once that I should have been a boy. Girls don't do the things I was doing.

In addition to their puzzlement over my ambition, Mom and Dad never understood a woman subsisting without a man. The rural Iowa culture, featuring well-defined roles for men and women, permeated their world. I was a worry to them because I didn't have a man to take care of me. As I went through my evolutions, their concerns deepened initially but eventually they decided that, although I was not what they expected, I was taking care of myself and my family on my own. That is all they really ever wanted anyway--for their kids to be okay.

LOSING DAD

Dad had a stroke at age 75. When I got word of it, I immediately drove to Iowa from Oklahoma and went straight to the hospital. He couldn't talk at all at that point, and we didn't know how aware he was of what was going on around him. He gazed longingly out the hospital window at the cars and trucks going down the road. I'm certain he was wishing he could ramble. I was wiping a warm wash cloth over his face and a tear ran down his cheek. I knew then that he knew I was there.

It is interesting to me to consider how Mom behaved in this circumstance. She was always all about her children, and through the years I often had the feeling that while Dad and we kids were up to our antics, she was hovering in the background, enjoying the show to the fullest but not really participating in it. She seemed rather on the fringe of things.

I had that feeling often when we were all gathered around Dad at the hospital taking turns caring for him. I recall being down the hall one day and her sticking her head out of the door of Dad's hospital room waving me to come. He was getting restless and she wanted me to help calm him. She was always so inclusive. She shared. I think the extent of her intense nurturing of our connectedness was unusual. To her we were first in all things, and she loved sharing us with others. We were everything to her.

Mom and we kids spent two weeks caring for Dad in the hospital, this big strong man who was suddenly helpless. I watched my brothers shave him, and we took turns feeding him. I gave him leg and foot massages when he got restless and combed his hair. And then he was gone.

A neighbor girl who worked as an aide at the hospital was with him when he died. She was giving him a bath. He had recovered enough to say a word or two at a time. She asked, "How are you doing, Ray?" He said, "Feels good." Those were his last words. Brother Kelly said at his funeral that we experienced God's grace that day, and I believe he is right. How many people's last words are "feels good"?

We all knew Dad was headed to a nursing home and how hard that would be for him, so it was better this way. It was time. Kelly did the service and sang a sweet nursery rhyme song about baby lambs that Dad sang to us as young children, one of the few songs that wasn't about getting drunk or getting out of prison. It would not have been right if there wasn't some irreverence at Dad's funeral, so Kelly also talked of roadkill, a smelly dead skunk to be specific, another one of Dad's favorite songs.

We had a private funeral, unheard of in Prescott. Funerals were typically a community event, but Mom wanted it that way. Outside of immediate family, only Dad's best friend and the neighbors down the road were invited to a service at the funeral home. As the funeral caravan went down the main street of

Prescott, I was surprised to see people going about their business as usual. It seemed strange. I thought: "Don't they know my dad died? Shouldn't the world stop for this moment?" The harsh reality that the world goes on seemed all wrong.

Mom and we kids went to the cemetery alone. Dad was cremated, and my brothers buried him themselves. There was a requirement that the burial team be present, so a couple of men stood to the side while the boys took up shovels and buried their dad. We stood there briefly, dark shadows on the sloping terrain of the cemetery in freezing cold Iowa weather--our father gone from us.

When Mom and I went through Dad's billfold we found a very old worn picture--my high school graduation picture. Unknown to us, he had carried it since 1962, thirty-three years, a clear indication that I was my dad's favorite daughter. I have never been back to the cemetery since he died except when we buried Mom. I don't want to be sad when I go back home, and it would make me very sad.

As I was driving back to Oklahoma, I thought about what was said at my friend Ron Mainer's funeral, that he invested in people, and we owed him a return on that investment. My dad invested in me, and I determined then and there to live in a way going forward that would make him proud. Fortunately, Dad's ornery nature and fascination with novelty provides considerable latitude for my behavior. At any rate, the idea of returning his investment gave me great comfort and considerable motivation then, as it does to this day.

Mom and Dad sold the 160 acre farm after we kids were grown. As empty nesters, they kept five acres and put a trailer on it. Interestingly, they paid very little on the farm mortgage all those years. The bank let them pay just the interest. It was a financial struggle raising five kids, and that is one way they got by.

During the farming years, the folks were never able to build a nest egg. Any year the crops were not good, they had to borrow money, often from Mom's dad, Grandpa Bray. Mom told me once that Grandpa loaned them money under the condition that Dad not go into the tavern any more--like that was going to happen. Grandpa was exceedingly righteous, and although he never gave up on his aspirations to save Dad from the clutches of the devil, I believe he eventually resigned himself to Dad just being Dad. Perhaps he concluded that wasn't so bad after all. I mean, you had to like my dad. Everyone did. He was good to Grandpa and Grandma, and they were often joyful subjects of his folly.

Without Dad to do the maintenance, we knew we had to move Mom off the remaining five acres of the farm and into town. The property was not worth much. The well didn't produce enough water, and the trailer had depreciated and required constant repair. There was too much land to mow and keep up but not enough to do anything with. For all these reasons, it was difficult to sell, but eventually a buyer materialized.

Dad had acquired a lot of junk, and the boys spent months hauling it off the place. They found someone to take the old cars. Dad had kept a red Farmall tractor he bought in 1944, the day I was born. I was told by several people that he had said proudly, "I got a new baby girl and a new tractor on the same day." The old tractor was too much trouble to move so it stayed with the farm. The boys threatened to transport it to Tulsa and unload it in my front yard since it had been tied to me since birth. I would have considered it an amazing yard ornament, but my city neighbors would have undoubtedly disagreed.

Years later, my nephew, Dray, who by then had a farm of his own and always had a special connection with Dad, asked the man who bought the home place if he could have the tractor. I can imagine him approaching the guy with nervous anticipation, wondering if he could pull off retrieving his grandpa's tractor. The guy was glad to be rid of it, so Dray fired it up and drove it off--an amazing feat. It was not red anymore; it was rust colored. Dray is fixing it up. The last time I was at his farm I drove it with him

Driving the old Farmall with nephew Dray

standing on the back just as Dad had done when I was a little girl. I used to set on Dad's lap to steer until I got big enough to reach the pedals at which time he stood on the back to keep me safe while I drove up and down the tractor paths. I delighted in pulling the hand throttle to give it power and feeling the surge as it accelerated. Experiencing that again with Dray, well, what can I say--it was sweet.

SAVING MOM

After Dad died, the boys and I focused on Mom. Some people said she wouldn't last long. I didn't think that. Other than arthritis, she was strong. She and I became girlfriends. I brought her to Oklahoma for long visits and took her on trips. We were roomies, compadres, and we were *Thelma and Louise*. My single guy friends teased her by asking her out on dates. I threatened to shoot them, reminding them that I was Louise, the one who shot someone. Some of the girlfriends I hang out with call themselves *The Divas* and Mom enjoyed being a part of that group, although she expressed considerable confusion about the definition of a diva, and she never did pronounce it right. I tried to explain it to her, which made her question whether or not she really wanted to be one. She thought she was being ornery when she was with *The Divas*, kind of like when I took her to the casino (she made me promise not to tell the girls back home that she gambled), but she enjoyed the good times.

In some respects Mom blossomed, not being under Dad's shadow. We moved her off the acreage into an apartment in town, and she engaged in social events with the widows there. They called themselves *The Bag Ladies* because they brought a sack lunch to their get togethers. One time I played cards with them. They played almost every day and were sharks. They had me begging for mercy in short order, and without a doubt, the ornery old gals enjoyed that more than they should have. They were fun--divas in their own right.

We called the five acres the trailer was on "The Farm." It wasn't worth much, but we kids pretended to fight over it for years. Some years before Dad died I was home for a visit and discovered shrimp in the freezer, a strange thing for Iowa farmers in those days. When I asked Mom where she got it, she said, "Gary gave it to me." This started a family feud right then and there.

I called my other brothers and warned them Gary was "sucking up" and trying to get "The Farm," and the feud was on. Mom milked this to the max, enjoying the ensuing competitive attention, although she always hated the term "sucking up" and took every opportunity to tell us so.

After Dad was gone, Gary took Mom on excursions. I topped him whenever I could. At one point I called him and told him I was taking her to Hawaii, and he would have to take her to Hong Kong to beat that. Mom ate it up. He took her in a limousine to a neighboring town to see the Christmas lights. The next year I scheduled a helicopter tour of the Tulsa lights, but she wouldn't go, so I took her to a craft store where I bought her plastic flowers, and we ate lunch at a nearby cafeteria where she stuffed her purse with sugar packets and crackers. Gary never bought Mom plastic flowers.

Mom and I had big adventures together. When we went on excursions in the car we were *Thelma and Louise,* me always reminding her that I got to be the one who shot somebody. She had not seen the movie and had no idea who *Thelma and Louise* were, but somehow she knew it was a fun thing, that some kind of adventure was in store, and she was game. I would say: "Come on, Thelma, let's go." We'd get in the car and head out to a cafeteria, the hobby store, Oklahoma City, or to Kansas City.

Dad was very spontaneous and was always surprising Mom by saying, "Get in the car, Virlee," and off they would go to some unknown destination, sometimes all the way to Oklahoma. They often called me from Joplin, telling me they were on their way, which was not always the best time for me. One tax season I had over 300 returns to do before April 15, and I got one of those phone calls. It never occurred to Dad to consider whether it was a good time on this end. When he was ready to ramble down to Oklahoma, it was going to happen. Mom, on the other hand, would have preferred to plan things out, but then she was not in charge. She kept a bag packed at all times and was ready for whatever adventure he dreamed up. I think our *Thelma and Louise* escapades reminded her of that. I'd come home from work and say, "Get in the car, Thelma." She'd grab her purse and we were off. She loved to ramble just as much as Dad did.

I found Mom quite useful when in the course of our travels we encountered the highway patrol. A small, plump, elderly woman who would remind you somewhat of Mrs. Santa Claus--short, round, white hair, calico print dress and old fashioned glasses--she was just the sidekick I needed to get out of a ticket. Here's the routine: When pulled over, I simply rolled down the window, pointed to her and told the patrolman, "She made me do it." They always leaned over to take a look, and I got to see the expression on their faces when they spotted Mrs. Santa Claus. Then I asked, "Would you take her to jail?" If that didn't get a laugh, I whispered, "You know, she kidnapped me."

> An Oklahoma patrolman called my bluff when I asked him to take Mom to jail. He said with a strong southern accent, "I would do so, ma'am, but I would have to tase her first." This produced an unpleasant spontaneous visual in my mind, and I decided to skip the kidnapping routine and allowed him the last word. I considered telling him we were *Thelma and Louise* and that I was the one who shot someone, just to get Mom off the hook, but I was fearful he would tase me. Not to worry. A few minutes later I thanked him profusely for a warning ticket. (I never got a ticket when Mom was along.) The patrolman did, however, suggest that my passenger looked suspicious, was likely a threat to any community, and I should get on down the road. I said, "Yes sir, officer. Have a good day, and thank you for your service."

Our escapades distracted Mom from her sorrow somewhat, but she cried a lot, especially when she left the farm. She had accumulated so much stuff that she had a lot of clearing out to do. She told me she burned fifty-some years of valentine candy boxes. I sadly imagined her tossing them into the flames in a barrel in the back yard, crying her heart out. Dad gave her perfume for birthdays and she disposed of many empty cobalt blue bottles and boxes of *Evening in Paris* products.

A "get it done" type of person, Mom did everything with determination. I went to Iowa to spend a week moving her into her apartment in Prescott and was shocked when I arrived to see the hard labor she had invested in moving. I made the apartment as nice as possible for her, replacing the carpet and furnishing it with new things. Everything in the trailer was old and some of it wouldn't fit. Mom rarely had nice things. Being extremely frugal, she couldn't deal with furnishing the apartment with new things, saying: "I don't need that." Consequently, I spread the acquisitions out so she could adjust a bit each day. Although the guilt of acquisition never completely subsided, she got with the program, commenting frequently on how spoiled she was.

Every day we went to a furniture store in a nearby town. She liked the guy who ran the store because her folks traded there. I locked into him, and each day he and I collaborated to convince her she needed something--a new kitchenette, new sofas, end tables, bedroom set, then came lamps and pictures. Kelly was with us when she picked out a water lily picture for the bedroom, and we joked about Mom having a Monet, something outside her scope of awareness. Very few furnishings from the trailer went into her new apartment, turning her into somewhat of a snob. She didn't have the insight to brag that she had a Monet, but she did occasionally comment on how other ladies had old stuff.

Quiet, rather introverted, and a product of the midwestern male-dominated culture of the time, Mom was in Dad's shadow. It was a revelation to me when her strengths began to shine after he died. I always knew Dad was smart, and certainly he called the shots. I never thought much about Mom being smart, but she may be smarter than any of us. She was also responsible, on time (actually, she was always early), following the rules, meeting requirements, keeping the schedule, and expecting everyone else to do the same. She aspired to be right and proper; nevertheless, I got her tipsy on Margaritas occasionally and into a few casinos when we were being *Thelma and Louise*.

In retrospect, the dynamics between Mom and Dad are revealing. Dad was such a card, and Mom reveled in that. She was always hovering quietly in the background, observing his antics. For us kids she was a lie detector. If we wanted to know if Dad was putting us on, all we had to do was glance at Mom. She wouldn't say or do anything, but somehow we just knew. Unfortunately, other people were not aware of this. They were on their own.

For sixteen years Mom stood on her feet all day grinding and wrapping meat in a meat locker for a few cents an hour. After school, five kids stopped in that locker looking for a quarter to buy a malt at the drug store, eating up a good portion of her earnings. We got to be like the other kids because she worked at the locker. We wore nice clothes, ate well, engaged in school activities, and had cars when we turned sixteen.

Mom was a church-going woman. I never heard her swear when I was growing up, but when she fell on my front porch a few years back she said a bad word. It was such a shock that I was more concerned about her going to hell than her physical well being. She was rolling around on the floor of my porch and I didn't say, "Mom, are you okay?" I said, "Mom, you swore!"

> When she visited Oklahoma I worried she would trip and fall on a curb or sidewalk. I worried her old dog would die while she was here. I worried she would trip over the dog, fall on it, hurt herself and kill the dog. It was stressful.

I am what I would describe as a thoughtful worrier, always anticipating a possible accident or other unfortunate incident and then endeavoring to prevent it. I come by this honestly. Mom was a worry wart; however, when the chips were down, she rose to the occasion and demonstrated incredible strength and resilience. You could count on her. Over the years when I needed encouragement and support, I could rely on her to provide it. She was stronger than she seemed--a rescuer in her own right.

Iowans embraced the requirements of midwestern conformity harshly when I was growing up. A fiercely independent youth, I railed against the conformity, and as I began taking charge of my life, I steered away from it at every opportunity. There were significant benefits to being reared in the environment of the heartland, and I am eternally grateful for them. They gave me a solid base of core values and a sense of responsibility that fortunately dampened the consequences of my independent nature. On the other hand, the narrow mindedness, judgement, and requisite conformity never set well with me.

Mom fit comfortably into this world. Although Dad participated in it to some extent, he had the moxie to rebel against it. He did not fit the mold, he didn't go to church, and he marched to his own drum. Unfortunately, he was so indelibly immersed in that highly structured world that he was often made to feel wrong for being who he was. I suspect he paid a huge emotional price for that. Mom confided in me that he told her she should have married a preacher, which reflects his feeling of not measuring up to the right and proper world of Mom and her parents. Dad was not a pillar of the community or a church deacon. Instead, he was a character, a realist, a humorist, and a bit of a rebel.

Although out of step with some aspects of the midwestern culture myself, I never felt a sense of being wrong. Instinctively I determined that the judgement, narrow perspectives, and limitations of the environment I was growing up in were not for me. I longed to graduate from high school and escape--to get out of there. That sounds harsh, especially given the love and support I experienced in my home and community and the many positives that environment provided, but that is exactly how I felt. I couldn't imagine fitting in, and I was really ready to go when I left. What is interesting about that is that I soon wound up in a small town in Oklahoma, a place brimming with prejudices, restricting conformity, and a tendency toward self-righteous judgement that makes Iowa look like a progressive maverick environment. Strangely enough, though, along with all its surface piety, propriety, and professed family values, Oklahoma also had the second highest divorce rate in the nation.

Prescott was a very small town of about three hundred people. Because it was so small and everyone knew everyone else, gossip was a favorite pastime among the women. After I moved away, I was home for a visit. Mom, Grandma, and Auntie Poll were talking about a neighbor lady's cold sore. They went on and on about it. I found it so funny that I had to leave the room and ended up giggling in the kitchen.

I finally got myself together and re-entered the room some time later only to find them still talking about it. I mean, how much can you say about a cold sore? I ran back into the kitchen. Finally, they moved on to a car accident that didn't happen. It was a near miss at an intersection and worthy of considerable discussion. They also gossiped about someone who didn't bake a pie for a funeral dinner and a Catholic family who had moved into town. I spent a lot of time in the kitchen that day. (The Catholic family did not stay in Prescott very long.)

While in high school I went on a date with a boy from a neighboring town. Turns out he was Catholic. Mom noticed the statue of Mother Mary on the dash of his car and made it clear she didn't want me going out with him. I was ignorant and when he asked me out again, I told him no and then told him why. I'd like a do over on that one.

Being prejudiced and having virtually no exposure to diverse cultures, Mom worried when I moved to Oklahoma that my children would marry Indians. When my daughter moved to California she worried she would marry a foreigner, and she did, a German fellow from Trinidad no less. Trinidadians believe that rum is a vitamin. Germans think beer is one of the four food groups. My son-in-law thinks I'm a frenzy with victims. He's a mess. I love him. Mom was quite taken with him as well, even though he was a foreigner.

Mom was a product of her environment. Prejudices are learned. Small children have no concept of them until someone teaches them that certain people are below them. Without that teaching, they just see them as different. Over the years Mom, like most people, learned new perceptions, and she softened considerably. I like to think my daughter, Mel, and I brought her along a bit in this regard, and there is some evidence of that. In her last days, her favorite aide in the nursing home was an Asian girl. Who would have thought that would happen?

Melanie, who doesn't have a prejudiced bone in her body, had an Asian girlfriend while living in California, and at the time of Mom's visit they were roommates. Mel and I decided not to forewarn her about this. Mom had a way of huffing and puffing when she disapproved of something, which she did when Mel's roommate walked in, and I rather enjoyed her obvious distress. She had never been this close to an Asian before. It was huge.

I watched her study the girl over the course of the visit. She was such a nice girl. It was impossible not to like her, and I think Mom got there, although I can't be sure. It was quite a leap for her. Months later when Melanie told me an African American girlfriend was living with her temporarily I thought, I have got to get Mom to California. I mean, I must see this.

When I took her to Hawaii, we had just arrived and were sitting at an outside cafe sipping pineapple drinks with umbrellas in them when Mom suddenly took on an expression of grave concern, eyes narrowed, shifting back and forth. Something was clearly concerning her. "Mom, what's wrong?" I asked. She looked both ways to make certain no one could hear her, leaned over the table and whispered, "All these people here are foreigners." She was dead serious and was genuinely stunned when I explained to her that in Hawaii she was the foreigner. It really was a concept beyond her comprehension and she was completely befuddled by it, but she managed to pull herself together enough to do some serious huffing and puffing and to finish the drink with an umbrella in it.

There were no minorities in southwestern Iowa when I was growing up. None. That is no longer true. I'd already left home when the first African Americans moved into that part of Iowa in the mid-sixties. A junior college recruited a few to play basketball. They apparently were not treated well, which is probably an understatement. At any rate, they didn't stay long, and they left suddenly, after which someone described the basketball team as "white and all right." Since then, Iowa, like most of the country, has come a long way, and so had Mom. With exposure, she mellowed over the years although, given the right circumstance, she could still get to huffing and puffing.

Now there are industrial plants around the area that employ people from other places, even foreign countries, propagating even more diversity. The influence of other cultures is particularly evident in the assortment of popular restaurants in the area. Is it possible that food, like music, is a major catalyst for mutual appreciation? I'm amazed by the changes; however, I'm not sure how much this turn of events reflects feelings. On the surface it appears there is an evolving concept of common humanity, but I suspect an undercurrent of pronounced prejudice. You can tell what adults are thinking behind outward political correctness by what their children say on the internet. This is admittedly an over-generalization, but if the kid says it, the parents probably think it.

Mom was not much open to anything different from life in Iowa. When I began taking her on trips to wonderful places she always had issues. In Salt Lake City she worried the mountains would slide in on her; in Hawaii there were surely sharks in the ocean. Everywhere I took her she would say: "I don't know why anyone would want to live here." Now this was coming from a woman who lived through incredibly harsh winters among the pig farms and feed lots of the great plains of Iowa, a wonderful place in its own right, but it is not Utah.

She wondered why anyone would want to live in the city and ramble around in big houses, and she grappled with the fact that there was no way to know where all the people driving around were going. In Prescott, when someone drove down the road, you pretty much knew where they were headed by their habits and the direction they were headed. Any situation outside of Mom's Iowa environment was interpreted by her as an unpleasant mystery, so on a plane bound for California, I advised her not to say bad things about California to my daughter whom we were visiting there. No doubt, Mom was not going to like California. I explained that Mel decided to live there, she liked it, and nothing is accomplished by saying bad things about it. She did pretty well and faced the challenges of the trip with good humor. Mel and I shamefully made certain there were challenges. Our plan was to broaden her horizons. Grandma was going to see a whole new world, outside of Iowa.

We took her to Venice Beach where wild and crazy people hang out looking like an extreme costume party or a *Rocky Horror Picture Show* event in progress. Here was my dialogue around this experience:

- Mom, how about we get you this tie-dyed muu muu?
- Mom, you want a tattoo? This skull and crossbones looks interesting. It's not about poison. It's about pirates. We love pirates.
- Don't worry about it, they are probably just making a movie.
- She's not naked as a jay bird, Mom. That's a thong and everyone wears them.
- It's not that odd. Many Indians wear mohawks.
- Body piercing is not a magic act.
- Yes, that is, in fact, a man walking another man with a dog collar and leash.
- You want a drink with an umbrella in it?

It was no surprise when in her Christmas letter that year she called it Weirdo Beach and wrote: "There sure are a lot of weird people in California."

Mom was simply an Iowa kind of gal and no place else, no matter how wonderful, ever appealed to her. For me, Iowa certainly held many wonderful qualities, and I love to visit there, but I never considered moving back, mostly for climate reasons. It is frigging freezing cold there in the winter.

I didn't grasp the extent of that until I moved south. Having not experienced anything any different, I did not realize how harsh the northern winters were. After moving south from Iowa and Chicago to Oklahoma, I experienced the alternative, and I liked it. Of course, Oklahoma is frigging hot in the summer. Everything burns up in July, literally and figuratively. There are signs along the highways that say: "Don't drive through smoke." Pick your poison.

> Dad had ancestors who moved to Oklahoma shortly after Indian Territory was open for settlement. Two brothers relocated to Cushing. One brother was a carpenter and eventually owned a furniture store. The other brother returned to Iowa, saying he would rather die trying to farm in Iowa than live trying to farm in Oklahoma. He had a point. Oklahoma soil cannot compare to that black Iowa dirt. Coming from Iowa to Oklahoma and expecting to raise corn is a losing proposition. I don't care what they say about corn in songs about Oklahoma, we don't grow corn here. It is frigging hot down here.

After Dad died Mom lived in senior housing. I have well-off Oklahoma friends who have second homes in places like Vail, Sun Valley, and Grand Lake. After I spent a week in Iowa moving Mom into her senior apartment, I announced to these friends that I had a second home. They were all excited and wanted to know when they could see it. Their enthusiasm waned when I told them I had an apartment in a senior center in Iowa.

I liked the place and enjoyed long visits with Mom there. We watched soaps, Lawrence Welk, and The Price Is Right. Teaming up, we worked jigsaw puzzles and word puzzles, and Mom yelled at me when I read into the night, telling me I would surely go blind. It was quite a fright to see her in the doorway in the middle of the night, hair askew, waving her cane, scolding me with enthusiasm reminiscent of one of Grandma Bray's fits. I was afraid she might lose it and box my ears with her cane.

At eighty-eight Mom was still mentally pretty sharp, but she did have her moments of confusion, as did ninety-one year old Aunt June. They lived in the same town for many years and called each other regularly. Considerable confusion ensued one day over who called who. This was important because in Iowa whoever called is the one who ends the conversation.

Steeped in tradition, Mom and Aunt June were determined to follow the required protocol. When they couldn't figure out who called who, it created quite a dilemma. Sitting on the sofa reading and possibly going blind, I heard Mom's side of a conversation in this regard, and even I became confused. Who called who? Without blatantly asking who initiated the call, both women were trying to figure it out. Apparently, neither wanted to admit they were so confused that they didn't know. I can only guess at Aunt June's end of the conversation but surmise it went something like this:

Mom: Well I'm glad we visited.
Aunt June: Yes, me too.

Mom: It was good to talk to you.
Aunt June: Yes, it was good to talk.

Mom: Yes.
Aunt June: Well, yes, it was.

Mom: Ah, well. I better get busy.
Aunt June: Ah, yeah, me too.

Mom: Sure is nice weather today.
Aunt June: Yes, it is.

Mom: Well it is nice talking to you.
Aunt June: Yes, it is nice to talk.

Mom: The squirrels are out today.
Aunt June: Really. How nice. Good to hear from you.

Mom: I'm glad you called, or I called. Who called?
Aunt June: I don't know. Did you call?

Mom: I think I called you the last time.

Aunt June: I called you the other day.

Mom: Yes, so I called you then?
Aunt June: Who called me now?

Well, you get the gist. This went on for some time. I don't remember how it finally ended, but Mom was tremendously troubled over the incident. When she hung up she asked me who called who, like I would know. I mean, I was mentally exhausted from listening to the whole episode. I couldn't remember if the phone rang or not, which had me concerned that I was losing it and possibly joining the club. I considered doubling my dose of Ginkgo Biloba and working more crossword puzzles. I could see my future through Mom and June. That was scary. In addition, I might go blind if I finished the John Adams biography I was reading. It was a nightmare. Then, there is the issue of hearing.

Mom's loss of hearing was an unfortunate handicap, and it has caused me to worry about losing my own hearing. The kids tell me I play the TV too loud, to which I respond: "WHAT?"

It is isolating to not be able to hear. When I stayed with Mom in her apartment she watched TV with both the mute and the closed caption features on. As a result, when Lawrence Welk was on there was no sound, but the lyrics popped up at the bottom of the TV screen along with music symbols, you know, little black notes sprinkled here and there amongst the words. I found *The Lawrence Welk Show* charmingly entertaining. For example, I once observed a quaint but stiff and properly costumed gospel singing couple sweetly crooning *One Toke Over the Line, Sweet Jesus*. (You can't make this stuff up.) One day, hoping for a similar treat, I asked mom to take the TV off mute.

Me: Mom, why don't you take it off mute so I can hear?

Mom: What?

Me: WHY DON'T YOU TAKE IT OFF MUTE SO I CAN HEAR?

Mom: WHAT?

Me: Never mind.

Mom: WHAT?

Like I say, I worry about losing my hearing.

Her hearing aids would squeal occasionally, "eeeeeeeeee." Sometimes she realized it and sometimes she didn't. When I attended church with her, hearing aides were going "eeeeeeeeee" all over the sanctuary providing interesting sound effects for the hymns and considerable distraction from the sermon. Some of the folks realized it and some didn't.

Once when I talked to Mom on the phone I asked her if she was watching much TV. She told me she wasn't able to get it to lather up good. Like I said, I worry about losing my hearing.

Mom never accepted the fact that medicine could not fix everything. As her hearing declined, she was determined to get to the bottom of the matter and hear like she used to. She asked her doctor for the umpteenth time what was wrong with her ears. In frustration he said, "YOU CAN'T HEAR." The eye doctor told her she couldn't see, and sadly she was sitting around waiting for the next things she couldn't do. Soon she was unable to walk, and that changed everything.

Those days with Mom in her little apartment were special, cozy, lazy times. When I was still working a high stress job, settling into her place for a few days was a de-stress opportunity. It felt good being her companion. It also gave Gary a break from the demands of care taking. I stocked her up on groceries, prepared food for her freezer, hauled her around to visit friends and relatives, and helped her decorate for every holiday.

We went someplace every day--*Thelma and Louise* heading out to some small adventure. The days of big adventures were behind us. I could tell she was declining. Medical crises began gaining momentum. I tried to get her mentally prepared for the impending nursing home stage of her life but, as is often the case, she had difficulty accepting the inevitable.

Mom went into a nursing home at eighty-eight when she could no longer walk and other things were failing. She was bummed about it, and I was trying to cheer her up. I reminded her that she had twenty-seven descendants, all alive and healthy (except the grandchild who burned his lip on a flaming blue drink in a

Costa Rica disco). All are productive members of society (except those of us claiming to be training for the Olympics). There are no tattoos of snakes or skulls (that we know of), most smokers have quit (those that do smoke at least don't lie about it), no one drinks much (although songs about drunken monkeys still resonate), race car driving is in the past, everyone has a job or had one and are now retired, babies and old folks are taken care of, dogs are fed, mortgages and taxes paid, no one is in Tijuana or jail, and we have a minister in the family praying for us. Grandpa and Grandma Bray would have been proud. Additionally, we all get along and have no family squabbles. Everyone is connected. This is highly unusual. Not only should this be a comfort to her, I said, but she can be proud because this is no accident. She must have done something right.

I don't think she got it, though. She was on a quest for her blood pressure cuff, mumbling something about how she can't reach her feet anymore, and that she sure hopes they don't serve green beans for supper. Mom suddenly hated green beans.

She complained about the food at the nursing home and seemed to have lost her appetite. Mom had always enjoyed eating and once she finished one meal she was contemplating the next, so this was a big shift. She may have lost her sense of taste which sometimes happens to the elderly. I ate with her at the nursing home several times, and it was good home-cooked Iowa food.

The ladies at her table were talking about their favorite desserts one day, none of which Mom liked. They commented on how much they enjoyed the ice cream, to which Mom responded that it was no good. I asked her what was wrong with ice cream and she said, "It's melted." One day on the phone I asked her what was on the menu for dinner and she said, "Nothing." Green beans was not the only thing Mom didn't like, and evidently she didn't like anything on the menu that day.

She had several stints in the hospital where she was constantly frustrated because they brought her a chocolate chip cookie every afternoon. She didn't like chocolate chip cookies and told them so, but they kept coming. Her doctor was there one day when the cookie arrived. She complained about it. Being well acquainted with her disposition, he snatched up the cookie and ate it, joking about timing his future visits to get one. She was quite taken back. When she told me about the incident later she said, "He shouldn't have done it," but she did have a twinkle in her eye when she said it. She got the joke.

Mom was well cared for in the nursing home. In small rural communities where everyone knows everyone else you cannot treat old folks poorly. Brother Gary and his wife diligently visited her daily. Still, she had a pretty rough go there. She was sick one day while I was there and asked me to help her take off her wedding ring. I thought perhaps her fingers were swelling, but when I asked her what she wanted me to do with it she said, "Keep it. I'm dying." When an aide entered, Mom was being sick and I was crying. The aide was very sweet and comforted both of us. The next morning I slipped the ring back on Mom's finger as she had decided she had to live another day to face green beans and melted ice cream.

Her temperament fluctuated. She was justifiably frustrated by the lack of control over daily life that comes with the nursing home setting, and she was saddled with gripping pain and declining physical abilities. It is a struggle when, as she said, "You can't walk so good, can't hear so good, can't see so good, and are no good." She had some vitality left as evidenced by her being in trouble with the staff for speeding in her wheelchair.

LOSING MOM

The end of Mom's life proved difficult for her and those around her. She suffered so much and was often grumpy. She aptly described herself when she said, "I'm madder than an old wet hen." Knowing that her whole life was devoted to making things better for her children, it was particularly sad as one of those children to witness her enduring so much at the end of her life. Being the rescuer that I am, it was frustrating that I was unable to fix her world, and she did not leave it easily. She died on October 2, 2010 at the age of eighty-eight.

I try to focus memories on the earlier years and what an awesome Mother she was. She was a happy, joyful, and devoted Mom. Chasing us children around the house with a yardstick and laughing along with us epitomizes her as a young mother. It is one of my favorite memories. There was no sacrifice she wouldn't make for her five children, and if she perceived any threat to them, she was all over it. It is important that we kids remember her as she was. I will always remember how her whole face lit up when I walked into the room, even in her last days. To have that kind of effect on someone sends a strong signal of relevance. Mom always made me feel as if I was somebody very, very special, her favorite. I have no doubt she made each one of the boys feel the same way.

Strangely, I realize I spent much of my life trying to not be like Mom. I understand this is not that unusual, but it has bothered me because she was such a wonderful mother. I now realize that this is because I didn't want the kind of life she had. It had nothing to do with my love for her.

Although her last years were difficult because of deteriorating disposition and health, we had a special bond, and I have many wonderful memories of our adventures together. I treasure them. I also know, without a doubt, that at one point in my life she literally saved me. I wish I could have saved her some of the suffering at the end, but I couldn't. I just couldn't.

After Mom was gone, the nursing home staff missed her. She occasionally gave them a run for their money as she dealt with her difficult decline, but they enjoyed her sense of humor.

Intensely private, Mom was always insistent that she didn't want any kind of service when she died, so we kids, Aunt Weezie, and a few others simply gathered at the gravesite. Brother Kelly did a short non-service during which he reminded us several times that it was not a service. Afterwards, we all complimented him on a fine and touching non-service.

Tiny great-grandchildren gleefully tossed handfuls of dirt in the grave as we huddled together there, our Mother and Father both gone. I felt unanchored, and that evening in my brother's basement I sobbed as I hugged my Mother's clothes hanging on a coat rack there, missing her, feeling regret that I didn't do more for her, and wondering if my brothers would now scatter to the winds without the force of this incredible mother nurturing our togetherness. The glue that held us together was gone.

Mom was always a binding force, and in addition to the impact this had on her own children, she left a legacy to my children that is invaluable. She told them often how lucky they were to have me as a mother. They needed to hear that, especially during the period of a divorce turned ugly. She left her mark on them, and for that I am eternally grateful. It has been a lesson for me on how as a grandparent I can influence little minds. The mother is gone, but the legacy remains.

A COHESIVE BUNCH

Over the years I've had the opportunity to observe the family dynamics of others and have come to appreciate something special about my family. We don't fight or argue. We are different in our life styles, political and religious affiliations, and our views of the world, but we have a similar style of interacting with others. We allow others to have their opinions, their quirks and unique qualities. If someone pops off, we ignore it.

We are not devoid of judgement, but we pretty much keep that to ourselves. In other words, we let everybody just be, and we often find humor in our differences. We may be put out with each other, and we have all said things we regret, but we don't fight. None of us are enticed by drama. I can't think of a single argument among any of us since we've become adults. On second thought, I can. After Dad died we kids and Mom were meeting with an attorney to settle some details. They didn't have

121

much, but there were a few items to divide up, and we kids argued about getting one of us to take something. (We never fought over who got anything.) The attorney looked on curiously as we argued:

> We know you don't want to, but we have decided you need to take it.

> But, I don't think it is right. You guys need to divide it up.

> You are going to take it whether you like it or not.

> But, I feel we already got our share.

> You are going to get it anyway. Just take it and shut up.

Brother Gary and his wife took care of Mom for several years, devotedly caring for her through many age-related transitions and health crises. They visited her every day and tended to her needs. Mom was a challenge and the rest of us were grateful for what Gary did. We supported him in all decisions. Many times over the years I have observed members of other families criticize the decisions of those doing the care taking. My brothers and I never second guessed Gary. Kelly put it so well when he said, "The only thing I am going to say to Gary is: 'Thank you.'"

I've also noticed that many families frequently engage in considerable drama, expecting it at every family event and preparing a drama-filled response ahead of time for some anticipated affront. This typically spawns a predictable outburst followed by a flurry of apologies and making up after everyone cools down. Iowans are not inclined to do drama and rarely does anyone get so crazy that they have to apologize for anything. I am grateful for that. It is one of the many Iowa values that has served me well over the years.

We kids stuck together tightly through Mom's end-of-life experience because, as Kelly so brilliantly put it: "The worst thing that could happen to Mom is for her kids to have a fight or falling out." We are a cohesive bunch, and although this sometimes frustrated Mom because we so often ganged up on her, she was primarily responsible for it.

Mom was undoubtedly the driving force behind our family being so connected, and brother Dennis sealed that connection with a family newsletter he published for many years. If we missed writing an article for the newsletter each month Mom was all over us. She pushed and prodded all of us to keep in touch with each other and to attend family events. Constantly and diligently she championed our staying connected. My son Marty called me one day because Grandma told him to, and she did so in no uncertain terms. She had asked me on the phone how he was doing, and I told her I didn't know. I hadn't talked to him in awhile. She was having none of that, and she called him and gave him a royal chewing out for not calling his mother. He said she tore into him pretty good, and that he was afraid of her. It may have been a fit or perhaps even a conniption. Whatever it was, it had its intended effect.

As I view Mom's life from my earliest memories to observations of her end-of-life phase, I can't help but notice the things that changed and, in contrast, those that stayed the same. The happy, playful mother of our early years transitioned into a determined, strong widow who was the perfect girlfriend and companion, and then into a vulnerable, frightened, understandably unhappy old woman trying desperately to deal with things she could no longer control. She progressed from blatant and intense prejudices to deciding an Asian girl was her favorite caretaker, and she came to embrace and even admire my independent lifestyle that troubled her so much in earlier years.

In other areas, she stayed the same, holding her position to the end. All her life she struggled with her weight, always worrying about what to eat but eating whatever she wanted. When she got into her seventies I tried to convince her to eat whatever she wanted without worrying about it, but worrying about weight (and anything else she could imagine) was an inherent part of her everyday life, and she wasn't about to give it up. Although excessive worrying was often a frustration to my brothers and me, her concerns often accomplished her intent to protect those she loved. It is impossible to speculate how many times her worrying saved us from some crisis or another.

Her devotion to Dad was constant and enduring. His bad boy image, at least in the minds of her parents, was probably part of the attraction. When he made bets in a bar that Reno, was west of San Diego and won, she reveled in the victory even though betting was a sin. Something else that never changed was Mom's determined focus on her children. She never wavered in that regard. She was, above all else, a mother, and that role defined her. We were always on her mind, always her primary concern, and always what she worried about most. I worried about something a lot. I worried she would outlive one of her children.

One of the things that worried Mom the most was friction between her children. Any sign of discord set her on a path of pestering us unmercifully to patch things up. As a mother-in-law she had her low moments. No one was ever good enough for her boys, but she lectured us if we exhibited bad behavior toward anyone joining our ranks. My brothers carried off my sister-in-law's Volkswagen Beetle and hid it. They got a scolding.

A sister-in-law asked me the day of a wedding if I would watch the person who was to help me cut the cake and make certain she didn't eat any because she was diabetic. I was contemplating my strategy for keeping this grown woman from eating cake and said, "Well, how big an old gal is she? If I have to wrestle her to the ground to keep her from eating cake, I need to know how big she is. I might need a five-gallon bucket of kick ass." My brothers laughed. Mom scolded me later.

After Mom died, brother Gary and I were going through the funeral arrangements she had made. The last instruction was: "You kids take care of each other."

5

FINDING MY STRIDE

Independence Day

At some point in my late teens I began developing an aversion to being like everyone else. I didn't fully embrace the structured environment in which I was raised, identifying more with my dad than my mother. She was a responsible, reliable, church going pillar of the community. Dad was, well, Dad was fun, a bit of a rebel. He didn't go to church, he didn't necessarily follow all of society's rules, and he was known to have a beer, which to many in the community was outrageous behavior. He might even pour a beer into your cap if you left it on a table and didn't keep an eye on it. Dad was never boring. Fortunately or unfortunately, depending on how you look at it, I related to that.

This is why I didn't go to Des Moines after high school and get a job with an insurance company until I got married, as many young girls who left our farming community did. I wanted to do more, something different. In my marriage I reluctantly acquiesced to conforming to the social norms of the heartland, but over time I became quite the independent spirit that my authentic self suggested, much to the chagrin of my husband and to some extent my parents.

I got married to my high school boyfriend, which is pretty much what everyone did in those days, finished my business school program, and moved to Chicago where he got a job with an airline, and we had a baby. I had filled my prescription for newly introduced birth control pills and was waiting until the appropriate time of the month to start taking them only to discover I was already pregnant. This was not in the plan, but there it was. I just missed the modern benefits of planned parenthood by one month.

We lived in an eight-foot wide trailer just off an O'Hare Airport runway. Building homes off the runway was prohibited, but trailer parks were allowed. The trailer was not air conditioned. We had to keep the windows open in the summer, and the airplanes overhead were loud.

This is rather historic. We occasionally ate hamburgers at the first McDonald's in Elk Grove Village, a neighboring Chicago suburb. They had a sign out front of how many hamburgers they had sold. I don't remember the exact number, but it was quite small, in the thousands. Still, we were impressed, not having any frame of reference related to the potential volumes to come.

Our moving to Chicago was a brave and unusual thing for young adults from our Iowa hometown to do. Most stayed in the area or went to Des Moines, Omaha, or Kansas City. I don't know anyone who went to Chicago. We didn't have visitors for awhile. People didn't travel as they do now, so we were alone in Chicago until the baby came at which time Mom rode up on the train to help out. We were happy and occasionally enjoyed exploring the city, but we were farm kids and were determined to save money every way we could in order to get out of there.

Being products of the plains of Iowa we could not imagine living permanently in the big city of Chicago. WE MUST HAVE LAND.

So we studied all the cities the airline flew into to target places where we might want to live. Our plan was to transfer to somewhere *out West*, a romantic notion in our minds. Our whole world for three years revolved around saving and planning to make that happen.

I was fairly isolated in Chicago, not knowing anyone. My world was the trailer park, and people were not friendly. I wrote regular letters home and learned to cook and keep house. I sewed a lot, making curtains for the trailer and clothes for myself. I earned money by babysitting and taking in ironing. We saved every dollar I earned and began making plans for the baby.

> I went to the Cook County Library and got a book on having a baby. It was written by a doctor, a man of course. All doctors were men. His message was that labor didn't really hurt, and childbirth pain was in the mind. As support for this premise, he pointed out that animals don't scream in pain during childbirth, and he described it as mildly uncomfortable if you had the right mindset. (You can't make this stuff up.) Women didn't talk about such things as childbirth as they do today, and being fairly isolated I had no one to advise me, so I believed it. I know. It is embarrassing to admit this, but I did believe it--that is, until the first contraction hit.

After Marty was born, having a baby was not something I wanted to repeat anytime soon. It took seven years to get up the courage to do it again. The delivery involved a sympathetic anesthesiologist who could not give me any anesthesia because of a blood pressure crisis and nurses who were mean to me for not getting up for days after the delivery. I could tell I was going to faint, but they were unsympathetic. Finally, it was discovered I was severely anemic. Incredibly painful iron shots followed which left huge bruises on my butt which were still visible on my son's first birthday. It was an ordeal, but the baby was such a sweet, precious little thing. I loved him immediately and delighted in everything about him.

I was home from the hospital with my new baby and a hovering Mom when the news came on television that President Kennedy had been shot. As the bad news unfolded, I eventually overreacted and became rather hysterical. Mom scolded me, insisting that I remain calm and focus on taking care of the baby, particularly since I was nursing. This was not the last time she was to calm my nerves and set me straight. She was always a stable, settling influence, a bit of a worry wart but a rock when the chips were down.

A few months after the baby was born, I got a job with an airline at O'Hare Airport as an executive secretary and was soon promoted to the executive offices. We saved every dime I earned. My husband worked overtime, and we saved a substantial amount of his earnings as well--socking it away to buy LAND when we moved out West. We worked different shifts so we could take care of the baby ourselves, me working days and my husband nights. This was fairly exhausting, and we were outrageously frugal, but I don't remember it as a struggle. We were in pursuit of a dream and had an undeniable sense of purpose and hopefulness. It was a special time.

GET DRUNK AND IRON

Because I was a working wife and a new mother, weekends were not restful. They were full of cooking, cleaning house, and laundry in addition to caring for the baby. Saturdays included washing diapers and clothes. I often washed things in the kitchen sink, hanging them on the clothesline to dry, weather permitting. Sometimes laundry was hung around in the trailer. This illustrates the level of our frugalness, although once I went to work we began using a laundromat.

We didn't have permanent press or synthetic fabrics, so I ironed everything, including jeans, sheets, pillowcases, handkerchiefs, and even t-shirts. This was quite a process. Many items had to be starched, a messy undertaking also done in the sink, that is, until spray starch showed up. Before ironing, I sprinkled clothes with a water bottle, rolled them up and put them in a plastic bag in the refrigerator overnight so they would be slightly damp. (We didn't have steam irons.) The next day I took them out of the refrigerator to iron. It was so much work that I wondered how Mom managed to do laundry for a farmer and five kids.

My neighbor Sharon and I hated ironing. We spent most of the day Sunday ironing, so we started doing it together. I dragged my ironing board over to her trailer, she opened a six pack, and we drank beer and ironed. I wasn't much of a drinker, so Sharon drank most of it, but it doesn't take much to get me snockered either. We were both pretty hammered by the time we finished. Get drunk and iron, that's what we did on a Sunday. Years later when permanent press fabrics were the norm, I became spoiled. If something came out of the dryer wrinkled, I threw it away.

We remained in our little trailer in Chicago until Marty was three, at which time we made our move. Having saved what we considered the requisite amount of cash and after flying around the country looking for where we wanted to live, we focused on Oklahoma. Once we hit Tulsa on a weekend excursion, we knew that was it. My husband's transfer request went through quickly. I quit my job, and we were off.

OKLAHOMA DREAMING

While pregnant and before I started working in Chicago, I babysat a four-year-old boy from Oklahoma. He had a strong southern accent and was always saying he was *fixin'* to do something, which I thought was so incredibly countrified. Little did I know that three years later we would be in Oklahoma *fixin'* to do things ourselves.

It was 1966 when, after three years in Chicago, we sold our trailer and transferred to Tulsa with an amazing amount of cash in the bank, especially for such a young couple. We were barely old enough to drink, but we had more money than many people accumulated in a lifetime. We lived in an apartment for a couple of months while scouting for a home with LAND in the green rolling hills beyond the city.

While I was visiting with a neighbor outside our apartment, her little girl and Marty, who was three, wandered over to the pool. Someone had left the gate open. Hearing a splash, I turned around to see the little girl standing at the edge of the pool by herself. I ran to the pool at a full sprint to find Marty underwater in the deep end, his little feet kicking like crazy. I went in feet first at a hard run and pushed myself up from the bottom, catching him on the way up. He popped up before I did. He didn't even cough. He had instinctively held his breath the whole time. If I had not heard the splash and turned around to see who was swimming that early in the day...I can't even say it.

We bought thirty acres outside of Tulsa with a nice house on it. We had LAND. It was an exceptionally beautiful place, exceeding any expectations we had. We realized our dream, and then some. The house was fairly new, high on a hill nestled into the trees. A Frank Lloyd Wright style, it was made of native stone with large windows and a huge rock patio. I am embarrassed to say that I furnished it in the Spanish decor popular at the time. We had an incredible view of the blue hills across the green valley below. The land was fenced, cross fenced and had fruit trees, a garden, two ponds, and two small barns.

We bottle fed a calf and a baby pig, raised hogs, chickens, ducks and had several dogs who had a propensity to kill chickens and ducks when the coyotes didn't get to them first. Other than the disappearing fowl, it was a great life for Marty. He and his dad did chores and went fishing. I cooked frog legs from the pond and squirrels from the trees, made jelly from the wild plum trees and blackberry bushes, and worked in the garden. We also had spiders and scorpions in the house, tarantulas and copperhead snakes in the yard, water moccasins in the pond, wasp nests in the eaves, not to mention the fact that it was a tick wonderland. Welcome to Oklahoma. These were not the only hazards.

> Marty was playing with cars in the dirt in the front yard one day when I looked out the window and saw a Chow dog stalking him, circling, crouched and ready to spring. I went out on the front porch and walked cautiously toward Marty instructing him to get up and walk slowly to me. He got up, ran to me and the dog sprung, tearing at his coat. I got to him, picked him up and faced a hugely pissed snarling chow. Backing my way into the house, I stared down that mad dog with the fierceness of a mother protecting her young. I was afraid, but the adrenalin was pumping, and I was contemplating how to poke his eyes out while he chewed on me if he attacked.

> Once in the house I screamed for my husband who grabbed a shotgun and was greeted on the front porch by a snarling dog who was swiftly and surely shot square in the face.

We paid a visit to the dog's owners, new neighbors who had recently moved in, and we weren't bringing cookies. We brought Marty's shredded coat. They were none too happy about what we had done and accused us of being cruel people. I thought: "Okay, I'll take that. I am cruel, but I still have my son." The dog owners had no children. They didn't get it, and we didn't care. We were thinking: "So sue us."

Marty started kindergarten at a little country school down the road. When a big yellow school bus picked him up for the first time, I let him walk down the long driveway to the road by himself like a big boy while I hid behind a tree and cried. I will never forget that little guy boarding that bus. He was so excited. Hiding behind the tree when it was time for him to come home, I watched the bus drive by without stopping and cried again while I raced to the school in a panic. I found him waiting there with the teacher who explained that he knew he was to ride the bus to school but did not understand he was to ride it home. I thought he knew, but how would he know if no one told him? Marty always seems to take things pretty much in stride and even as a little fellow he did so. To him it was no big deal.

THE DREAM FADES

Four years later our lovely place in the hills of eastern Oklahoma was no longer ours. My husband wanted to sell it and get something else, something more rural, not as nice, and completely paid for. I never understood why he couldn't settle in there, and I still don't.

I am just guessing here, but I think it was too much of a step up from the trailer in Chicago and how we lived growing up. He never felt comfortable with something that nice. He is a simple man and wanted something more modest. Unfortunately, living like you are poor when you are not poor was contrary to my basic instincts, and I felt the sting of the loss of our dream home intensely. It was what I thought we had worked so hard for, and I couldn't apprehend his discontent.

We were so set up. He had a good job with the airlines, and I worked as a bookkeeper for a CPA in town and as a secretary for the city schools. The place was almost paid for because we had such a big down payment. Since I worked, we were able to pay extra on the mortgage principal every month and still save money. When we bought it, I thought we would live there the rest of our lives and raise our family there. I had settled in, but I wanted my husband to be happy, so I gave in and it was done. It sold quickly. I didn't realize it then, but this loss put the first nail in the coffin of our marriage.

I had a baby girl just before we left the country place, and looking back, I think a bit of postpartum depression left me psychologically weak. I didn't have the spirit to buck up and insist we keep our home, and in the time and culture in which we were raised, women didn't do much bucking up.

There was little focus on women's needs, and wives often assumed self-sacrificing roles. Although being a martyr is not my nature, it was my frame of reference, and it posed some novel implications. For example, I was often anemic and recall being exceedingly tired and wanting to take a nap. This seemed strange to my husband who was puzzled by this need. He perceived my taking naps as being lazy and pointed out that his Mom never took a nap and neither did mine. That was true. I felt inadequate because I really wanted that nap.

We moved into a rental place when the country home sold, and I couldn't get my husband out of it. We looked for a place to buy but nothing suited him, unless it was so remote and shabby that I refused to raise our children there. One of the places that interested him had creepy neighbors and roads that were impassable in bad weather. I thought: "You've got to be kidding."

I came to realize his vision of rural living was very different from mine. Apparently his idea of LAND out west was a wilderness, Grizzly Adams, mountain man thing. When we did find a couple of compromise properties, he could not make a decision to act and we lost out on them. I was becoming hugely frustrated and began to think we would be living in the rental house forever.

The rent house had a suspect furnace and cold floors. Marty was shooting out street lights with the neighborhood rabble-rousers. They were actually a delightful gang of boys, but wild and wooly and a bit too adventuresome for my comfort level. As we approached our second winter there, I decided I was not going to have my baby crawling around on the cold floors all winter, nor was I willing to risk us all burning up in a furnace fire. I was also not up for rescuing Marty from juvenile hall.

After subtly exerting considerable influence to get my husband to act on something suitable, I determined he never would unless I forced the issue. I went house hunting on my own and found what I thought was a suitable place, arranged for a cash contract on it, told him the kids and I were moving into it before winter, and we hoped he would come with us. He did. This was a brazen thing for a wife to do, and you have to know I was tremendously frustrated to do it. Even more surprising is that he went along with it. I couldn't take a nap, but I could buy a house.

After giving up the homestead, I began working on a college degree. My husband wasn't too keen on my getting an education, but he allowed it as long as I kept up with the housework. This was the same mandate I had when I had jobs. I worked as a secretary and bookkeeper throughout our marriage except for a time after Melanie was born. Though few women worked outside the home at that time, I liked to work and was driven to do so primarily for the stimulation. I made good money in Chicago, but was not paid well in Oklahoma. It was barely worthwhile to work once we had to pay child care costs for two.

In those years women who worked outside the home were the exception and took criticism for doing so. There were many magazine articles and news stories on the controversy. Now most women work and the stay-at-home moms are often on the defensive, a scenario I never could have predicted

My husband and I had some good years and created a nice little

family. The early years were especially good with both of us wanting the same things. Eleven years later we were headed toward divorce. If I had stayed the Iowa farm girl he married, the marriage would probably have survived. Most of his behavior was in response to my changing.

My going to school irritated him. I was not allowed to study when he was present, and I couldn't leave my books lying around. My career choice once I got a degree was limited to teaching school, an acceptable job for a woman in his mind. In the back of my mind I had bigger ideas but they were cloudy and undefined. Women didn't have serious careers, but I secretly had thoughts of not doing what everyone else did, although I had no idea what that would be. This was the 1970's; the feminist movement was ramping up. Women were beginning to aspire to careers never dreamed of before. This prospect was enticing to me. I was a bookkeeper. I asked myself, Could I possibly be an accountant? Becoming a Certified Public Accountant was not on my radar yet, but it would be within a year.

My poor husband was trying desperately to reel me in. My working was always problematic for him. Although he appreciated the extra income, he did not like the distraction and the implications of my independence. My going to college compounded his anxiety, and he put considerable effort into putting me in my place. He was a man trying to control a woman who was, no doubt, out of control. I began to feel his intense disapproval of me and everything I did. I understand now that this disapproval most likely stemmed from insecurity which was expressed through attempts at leveling--putting me down and keeping me in my place--but I had no sense of that then.

His distress was compounded by problems at work which had an intense impact on his disposition. I observed the union turn this hard-working Iowa farm boy into an unhappy, discontented, abused victim. He seemed to be mad at the world a good part of the time. He came home from work every day mad about something. This was in contrast to the positive reinforcement and upbeat environments at my jobs and the university. Finally, I could not take the negative barrage, angry disposition, and cloudy omnipresence anymore. I shut down and love died.

I hesitate to speak for him, but I think he felt he had lost his dream when he was not able to live the remote wilderness life he wanted. That was probably his romantic vision of what moving out West meant. He made a comment one time that drove home that point. We were driving back from a deer hunting trip in the wilderness of southeastern Oklahoma when he spotted a cabin up in the trees on a hill. He said, "If I didn't have you and the kids, I could live in a place like that and hunt and fish every day." I suppose that pretty much summed up his lost dream.

We spent a short stint in marriage counseling where the objective in my husband's mind was to straighten me out. He thought the problem was all about me, and frankly, at that point, so did I. There must be something wrong with me for wanting out of the marriage. The counseling didn't help much, but the experience connected me to someone with rational thought who proved invaluable later. I never did get "straightened out," and we got a divorce after a little over eleven years of marriage.

D-I-V-O-R-C-E

A few years before the marriage fell apart, I read Bette Davis's autobiography. She faced tough times in her early career fighting the contract studio system in Hollywood, getting divorced, suffering abuse, and being financially devastated with children to support. Yet she persevered and rallied over and over. Her world and experiences were so foreign to me that I was mesmerized by them and, more importantly, how she coped with them. Her strength and fortitude were fascinating to me because my life had been so cushy.

My Iowa world consisted of stability and intense support systems. No woman would be left to her own devices in that world, and I never observed women with gumption. I saw strong women, but they got things done more by patience, persistence, and perhaps some degree of manipulation. Bette had moxie, faced problems head on, and took no crap. After my divorce, when my world got rather crazy, I often thought about her desperate struggles and how she ultimately prevailed. It was my only frame of reference for dealing with chaotic change and facing unknown challenges as an independent woman with limited resources and burdensome responsibilities. I drew on her experiences for inspiration during that dark interlude and during other difficult times throughout my life. This illustrates how another person's experiences, once shared through biography, can profoundly influence someone else's life.

I mentioned in this *Introduction* how growing up in the stable, structured environment of rural Iowa left me ill-prepared for some of the situations I encountered. This was where this issue surfaced. The areas I was unprepared for were being single, raising children alone, and having a professional career. In the 1960's when I started out, I could not have anticipated encountering any of these situations.

I recall a man telling me after just a few dates that he loved me, and I believed him. He was as screwed up as I was, and he believed it as well. That is unfathomable to me today, but that is how naive I was. In the career arena, I was ill-prepared for the tough environment, blatant discrimination, and broad range of foreign experiences that were forthcoming. As for raising children alone, well, I was really feeling my way along on that one. Nevertheless, I can say that because of the positives of my Iowa beginnings, I had a responsible nature and the fortitude to navigate these experiences and to eventually acclimate successfully to all of them.

ON MY OWN

The post-divorce transition was a hugely traumatic turning point which eventually evolved into a life transforming milestone. The process, though, was brutal and precarious. I feel fortunate to have survived it. I had a year of college left when the marriage fell apart. We owned our home outright. I took out a mortgage to give my husband his share of the equity and to provide me with enough cash to get through the last year of college. Doubling up on courses, I carried a heavy load of twenty-one hours per semester to finish as soon as possible. I desperately needed to work and bring in some income.

At undergraduate colleges in the seventies there were very few older people taking classes. I was thirty and an older person by the standards of the day. If it weren't for teaching, there would have been hardly any women. I remembered Shuppy starting college at the age of forty, a whole generation ago. I wondered what that must have been like for her and considered how brave she was to do it. When I went on to graduate school there were few women in that program as well. Times have changed. Today older students are no longer a novelty, and more women than men are enrolled in many programs.

While completing the last year of my undergraduate studies, I worked part time at the college for one of the professors. He was writing a book, and after several disappointing experiences with young student helpers, he was delighted to discover in me a seasoned secretary as well as an exceptional typist and editor. Today everyone can keyboard. Back then good typists were rather rare. One day he playfully brought a pitcher of water into the office to pour over the typewriter, saying I was burning it up.

I minored in journalism, joined the journalism fraternity, worked on the university newspaper, and had several articles published. Graduating summa cum laude, I received the outstanding student teacher award. In the midst of all this, I had a nervous breakdown, if you can call it that. I don't know what psychological label is appropriate, but I crashed--big time.

The divorce turned ugly and I got little support from my family initially, although they came through in the end. Divorce didn't happen in Iowa, and since I was the one who wanted it and my husband didn't, I was the bad guy. My family was embarrassed by it. I am certain my husband's family was as well.

To that small community in Iowa where everyone knew everyone else, our divorce in Oklahoma was a bit of a scandal. My husband's distorted communications to my family and others on what was going on contributed to the gossip and speculation. It confused my family. They didn't know what to make of what was happening. They were told I was crazy, among other things. Divorce was a mystery to them. I talked to them regularly on the phone, and they were on my side but seemed paralyzed by the whole thing. It was clear they were hoping I would come to my senses, and it would all just go away. Once the divorce was on the table, I never contacted my husband's family. The way I saw it, they should take his side no matter what. He clearly didn't feel the same. Fortunately, his attempts at alienation failed.

If I had to say why I wanted a divorce, it would have been because I simply couldn't live that way any more. I didn't know how to articulate this to my family, so I was unable to help them understand the problem. They were looking for a smoking gun and there wasn't one. In their environment, there would have to be a very big bomb for someone to get a divorce. I just wanted to get out. I thought about running away, but I had children, and they needed me. I couldn't imagine living without them. At school I received positive strokes which gave me a taste of feeling good about myself. At home, I was always a failure, no matter how hard I tried. How do you articulate that?

During the married phase of my life I sewed, knitted, baked, did crafts, and was active in the community. I was nominated by the neighbor ladies for the *Homemaker of the Year Award* at the county fair where each year I won many ribbons. When I told my husband about the award, he said, "Well, they don't know what you're really like." I remember thinking: "What am I really like?" I sponsored a boy from Marty's class in a Cub Scout Den and my husband questioned my motives for doing that. I did it because the kid's folks couldn't afford it, plain and simple, but he just knew there was some ulterior motive. I questioned myself: "Why was I doing it?" It must be for some selfish reason.

As I began pulling away, my husband told me I could never make it on my own, that I was smart but had no common sense. My self-esteem was low. I became convinced I was a terrible wife and mother, and I was evil for wanting out of the marriage.

I couldn't measure up and was under constant criticism for what I now see were very minor housekeeping issues, things such as ring around the collar, lint on clothes, and too much Tupperware in the refrigerator. I didn't know how to solve these problems. These sound like little things, and they seem ridiculous in retrospect, but they represented the global dilemma I faced of being inadequate. They were my failures. I was constantly reminded of them, and at one point the barrage of grievances drove me into the fetal position. I knew then I had to do something. I felt weak and vulnerable but still driven to action.

I held on for a long time because I knew divorce would embarrass our families and traumatize the children, but finally nothing mattered but saving myself. I was going to go crazy or get out of the marriage. Because of the kids, I had to save myself. I got out, but I also went crazy, and I began having thoughts about ending it all as a way out of the whole mess. I thought there was something bad wrong with me, that I was a failure, and I was letting people down. I concluded that I didn't deserve to be here, and people would be better off without me. A multitude of negative thoughts permeated my mind.

Looking back it is hard to imagine that I got into such a state. As spunky and spirited as I can be, I somehow lost all sense of self. I don't know how to explain it. Given how productive my life has been since, I can't help but think how sad and unfortunate it would have been if I had not made it through that time, and I almost didn't. What a shame and a waste that would have been.

> I've run across women in similar predicaments throughout the years and have championed and supported them whenever possible. I found them working for me, sitting next to me on airplanes, and in the college classes I taught. I shared my experiences and advised them not to let someone else define them. Few people, including many counselors, understand the toll pervasive verbal abuse has on a person's psyche. Words can destroy you.

> I served on the board of a domestic violence intervention organization and tried unsuccessfully to hire women breaking away from abusive situations. Since verbal abuse and physical abuse commonly go hand in hand, I had to stop. Giving women work helped them get out of a bad situation, but their men were often so threatening that doing so jeopardized the safety of other employees.

I convinced my husband's best friend, who was single, to take him in, and once I got him out of the house, an intense sense of relief set in. This was offset by the fear of being on my own, concerns about his well being, and constant challenges from him. He clearly wanted me to fail so he could get back in. It was quite puzzling to me that he could disapprove of me so intensely and still want to hold on to me. I was told over and over how crazy I was. When the intimidation didn't work for him, he intensified his efforts and words turned into action.

I realize now the threat my husband must have felt when confronted with my evolution. We were both victims of our culture and the times as well as the natural changes people experience in their twenties as they find out who they really are. I was breaking out. He was regressing and trying to maintain what he had always known. We were polar opposites to start with, and our changing in opposite directions made the viability of our marriage a hopeless proposition. It had to happen. We had to go our separate ways. People who know us both, including our children, are amazed we were ever together.

I have to wonder if my actions were the result of my moving away from something or going toward something. Oklahoma had the second highest divorce rate in the nation, after Nevada-- a curious statistic, particularly given the more fanatical religious characteristics of the southern Bible Belt region. Did the fact that divorce and a career were viable alternatives in Oklahoma draw me toward striking out on my own? Probably. Had my husband and I stayed in rural Iowa where divorce was not an option and fewer career opportunities were available, would our marriage have survived? Who knows? Most likely, divorce was inevitable under any scenario. We were not a good match.

THE FALL AND THE RESCUE

The divorce was traumatic for everyone involved. I became so depressed that I asked my doctor for medication to help me cope. It seemed to make me worse instead of better. One day I took too much of it, and I must be honest and admit that I did it purposefully. I immediately regretted it, thinking of the kids, how much they needed me, and how my actions would hurt them. I recall wondering who would fix my daughter's hair, put it into a pony tail, braid it and make it pretty, and I knew it must be me. I ended up in the hospital, not for me, but for them. I had to make it through for them. Perhaps my actions were a desperate cry for help. I was pretty crazy with emotional pain so deep I felt like someone had reached in and ripped my guts out leaving a gaping, hemorrhaging hole. I just wanted the hurt to go away. This was the lowest point of my life, and once I got past it, I never, ever went there again no matter how down and out I was, and I know I never will.

At any rate, the crisis rallied my folks to my side, and they spent time in Oklahoma giving me support. They realized that if they didn't, they could lose me. It was a scary and puzzling time for them. I recall sitting on the couch beside Mom and crying so hard that she started rocking me. She held me and rocked me for hours. I finally slept with my head in her lap, her stroking my hair. I felt like a child. (Thirty years later, she would do it again.) How difficult that must have been for her. Dad tried to convince me to move back to Iowa. That was not going to happen.

Divorce was extremely rare and rather scandalous in Iowa in the seventies. I knew as a divorced woman I would be incredibly lonely and unhappy going back home no matter how much family support was available. I couldn't imagine fitting in there, and I was beginning to see the possibilities of a serious career, which could not be realized in rural Iowa.

As the folks began to intervene, I know Mom was afraid she couldn't save me, but she was, by god, going to do everything she could to do so. Mom and Dad visited me often, and Mom stayed for weeks at a time. They were lifesavers, literally. Somehow I continued intern teaching, graduated, got a job, and went to work every day throughout all this emotional distress.

Mom and I were struggling. I couldn't sleep and roamed the house at night. I was exhausted and had trouble concentrating which made school a challenge. Still, I graduated with a 4.0 grade point average, an amazing feat under the circumstances. It is a wonder to me now that I did that. Concentration was elusive, as was sleep. When I did sleep I was often curled up in bed with a kid, holding on for dear life. They kept me going. I never missed a day of school or work, but Mom and I were a wreck.

A friend suggested we drink wine at night to relax. So we bought wine. Neither of us had bought wine before, and it didn't occur to us we needed a cork screw. We were two desperate women in the kitchen with a hammer, pliers, and a screwdriver trying to get to our wine. I thought of Dad and all the tools it took him to charcoal. It took a lot of tools for us to drink wine.

Mom and I ultimately added a strainer to our collection of tools to eliminate the cork debris and had our wine. We hated the taste but drank it down, having no concept of sipping, and went to bed dazed and wasted. We woke up at 2:00 in the morning restless with headaches. That was the last time we consumed any prancing grapes, although we both later developed a taste for frozen drinks with umbrellas in them.

I went into counseling with the therapist who did our marital counseling. Something he said really hit home. I was so afraid and felt like I was fighting a raging battle all day every day. I was trying so hard to make it. When the therapist suggested I give up the fight, I was shocked. "Give up," he said, "Just lean into it. Flow with it." Giving up was such a strange concept to me, but he maintained that if I would just chill and let things play themselves out, I could cope better. He was right.

I let go and began taking things as they came rather than trying to solve all the problems in my world. This was an important lesson, and I've used this giving up the fight approach to coping throughout my life. Sometimes we just try too hard.

In addition to the coping element, there are other benefits to giving up. In a sense you are admitting that you lost, and you surrender. When the game is over and you accept the loss, an interesting thing happens. You now have nothing to lose. The only way to go is up. It is like starting over fresh. Giving up sets you free, and you have the energy to run your own agenda with courage and bravado. I lost, and I gave up. Freedom!

I moved into a one-day-at-a-time approach to things while keeping my eye on becoming independent and providing for my family. For awhile it was all about survival, but gradually I began thinking about a serious career and the good life for my children. I began to think about the prospect of life being fun.

There were about three rough years after the divorce before I got my land legs and felt a solid sense of security. This post-divorce period was fraught with fear, emotional turmoil, and daily struggles. When I look at pictures from this time period, I see this dead man's stare in my eyes that vividly reflects the state I was in. This is a woman on the edge, hanging on by her fingernails. Over time, the wear and tear is reflected in the kids' faces as well. Their innocence seemed to disappear.

THE RALLY

Gradually I moved into the world of divorced singles. At the advice of my counselor I attended a seminar for people going through divorce. When the holidays rolled around, those in the group who were experiencing their first Thanksgiving alone collaborated to convene at a friend's house for dinner. My classmate, Max, had been to the home and offered to drive me there. I took a homemade lemon pecan pie, and he brought the requisite sack of store-bought rolls men contribute to dinners. Max was sure he knew where our friend lived. He didn't.

We rang the doorbell and the nice folks let us in, took my pie and his rolls, and we began to mingle. I wish I had noticed sooner that there was no one there we knew, before I gave them the pie. By the time I realized we were at the wrong house, the residents were happy to relinquish the rolls, but there was a bit of a tussle getting the pie back.

Anyway, as Max and I slunk to the car, I looked back and noticed several people sitting at the dining room table, looking out the window obviously roaring with laughter. You can be sure this incident was a topic of conversation at that family's Thanksgiving table for many years. At any rate, Max and I were were back on the road meandering around looking for dinner.

Me: Well, that was embarrassing.

Max: I have a feeling we are in the right neighborhood.

Me: You do that again, and I will kill you.

After the divorce I remained in the town outside of Tulsa for a few months. A widowed girlfriend was trying to boost my spirits and suggested I go with her and her date to a club in a nearby town to hear a popular band. It was her first date with the guy, and she knew little about him except that he was a welder by profession. On the way home he pulled his pickup off on a dark side road, got out and went around to the back of the truck. We were petrified, certain he was a serial killer retrieving an axe or tire iron from the bed of the truck. We locked the doors. Then we unlocked them when my friend took a peek and reported that he was peeing along the side of the road. What a relief.

Learning from this experience, the next time my girlfriend and I got foxy and felt like prowling we went to the big city of Tulsa. There, at a popular nightclub, we discovered among the flashing disco lights men with mustaches and blow dried hair dressed in leisure suits, gold chains, and loafers doing a dance called the hustle. This was the first of many times that I experienced an environment where it was raining men. I mean, it *was* raining men. Hallelujah! I had never seen anything like it and was encouraged to contemplate some level of sophistication. I could not envision any of these men peeing along the side of the road behind a pickup truck, although I do recall being intrigued but terribly afraid of them.

After finishing my degree, I found work as a petroleum accountant in Tulsa. Tiring quickly of the long commute to work and having identified a clear preference for leisure suits over dirt roads and pickup trucks, I moved there. Divorced women didn't fit in well in the small town where I was living. Married women were understandably no longer friendly to me. (A couple of husbands were a bit too friendly.) More importantly, I needed to get some distance between my ex and me. All this considered, the move from the rural town to Tulsa was an obvious positive change, and it ended my country life forever. From then on out, I was a city girl. I've always felt at home in Tulsa.

The kids and I settled into a nice neighborhood in south Tulsa. I could barely afford it, and to save money I rode the bus downtown to work. It took every dime I had to get into a house in a good school district, and we struggled financially. I raised my kids on the four basic food groups of goulash, Cheerios, tomato soup, and grilled cheese sandwiches.

Marty learned to cook, and one day after school Melanie called me at work all hyped up telling me he had baked a giant cookie. I wondered just how big this cookie was; she was pretty excited. I told her to put her brother on the phone while I contemplated just how big a cookie could get. He explained that he had simply made one cookie out of a batch, something most of us have tried only to realize you can't get a big cookie crispy. Marty always learned by doing, and he had no reservations about doing. He was always doing, and this particular day he did a giant cookie.

It was scary to me to realize the weight of the financial responsibility I was facing, especially having been told over and over that I could never make it on my own. What would happen if I couldn't? A lot was at stake, and I knew it. I couldn't count on child support and had to repeatedly spend money on an attorney to get it. In those instances, I netted very little. I hadn't asked for alimony in the divorce settlement. Had I known how things were going to be, I would have. My attorney told me I would regret that decision, and I did.

I applied at several banks for a credit card because of the irregularity of child support, but banks were not giving them to divorced women. One of the men I worked with advised me to call the bank, accuse them of discriminating against me for being a divorced woman, and they would give me a card. They did.

Until I got that card, it was literally paycheck to paycheck. When the money was gone, there was simply no money. I got creative at preparing meals with whatever food was left in the cupboards until the next payday. I recall serving lima beans with ketchup and biscuits. I watered down milk. I learned I could buy enough soup for a meal with just the change in my purse, that potatoes were the best food bargain, and the concept of layaway worked for school clothes, but it had no advantage when it came to gas or groceries.

We went without air conditioning one summer because it broke, and I couldn't afford to fix it. Our washer broke, and I had to go to the laundromat because I couldn't replace it. Marty didn't get to play football because I couldn't afford the gear. He needed a blazer for the school jazz band, and child support didn't come that month. When I got the credit card, I was able to get through such crises. My priority was always to keep the kids in a nice neighborhood with good schools--a challenge, but it got done.

At several points during this period of struggle, I had to decide whether to get a second job to ease the financial pressure or invest in my career, which meant getting an MBA and becoming a CPA and Toastmaster. I took the long-term view and decided to pursue the credentials. This ultimately paid off big time. Over the years I've observed others at similar crossroads make the decision to work a second job rather than focusing on professional development. Years later they are still struggling financially, one working two jobs to this day. My decision required intense sacrifice at the time, but it paid off later.

Getting an education and obtaining credentials was not just about making good decisions and earning money. Once I entered the corporate work force, the primary driving force behind what I did to get ahead was that I was exceedingly frustrated, and I wasn't going to take it any more. Discrimination and the good-old-boy network were alive and well in the seventies in spite of legislation otherwise. The unfairness of this did not set well with me. Two of my internal buttons were pushed--the one that responds intensely to *it's not fair* and the one that has *something to prove*. What would happen next was inevitable. I was going to make it happen. And I did.

I could see that it was going to take some serious strategy to move up in the business community in Tulsa, and I set out to do it. I was going to get so credentialed, work so hard, and deliver the goods so well that no one could turn me down when I was eligible for promotions. In other words, I was going to mitigate the excuses of why I didn't get a job and a less qualified man did. I attended Toastmasters meetings at six in the morning, joined The National Management Association, enrolled in an M.B.A. program, and began studying for the C.P.A. exam.

On the home front, things went well once we moved to Tulsa. I bought a membership in the neighborhood pool every summer, and we swam on Saturdays and Sundays. I made a list of chores for each one of us to do on Saturday mornings. The kids did their own laundry, and we did housework and yard work together. When we moved to Tulsa I heard that neighbors were concerned about a divorced woman moving in and not keeping up the yard. Not to worry. Marty and I landscaped, gardened, planted flowers, and had the most manicured yard on the street.

Once the kids' Saturday "To Do" lists were completed, they were free for the rest of the weekend. Marty's friends helped him with yard work so he could play. Their fathers teased me about how I got them to do work they couldn't get them to do at home. Both Melanie and Marty worked hard, and we were a team.

I couldn't meet my career goals and keep up with multiple activities for the kids, so I allowed each of them just one extra-curricular activity. Marty played the tuba in band. At high school football games, kids in the stands threw things, aiming for the hole in the tuba. M&M candy was one thing, an orange was another. It bloodied his lip. He quit with my endorsement. His priorities were shifting anyway. He had a job and after experiencing money rolling in, all he wanted to do was work.

Mel's activity of choice was Girl Scouts early on and then synchronized swimming. When I went to her first performance, all the girls wore identical swim suits and nose plugs. Someone had braided her hair. When the grand finale was introduced, I wondered why she hadn't been in the show. She was there all along. Her own mother didn't recognize her.

Raising children as a single mom presented challenges that at times were almost overwhelming. I had no family support in Tulsa but developed a backup support system of neighbors that I don't think exists much in the country today. Everyone looked out for each other's kids, who could pretty much roam the neighborhood. Melanie found a second mom in the mother of one of her friends. Marty became the neighborhood bike mechanic which endeared him to many parents. Good friends lived across the street. It was a safe, nurturing neighborhood environment. We were friendly with an elderly lady nearby, and when it snowed Marty scooped her sidewalk and got her mail. She got fairly senile. One day when I was visiting her, she began gossiping about the divorced lady across the street. Of course, that was me. I didn't want to embarrass her by stopping her so I let her go on and got the whole scoop on what was going on in my life. This was when I learned I was a heathen.

I had to leave for work in the mornings before the kids left for school, which meant they were responsible for getting themselves to school on time, and they did. They were in their pajamas eating cereal when I left. Fortunately Melanie's bus stopped in front of our house. Marty rode his bike to school every day and rigged up a trailer in which to haul things. One of his counselors told me he observed him after school in an ice storm chipping ice off his bike, which was frozen to the bike rack, so he could ride home. It was the only bike there. I was stuck on a bus in traffic, and we had no cell phones. He was on his own. You have to give it to him. He did what he had to do.

Marty was a remarkably skilled bike rider. (He was also proficient on a unicycle). All three of us rode around the neighborhood almost every day. From riding with his buddies, he knew where the dogs lived that would chase us. As we approached he took the lead, enticed the dogs to chase him, then lifted his bike up, swung the back wheel around and whacked them. They would roll from the blow. Mel and I had a wreck once because a dog chased us, so we had no sympathy for them, further evidence that we were heathens.

When Marty couldn't ride with us, he taught us to stop and look at any attacking dogs. They didn't know what to do with that. They wanted to chase, and we weren't cooperating. Usually they slink back to their yard, occasionally looking back at us like a pouting child. We had to walk our bikes down the street very slowly or the dog would resume the chase. A neighbor's dog used to chase our car when I lived in Iowa. We often stopped the car, and he jumped up repeatedly, looking in the window while we giggled. (I had a boyfriend do something similar once.) Occasionally Dad opened the car door and growled. The dog tucked his tail and ran. Otherwise, he resumed the chase once we started up again. We might stop again and start the process all over. This could go on for awhile.

If the kids had issues at school, I coached them on how to approach the teacher or classmate, but I did not run down to the school to solve all their problems. Taking the bus to work downtown, I simply could not do it. They did a fine job of fending for themselves, becoming unusually independent for their ages. My work in accounting required an unrelenting commitment. At one point I missed so many days staying home with sick kids that I was put on probation. If I missed another day I would lose my job, so I let the kids stay home from school to take care of each other when they were sick. This was a desperate measure for certain, but a lot was riding on me keeping my job.

> In later years as I moved higher up into management, I implemented *no fault* sick leave and other policies to allow parents working and raising children to take time off and make it up later. No parent's job should be in jeopardy because they have to stay home with a sick child. It is as simple as that.

In response to some victim mode whining, you know, the "all the other kids have one" story, I sat the kids down and went over the budget with them so they understood why they didn't have things their friends had. I remember one time they both complained about something I couldn't take them to because I had to go to night class. I asked them if they liked the new bikes in the garage and made it clear they wouldn't have them if I didn't do the things I was doing. That seemed to settle the issue. We each had a stake in the game, and they got with the program.

Although they have admitted to having some envy of friends with stay-at-home moms, they valued the freedom and independence of our rather non-traditional lifestyle. Given the choice, they will tell you they will take how we lived over freshly baked after-school cookies. I'm well aware this means there were after school shenanigans I didn't know about which would cause them to say that--experiences outside the scope of giant cookies. Although parents find out about many of these things when the kids are grown and bragging about their childhood escapades, I have no doubt there are still untold tales out there.

The important thing is that my children reflect on their childhood with joy. I know from my own reflections that you can pick out unfortunate behaviors of your parents and make a big deal out of them, even use them as an excuse to ruin your life, or you can recognize that they did the best they could with what they had and what they knew and let it go. Take your pick.

There were times during this difficult transitional post-divorce period when I couldn't hide emotions from my children. They saw me suffer. I felt bad when I couldn't shield them from those experiences, but in later years I came to believe that their participating, at least to some extent, in the emotions of what was happening helped them develop empathy and sensitivity to the feelings of others. They were protective of me, and I felt their caring and support.

Observing friends who were determined to shield their children completely from divorce, I noticed the kids were bratty through the whole thing. Mothers and children were pulling against each other. They were not a team getting through the crisis together. Heck, the kids hardly knew there was a crisis. They were enjoying the over-compensation experiences from both Mom and Dad. I wondered if maybe they needed to see a bit of their mother's pain so they could support her and learn to be sensitive to others. I don't think they had a clue about any of that. They were so protected that they were just thinking about themselves.

My twenties were spent discovering myself, becoming a mom, gaining independence, and finding my stride. I went from being a married woman in an eight-foot-wide trailer at the end of an airport runway in Chicago to being a thirty-one year old divorced metropolitan career woman and single mother in Tulsa, Oklahoma, living life on my own terms. I found my stride, and I was liking it.

I sold my sewing machine and tossed out the knitting needles, blue ribbons, and canning jars. I bought a new Thunderbird, painted the house a happier color, built a sunroom on the back, and got the kids a dog. I had permanent press clothes, a washer and dryer, a cupboard full of groceries, a microwave named Wilson (the heart of our home), a self-cleaning oven in which you could bake goulash and giant cookies, and I could buy groceries and Snickers by the bagful. I also had a new stereo, books, business suits, and briefcases.

Going forward into my thirties, I blossomed. It was my life. I owned it. I was going to live it full out, and that I did. Certainly happier times were in store for the kids and me. The blank stares on our faces in those photos after the divorce turned into twinkling eyes and gleeful smiles which reflected the prospects of a bright and, as it turns out, rather remarkable future.

6

THEY GREW UP

You are never free of your children.

Rearing children is both a rewarding and a challenging experience, and I'm grateful for the role my Iowa connections have contributed to this effort. I shipped the kids off to Iowa for long summer vacations where they spent magical times with grandparents, aunts, uncles, and cousins. They fished ponds, shot birds and critters, drove four wheelers, and helped with chores. These adventures exposed them to the values and traditions I grew up with, and I witnessed these positive influences in their behaviors as they progressed into adulthood.

In my family we sometimes call me *The Nik*, my daughter *The Mel* and my son, *That Marty*. Then Damien came along, a young man I raised from the age of two. I called him *My Damien*. What he called me took a while to figure out. He has been in my life since he was two, but his dad and I never married. I was not officially a stepmom and was not fond of that label anyway. Because of the unfortunate circumstances around his mother not being there for him (I'll get to that later), his calling me Mom didn't resonate. I felt I could never take her place.

The first time I picked him up at the nursery, a playmate asked him if I was his mom. I could tell he didn't know how to answer that and, frankly, neither did I. He did a good job of coming up with an answer, though. He said, "Sorta." The label stuck, and I became his sorta Mom. Along with me came a sorta brother, a sorta sister, and a whole host of other sorta relatives. We were Damien's family without any implication that we were replacing anyone else. The sorta label may have confused others, but it worked for us. Over time, each of us defined our relationship in our own way, and he found his place. Damien became mine, and he became the younger brother to The Mel and That Marty. He was ours and we were his.

Nothing in life can surpass the special nature of the mother and child connection. I know people who have lost children, some who don't get along with their children, and others who have children who are a mess. I still have my children, we all get along, and they rarely require any parental damage control these days. Of course, this could change at any moment. You are never free of your children.

Each is very different from the other as well as from me, thereby exposing me to generous doses of unanticipated experiences beyond the scope of my imagination. Certainly they've broadened my horizons. Although they have at times created considerable angst in the process, in the end they all became impressive adults, generous to a fault, and solidly productive. That outcome is reminiscent of my own siblings, particularly in how they are each so unique but bound together in a solid attachment. I admire each one of my children immensely. We have met the challenges of the past together, and I know without a doubt we will face those in the future as a cohesive unit. (However, my plan is that when I can't take care of myself, I will go into a nursing home, and I will tell them not to be coming down there and bothering me.)

There may be some luck involved in this blessing but clearly, like my folks, I've done many things right. I'm going to blatantly take credit for shaping these three souls. I put considerable work into them, and each one has put me through a living hell several times over. Here are just a few of the more memorable examples of parental anxiety with which many parents will relate:

> While still in high school Marty didn't come home one night. I was a wreck. Then I saw on the morning news that a young male adult was found dead under an overpass. After many frantic phone calls by me and others, one of his friends located him sleeping on the couch at a friend's house. I threw a royal, wide-eyed, raging and ranting fit when he got home.

> Melanie didn't come home one Sunday from a visit to her dad's and was nowhere to be found. Her dad was driving the roads on his end looking for her. I was hiring a private detective since the police are unlikely to do anything meaningful for twenty-four hours. She finally showed up, having spent the evening with a friend, thereby demonstrating why the police hesitate to do much for twenty-four hours in these circumstances. I threw somewhat of a fit when she got home.

> When Damien was a teen I answered the phone late one night, and a Tulsa policeman asked me to hold. I could hear chatter on his car radio and, looking over at his dad on the couch, wondered how I could possibly break the news to him that something awful had happened to his son. The policeman finally came back on the phone to tell me Damien was among a bunch of minors at a beer party in a park, and we needed to come get him. Fearing the worst and then realizing the immense relief that he was okay was by now a familiar experience. I considered us *somewhat lucky* and didn't throw a fit. I had mellowed.

In spite of the traumas of parenthood, it has generally been a wonderfully rewarding experience, and I've managed to wrangle three amazing children out of the years of challenges, sacrifices, angst, fear, worry, frustration, anxiety, concern, apprehension, tension, confrontation, strain, struggle, panic, stress, trepidation, effort, chaos, love, pride, and the heebie-jeebies. (Sorry, I had a George Carlin moment.)

It amazes me how each child is his or her own unique person from the moment they are born, and how much my life has been enriched because of those differences. As Dad used to say: "It's a good thing we're not all just alike." He also said: "It's a good thing we don't all want to live in the same place," and he quoted Yogi Berra with: "If you come to a fork in the road, take it." Dad was somewhat of a philosopher (emphasis on the somewhat). That last quote has no practical application whatsoever that I can interpret, and it reminds me of the degree of Dad's idiosyncrasies. I digress. This is about the ambiguities of child rearing and the challenges they represent.

THAT MARTY

Marty was around ten years old when I got a sense that I needed to quit kissing him, that maybe he was too big to be loved on by his Mom. Having not kissed him goodnight for some time, one evening I got the urge to sneak in and kiss him while he was sleeping. As I was leaving his room, I heard: "Thanks Mom."

There is something special about the first born. I know this because everyone has more pictures of the first one. Parenthood is fresh and new, and the bond is uncomplicated by the distractions of other children. That is how it was with Marty.

A question I have often asked to stimulate dinner conversation is: If you could live one awesome incident in your life over again, aside from the obvious ones of childbirth, marriage, etc., what would that be? My choice is a moment with my Marty.

I had a fancy for a '57 T-Bird, the one with a little round window in the back like in the movie *American Graffiti*. Marty called late one night and asked me to meet him in my driveway. What a strange request, I thought.

154

Standing there, I saw a yellow '57 T-Bird coming down the street, shining brightly in the street lights as it pulled into my driveway. Marty got out of the car, with a big grin on his face, and tossed me the keys. I will never forget that grin. I tell you, it was a moment, one I would pick to live over again, not because of the car but because of that smile and the twinkle in his eyes.

I drove the T-Bird to work one Veterans' Day. After finishing lunch downtown I was weaving between barricades on streets blocked off for the parade, trying to get back to the office. An accommodating policeman stopped traffic at an intersection to let me in. Next thing I know, men on mini scooters, decked out in costumes as bowling pins, were circling my car while being chased by a guy dressed up as a bowling ball. (You can't make this stuff up.)

Driving around in the atmosphere of a bowling alley is a pretty strong clue that something is up. I then noticed an old Model-T Ford in front of me with flags sticking up all over it, and in my rear view mirror was a convertible full of Shriners followed by a marching band about to play at any moment. Since the parade was going in the right direction, I was willing to flow with it, so I rolled down my window, rested my elbow on the window sill, and was in the parade.

I was glad I wore my yellow suit that day. It matched my car. Occasionally, I waved. Too bad, I thought, that I didn't have time to take the top off. I was having a high old time, but as we approached the intersection where I needed to turn off to get to the office, I became anxious. I sure didn't want to lead a marching band into the company parking lot. Everyone would know I took a long lunch.

That Marty is a car guy. Always was. Always will be. Hot Wheels were his thing as a child, and street rods are his thing as a man. His business is cars. He has built them, repaired them, drag raced them, stock raced them, and showed them. He tears them down, builds them up, soups them up, and shines them up, hauling them around to car shows in a camper trailer the size of a semi. Driving for him is fun. When he is stressed, he drives. Like I said, he is a car guy. He always was a car guy.

When he was three, Marty was the ring bearer at his uncle's wedding. Dressed in his little tuxedo, he was about to enter the car to go to the wedding when I noticed his suit bulging and removed close to a dozen Match Box cars from his pockets. I let him keep one. During the wedding ceremony, he began running it along the railing of the altar, making that car noise little guys make with their lips. Uncharacteristically for a small child, he had some sense of decorum. There was not the normal honking, crashing, or peeling out.

As a child Marty was always taking things apart and putting them back together. When he was ten, his dad and I were up till three in the morning putting together a new bike for Christmas. Later in the day I went into the garage to call him to dinner and discovered the bike completely dismantled on the garage floor. He was so proud that he was able to do that. His dad and I, on the other hand, were astonished and devastated. Not to worry. He soon had it all put back together. A few years later he custom built a chopper bicycle that was the envy of the neighborhood and had modified a skate board. I don't have the verbal dexterity to describe a modified skate board but, trust me, he had one.

A pizza place where he was working when he was just fourteen was robbed. Of all the people in the store, it was Marty who was able to supply the police with a detailed description of the getaway car from the make, model, and year down to the type of tires, wheels, hubcaps, window tinting, and pin striping. The perpetrators were soon caught.

When he was a teenager, I often came home from work to discover a car dismantled in my garage--car seats, dashboards, and other miscellaneous interior parts strung all over the driveway. He and his friends could completely gut a car in short order. When I asked what they were doing, it was something like installing new speakers. That was not always the case. They installed a whisky dispenser in the dashboard of at least one pickup truck that I know of. My memories of him and his friends during this time were of feet sticking out from underneath a car and butts from under a hood. I used to carry pictures of my kids in my wallet. The one of Marty was of his feet sticking out from underneath a car because that is how I most often saw him.

The young mechanics tracked so much dirt into my house that when it was time to replace the carpet I cut out the dirtiest swatch, took it to the carpet store and told the salesman, "I want carpet this color, the color of dirt."

In his forties now, That Marty has had his own business tinting car windows since he was nineteen. He drives around the Tulsa area in a 1938 Ford street rod, bright orange with royal blue pin striping, tinting windows on car lots and in garages.

Marty wasn't much into school. His grades were erratic. Report cards were what I described as interesting. When he got a low grade in one course, he pulled it up but dropped down in another. Although his grades were all over the place, teachers loved him. They gave him a D or an F on a report card with an accompanying note saying something like: "If I could give Marty a grade for attitude alone, I would give him an A." I wasn't sure what to think about that. I suspected a budding con artist.

Once he turned thirteen he lied about his age to get a job. From then on, all he wanted to do was work and make money. At sixteen, he got a car and began skipping school. Finally, I took it away and personally deposited him at school. Still, the school called to tell me he was absent. How can that be? I dropped him off. The emerging con artist was successful at talking a mother from the neighborhood, who had taken her kid to school, to give him a lift back home. I was incredulous. He was on the slippery slope to becoming a high school dropout, and I became determined to do whatever was necessary to get him a diploma. This is evidenced by the fact that I sent him to live with his dad his senior year, one of my many parental acts of desperation.

Although I don't believe any of them do it anymore, shortly after getting out of high school Marty and his friends converted from Crown Royal whisky to smoking themselves some pot. I came home early one night, opened the door to a smoky sun room full of young men, and immediately got a gray contact high from the secondary smoke. I asked them for a hit, just to shock them, and was glad I did. It kept my house from burning down as joints were retrieved from hiding spots among the rattan furniture.

I didn't like their smoking, but I didn't like their drinking either. I could throw all the fits I wanted, but no doubt they were going to do one or the other. Either one was not good and could put them in jeopardy in the right circumstance. The distinction was that liquor might cause them to fight over a chair while weed would cause them to sit on the floor and say: "A-W-E-S-O-M-E." I reminded the foggy, jolly tokers that what they were doing was illegal and that no one should drive under the influence. The boys (actually they were men at this point), were welcome to detox in my sun room as long as they didn't set it on fire and eat all the food in the kitchen.

We were visiting Iowa one summer when, in passing, Dad commented that he needed to cut down the marijuana weeds  growing up along the fence line. It grows wild in Iowa but does not produce anything worth smoking. We used to cut it out of bean fields and gardens. Marty didn't know that, and he perked right up at Grandpa's comment and was eager to help clear out the weeds. Consequently, we have a picture of us with a robust looking weed crop. Even though it was not a viable product, Marty wanted to take it to Oklahoma for "show and tell" for his buddies. He settled for an incriminating picture. I wasn't up for going to prison for transporting drugs across state lines just for the fascination of a bunch of redneck toking party animals and was not much up for ticks in my trunk either.

Marty has my dad's talent for figuring out creative uses of things and has been known to clean his house with a leaf blower and scoot around on roller skates to sweep his shop, which is full of all kinds of contraptions. He can fix just about anything with just about anything. He has a rare combination of artistic flair and mechanical aptitude. Unique features in my townhouse include art deco windows that Marty designed.

He has a shop where he builds street rods and mechanics cars for himself and friends. Mustangs are his specialty. I have heard friends refer to him as Mustang Marty. His shop serves as sort of a club house for car guys. He can do anything to a car. When he was stock car racing he often wrecked his car on a Friday night and had it looking like new the next Friday.

It was scary to watch him race. I was frequently in the stands with his fans. During the warmup lap, when he passed in front of the stands he always gave us the thumb up, and everyone hooted and hollered. I would say: "He's so cute." This tickled his friends. I was always extremely anxious before the race, but once it started I could get into it.

He was good and won many trophies. His combination of mechanical and driving skills were the perfect mix for racing. It was quite a thrill to watch him work his way from the back of the pack where the high-point racers started to the front and often to victory. The deathly quiet in the stands after a wreck where he was knocked senseless paralyzed me, but eventually the thumb up came out of the car window, the crowd roared, and I could breathe again.

Marty was always a fearless risk taker, which I find both fascinating and terrifying. He is a fireworks aficionado and once rappelled down a high rise building for a charity event. I watch his antics when I can, going to drag races, stock car races, pool games, or whatever, always recognizing that it is his world, and I am just visiting. Sometimes I was more a part of his world than I bargained for:

> I dropped my new car off at his shop to have him tint the windows, and he gave me a loaner. Little did I know it was one of his drag cars--revved up, rocking, and ready to roll. I sat at the end of the shop driveway, waiting for a break in traffic, and when I got it, I pressed the pedal and peeled out, fishtailing all over the place. I was thinking: "Wow!" However, I still had not grasped the magnitude of the situation.

> Idling at a red light down the street, I noticed how loud it was. Chug, chug, chugging away, and bouncing. The frigging car was bouncing. I glanced over at a man in the car next to me who was clearly amazed that an old woman was driving this hot rod. Then it died. I mean it just coughed it up and frigging died. I started it back up, turned around and headed back to the shop. When I walked in, Marty and his friends were rolling with laughter. "Hey, Mom, if you need more power there is nitrous in the trunk." Humor at my expense was common among them, and I played my role, pitched a fit, and left with a suitable car.

Marty is a mean pool player, playing on Tuesday nights for fun and Thursday nights in tournaments. I go to the fun nights occasionally, stepping into his world. When he has an unsuccessful shot, I like to tell him: "That sucks." When he does good I tell him: "That doesn't suck." (This is why I don't get to go on tournament nights.) When I am not there, his friends fill in for me. Sometimes he calls me late at night to give me a report on how he did: "I got beat by a girl," or "I didn't suck."

Marty has a good-old-boy mentality and is always ready to help an acquaintance or neighbor. When someone slid on the ice and wiped out his new neighbor's mailbox, he rang their doorbell, introduced himself and advised them their mailbox was down. A few days later when a man ran into Pokey, another neighbor's donkey, he heard the crash and ran to the rescue. Once he determined the driver was okay, he checked on Pokey who was dying in his new neighbor's front yard. This time, he rang their doorbell and told them they had a dead donkey in their front yard. "His name is Pokey," he said. When he left they said, "Marty, don't ring our doorbell anymore."

Marty tricks out his street rods, and I like to go to the car shows and see his handiwork all shined up. He had a car that hung so low he installed a mechanism to flip up the license plate when driving on bumpy roads or over speed bumps. He installed a button on the dash to raise and lower it. He had forgotten to lower it one day, and a policeman pulled him over for no license plate. Marty waited until the cop got past the back of his street rod and approached his window before pushing the button to lower the plate. He then watched in his rear view mirror as the cop got back into his police car to call in his driver's license information. The cop's double-take reaction when he saw the license plate was reminiscent of Barney Fife.

We almost lost Marty to a heart attack a few years ago. He was in his mid-forties when I got the call at my office and rushed out to the hospital, telling my secretary, "Well, it has happened." I was always a bit of a worry wart when it came to my children, and this is one of the things I worried about. Marty had several risk factors, and I was braced for the consequences. I mean, I could see that train coming down the track.

The doctor described his blockage as the widow-maker. If he had been alone when the attack occurred he would not have survived it. Fortunately someone was there to call an ambulance when he went down, and the surgery staff was immediately available when he got to the hospital. They got him right in. He experienced a remarkable recovery. I continue to worry but encourage him to enjoy life full out every day, and I relish every day we have him. It could have easily been different.

Looking back at all the years as Marty's Mom, certain things stand out. I recall when he started making good money after he got out of high school. We went out to dinner one night, and he proudly insisted on paying for it. It was strange to see him pull out his wallet and have so much money in it. I still didn't see him as a man, though. I remember to the minute when I faced that reality some months later, and I viewed him differently from that time forward. I felt comfort from that realization, knowing what kind of man he had become. He was freshly out of the house and on his own when this incident occurred.

I took him and his sister to San Francisco on vacation. One morning in Chinatown a man grabbed Mel and was pulling on her. It is hard to believe that he was actually going to take her. Who knows? At any rate, Marty ran him off. Later that day, as he was driving us down a coastal highway on a curvy, somewhat treacherous stretch of road in full command of the situation, I looked over at him. Watching him drive so competently, I thought: "My god, he's a man." I felt safe--and proud.

Because he was so different from me, I always worried about his path in life. It was also at that moment that I recognized that his path was a good one. That Marty was his own person. He was beautiful, and I loved him unconditionally.

THE MEL

When people ask me who is the woman I admire most, I used to say Tina Turner. Now I say my daughter, The Mel. She is just the most amazing person. A mom extraordinaire, a friend like no other, a smart, sharp, strong, intuitive, sensitive, loving, resourceful woman. I am in awe of her.

Bossy as a child, she once posted kitchen rules with an accompanying kitty where fines were to be deposited by violators. She marched through the living room one day, the kitty jar in hand, headed to her older brother's room to collect a quarter for a violation. Thinking, "I've got to see this," I sneaked along behind. Striding confidently into his room, she advised Marty of his violation and fine. His response was: "Yeah, well, how would you like me to re-arrange your face?" I scurried back to my chair and settled in just as she marched, a bit less purposefully, back through to the kitchen stating: "Maybe I won't make Marty pay this time."

Her second grade teacher called me once and asked if she was always good. She had concerns because Mel was so perfect at school. I assured her she was not perfect at home, but she was darn close--so good that it made me just want to buy her a pony.

She loved animals and babysat them for people. I often came home from work to find a strange animal in our house. One day I was shocked to discover a bird fluttering around. Taking a stand, I made it clear a loose bird in my house was not happening. I was not up for Polly flying into a ceiling fan or dropping doo doo on the furniture, carpet, or my bowl of chili.

The Mel once celebrated her dog's birthday by gathering up dogs in the neighborhood for a party. I came home from work to a backyard full of dogs. Can you imagine having a little girl knock on your door, ask for your dog, and you actually give it to her? I can't, but she pulled it off. Everyone knew her and they knew she loved their dog. I was thinking: "What if the dogs had gotten into a fight?" They didn't, and a good time was had by all.

The Mel was always, as far back as I can remember, incredibly resourceful. If I had to describe her in one word, that would be it--resourceful. At the age of ten, when a house came up for sale across the street from her best friend, she decided we should live there. She went into action, called the real estate agent, and booked an appointment to tour the home. She then called me at work to inform me when and where to show up. I had her cancel the the appointment, much to her dismay.

I was in a budget meeting with the president of a large Tulsa corporation when his secretary came in and said I had an emergency phone call. Melanie called to inform me we received a coupon in the mail for 20% off any dog at the pet shop. When I returned to the meeting everyone was curious about the emergency, so I told them and they got quite a chuckle out of it. This was early in my career when women were just starting to play a meaningful role in the business world, and this incident was quite a novelty to the men in the meeting.

I was at the airport about to board a flight when an intercom voice directed me to a white courtesy phone. I had a message to call home, a worrisome thing to hear. Not to worry. Melanie had a question about what kind of pizza to have the sitter order. The big question, though, is how does a twelve year old girl figure out how to page someone at the airport? As I said, she was resourceful.

When The Mel started running around as a teenager, boys began calling. Once at about 2:00 a.m. a very inebriated boy named David rang her up. Back then kids didn't have their own phones (imagine that), and I answered. He asked for M-e-e-e-l-a-a-a-n-i-e. Not only was he drunk as a skunk, it was after 9:00 p.m., the cut off time for phone calls in those days (imagine that). So I said, "David, if you ever call here again after 9:00, I will kill you." The next morning I told Mel that David called and he probably won't call again.

The Mel went to Oklahoma State University, a party school with a football problem, and about partied herself to death her freshman year. I know this because when visiting the campus I heard her classmates bragging about throwing up and sleeping on grass. After college she moved to Dallas, then California, Salt Lake City, Boca Raton, Florida, and back to California. I lost count after moving her eleven times. I am not exaggerating.

She had quite a career, mostly in marketing with start-up companies, a couple in which she had some ownership. Building a solid reputation in this niche, she was much in demand and flew around the country on corporate jets. She was on the floor of the New York Stock Exchange when one of her companies went public. (I was in Dallas moving her into a new apartment.) She also did some satellite broadcasting.

When she left college, I was disappointed she didn't come home to Tulsa. She was aware of my experiences in the business community here and wanted no part of it. So she headed to Dallas where she discovered things were not much better. In spite of her accomplishments, she was viewed mostly as a cute little blond girl looking for a rich husband, so when recruited by a company in California, off she went and that was the end of that. She become a California girl.

While in Dallas she dated a lot and had a couple of incidents where she had to call the police because guys behaved poorly

after a break up. She had a similar experience in college so I was not surprised when she called me one day from Dallas complaining, "Men are like gum in my hair, Mom, like gum in my hair."

Guys did stick like glue. Twice she had to call the Dallas police to run young men off who were sitting on her doorstep and would not leave. The second time the officers responding were the same ones who answered the first call. When the incident was over one of the policemen asked her, "Melanie, what do you do to these guys, anyway?"

She had lessons to learn about the kind of guy to take up with. I knew she was catching on when one showed up late for a date looking somewhat slovenly because he lost track of time playing video games with his roommate. This was a strong signal that someone was stuck in the frat mode and unlikely to leave it soon. She got it.

After my first weekend visit to Dallas I realized that The Mel living away from Tulsa was not necessarily a bad thing. I got to buy a lot of clothes there because the racks were overcrowded and I was concerned they might collapse. I do what I can. I got to dance with the best two-steppers in Dallas. In Florida, I spent a Christmas Eve in a Cuban home in Miami where the men wore silk turtleneck shirts, taupe dress pants, leather belts and shoes, and nice watches in contrast to the float trip attire and hunting garb common to many Oklahoma men.

If it were not for The Mel moving around so much, I would have never known that El Niño makes me shop. During this southern California wet weather phenomenon I found myself in peculiar circumstances--a Harley Davidson store. It was pouring outside, and I had to be somewhere. While there, I purchased a t-shirt which I mailed to my biker brother in Iowa with a note that read "El Niño made me shop." I am relatively certain he thought: "Who is El Niño?"

Not all was good, though. It was exasperating to have to search for frozen margaritas in the dry state of Utah and to experience an old hairy dweeb in a wife-beater t-shirt crowd in front of me in line in Boca Raton, Florida. More important than challenging his manners, I wanted so badly to say, "Oh, just cover that up already." I didn't need to see that.

Mel worked for a company that moved its headquarters from California to Florida where she discovered a whole new culture of transplanted north easterners. She was in the waiting room in her new doctor's office when she heard "Hello" and noticed a parrot in a cage in the corner. The bird kept repeating the word. A little old lady went up to the cage to engage the bird in conversation by saying "Hello" in a particularly heavy nasal Brooklyn accent. She and the bird continued communicating and in no time at all the parrot was saying a very nasal "Hello" just like a true New Yorker.

Mel noticed a difference in temperament between people in California and Florida. In the office building in California, the deli workers knew her staff by name and were always happy to see them. In Florida the deli staff were curt and unfriendly and were soon labeled The Deli Nazis. Mel and her employees set a goal to win them over. They were not successful.

When I visited her in Florida I noticed people often treated waitresses and clerks rudely, and I observed many examples of discourteous driving. A guy yelled at us out of his car window apparently because we were walking too slow in a parking lot crosswalk. This was a new experience. Texas drivers are maniacs, but they don't yell at you, give you the finger, or intentionally keep you from merging. They may dart across three or four lanes in a heartbeat to get away from you or get ahead of you, but they won't purposely get in your way. In Oklahoma, drivers let you merge. You are expected to give them a friendly wave after they do. When moving to Tulsa from Chicago, it took me a while to figure out what all the waving was about. Oklahomans are a hospitable bunch. Even California drivers display a reasonable level of courtesy.

The Florida experience puzzles me. I've been all over the northeast and didn't observe people behaving that way. I did have a young woman in Philly in a flannel shirt and work boots, a cigarette hanging out of the corner of her mouth, slap the hood of my taxi and issue a rude hand gesture. I assumed she did so because she perceived the car was in her way, but perhaps she was practicing for a trip to Florida. I can't imagine slapping a car. That is so far outside of my realm of possibilities that I cannot comprehend it. I told my Russian taxi driver (who was suggesting that I help him relocate to Oklahoma, like that was going to happen), that the girl needed a Snickers bad.

For some years, Mel and her sophisticated, jet-setting friends flew all over the place for business and fun--New York to ring the bell at the stock exchange, Vegas for Halloween, Tampa for New Years, and Trinidad for Carnival, etc. Then in her mid-thirties motherhood happened, and that changed everything.

She is now settled in California with her little family, and our shopping strategy has shifted. We used to doll up, be looking good, and shop and dine at marvelous places. Now we shop separately while one of us is home with the kids, or we divide and conquer, each one of us taking a child.

We don't dress up nice anymore. I usually look like a bag lady with a human appendage. My shopping venue is the nearest dollar store where the objective is finding the diaper aisle and locating a toy lawn mower while managing a toddler who does not want to move past the gum machine. As for dining in marvelous places, that ain't happening anymore, that is unless Chuck E Cheese qualifies. It is a sad, sad, sorry situation that has left me wondering what the hell happened.

One of my greatest joys has been observing Melanie as a wife and mother. She and her husband, Chris, complement each other, and I've watched them grow in their relationship with great delight. Chris does volunteer work in search and rescue, and Mel is an advisor to a mothers' support group that assists families with babies in medical crisis. I am constantly amazed at the positive contributions they make to others.

When babies came along with accompanying crises (more about that later), I saw Melanie in a whole new light. The strength, fortitude, patience, and pure unmitigated love flowing from her was absolute bliss to behold. Add to that the generous support both she and Chris have given me over the years, and I'm overwhelmed with awe that I did this. I created and shaped this powerful, generous, loving woman who every day makes a difference in so many ways. She is a gift to so many people-- making her mark. You have gotta feel good about that.

I never experienced a defining moment of realizing The Mel was an adult as I did with That Marty. She just always was one. I never, ever had to ask her to study. She made good grades, had a night shift job in high school, bought a new car, and paid for it and all related expenses herself. She never violated curfew except for the few occasions when she drove someone home who was wasted. She never got into trouble--that I know of. Recognizing the requirement to qualify positive statements about a teenager, I temper these remarks. I'm sure there was some nonsense in there somewhere. I do know that wine coolers were in fashion, and who knows what happened on spring break. At any rate, I didn't worry much about her.

This is in contrast to Marty who had a series of speeding tickets, never grasped the concept of curfew, and came home with a bullet hole in his car door after a late night lake party. (It's an Oklahoma/Texas thing. There is a gun in every pickup, and there are lots of pickups.) The bullet went into his car seat just inches from him, proving that nothing good happens after midnight.

Every child brings something different to the table. The first two were what I'd expected all my life. The next child was quite a surprise, not only because he was so different from the other two, but also because he was at the table at all.

MY DAMIEN

I was looking forward to empty nesting when Damien came along. He brought along with him his own special series of worries and concerns which I wasn't sure I was up to taking on. I wanted so much for him, especially since the one thing he deserved the most in the world had been taken from him--his mother. If he couldn't have that, how could I ever fill that gap? Stepping up to that was huge, and had it not evolved one day at a time, I probably wouldn't have done it. The kid grew on me.

I started out as Damien's sorta mom, but over time he began calling me My Nikki. Marty was out of the house and Mel was pretty much raised when Damien's dad and I started dating. I wasn't interested in raising another kid, especially a two year old. In fact when I first started seeing his dad, who was raising the boy alone, I was reticent about the relationship for that reason. Little did I know at that time how all this was to turn out--that I was to keep the child and lose his dad. That's another story. Anyway, when I finally met Damien, it was obvious his dad, who wanted this introduction to go well, had played me up pretty good because the little guy was bursting with anticipation.

He darted through my front door all excited, squealing "Nikki! Nikki! Nikki!" and holding his crotch because he had to pee. He ran to me, threw his arms around my legs and kissed me right on the...well, you can figure that out. Thinking oh my god he's just like his dad, I

169

wrestled him loose, picked him up and fell in love. He was so-o-o-o cute. A few minutes later I fell out of love as he jumped up and down on the coffee table.

Damien's mother had been murdered by a serial killer when he was eighteen months old, and his aunts and grandparents were evidently over-compensating. He was a bit of a pistol. His dad understood that and let Melanie, a teenager at that time, and me work with him. She took him to the mall and didn't buy him a toy. I took him to the grocery store and didn't buy him a toy. We played games and didn't let him win every time or take our turns, a huge shift for him. Mel took him out of a restaurant and sat with him in the car while his dad and I ate because he was naughty. I guess we abused him thoroughly because in no time at all, he was a good kid. The only problem was that at the mall he called Melanie "Mommy," devastating her dating prospects.

I took him on a trip to Iowa and didn't warn Mom and Dad I was bringing a small child. Dad woke up from a nap on the couch to a little guy in his face asking, "You got any toys?" He was a city boy. When he saw ducks on the farm, one of them was sitting on the ground and he said, "Look, a duck with no legs."

We often called him Rambo, a ridiculous name for him. There was nothing rough and tough about him. He was a creative spirit, and if you put him on a skate board, bike, or in roller skates he was just as likely to hurt himself as not. This was a revelation which required considerable adjustment on my part because I was accustomed to Marty's reckless, adventuresome, and wandering ways. Damien, on the other hand, spent most of his time in his room.

He could draw, play music, and write. In fact, his writing in junior high was so expressive we accused him of plagiarizing. It was difficult to believe he could write like that at his age. Just a few months after getting his guitar we heard music coming from his room and thought it was the stereo. It was him. Rambo he was not. To my knowledge, Rambo didn't play guitar or write eloquent essays.

It was a major adjustment to take this small child in when I thought I was through raising children. When he got into the Batman phase, he drove me insane. I related to the store that had a sign in the widow that said:

We don't have any Batman paraphernalia,
We won't be getting any Batman paraphernalia, and
Don't come in here with any of it on.
Zap! Boom! Biff!

Damien went through the phase most boys of that era experienced, a fascination with action figure characters. This completely mystified me. I was accustomed to Marty's miniature cars, and the ugly little muscled-up, armed, crouched, ready-to-chop-your-head-off or laser-your-guts-out, nightmare-inducing people creatures were quite a shock to me. He held them up to my face with pride and delight while I thought: "What is up with that? How much is that ugly, distorted monster thing going to warp his little mind? Who makes such things for children?" The more I reacted in horror at the little perverted creatures, the

funnier he thought it was and the more they showed up in my kitchen, on my makeup counter, or in my face. I tried to make the best of it for the little guy's sake. I even took a stroll down loony lane and cheerfully tied close to a hundred of them to a Christmas tree with brightly colored ribbon, proving that I was irrefutably losing it, but he was a happy camper. The tree definitely had the wow factor for his little friends, and I had fewer savages loose in the house.

There are lessons to be learned from these awful characters. Throughout the years I've occasionally taken on the action figure persona in my mind. It provides a fresh perspective, you know, shines a new light on things. I never assumed the crouching, ready-to-strike position, nor did I wear capes, except I used quilts and fluffy comforters as capes once during a severe hail storm as I ran about covering my daughter's new car, all the while singing a song from *Rocky*. I digress.

I speculated about how the brawny characters would react in certain situations, especially if they had a laser weapon or something resembling a machete. I deliberated on that perspective when a couple of inconsiderate bastards sauntered in and stood in front of us while we were sitting contentedly on a blanket at a concert in a park. Of course I didn't act on that thought. I am not an action figure.

I did yell "Down in Front!" in a similar Fourth of July incident, but that didn't set too well with the violating revelers who were three sheets to the wind and evidently in an evil-action-figure-state themselves. It didn't work out too well for my boyfriend either, although it did give me an opportunity to apply one of my rescue techniques, which in this case consisted of yelling "Stop it!" Lesson learned: It is best to just move your blanket, or, better yet, put it on like a cape and go stand in front of the perpetrators and act ignorant, rude, and inconsiderate. But, if I were an action figure...

Damien was always good in school and, like Marty, he had a knack for charming teachers. When he graduated from junior high he received no less than seven awards, including the president's and principal's awards for academics, a library award for being a helper, a talent award for art, and a citizenship award for conning teachers.

He has a delightful, upbeat personality, a deep and sincere attachment to people, a talent for music and writing, and a very messy room. He is a bit of a peace and love kind of guy. When he was a teen, his car looked like a homeless person lived there, and he didn't care. He didn't even notice. Actually, it served as somewhat of a storage unit for his friends. When we tried to help him clean it out, we couldn't get rid of much of the stuff because it belonged to someone else, or it was some kind of keepsake. We'd say, "Whose trombone is this?" and he'd scratch his head.

Same thing with his room which, when he got a mandate to clean it up, he did so by moving the piles around. After hours of picking up, it looked just like it did before. Finally, curiosity got the better of me. I had to see this process in action. How does this happen? I watched him, and he picked something up, looked at it, contemplated who gave it to him and what meaning it held for him, and then he put it in another pile of things totally unrelated to the item. He was fortunate Marty had already taught me that my children don't have to be like me.

When My Damien went off to college, I cried so hard he asked his dad if he thought I was going to be okay. When I dropped

Mel off at OSU some years before, I cried all the way home. Perhaps the hardest part of raising children is the letting go. I packed extra underwear for Damien, and when I mailed food packages, I included underwear, knowing he would not be able to manage to do laundry. I predicted he would run out of clean underwear and then wear them wrong side out, not wear any at all, or steal some. Home for Christmas break, he came down for breakfast in a swimsuit. I couldn't imagine where he could swimming in December. He wasn't. He was simply out of clean underwear, and that was his solution. I thought it was brilliant.

While visiting Damien on campus, I spent an entire afternoon in the laundry room. When word got out in the dorm that a mom was doing laundry, several students appeared with baskets of laundry. Damien showed up to check on me and I said, "We're going to need more quarters."

Damien's great-grandmother on his dad's side was Choctaw Indian. When he applied to colleges he was able to get a scholarship to a prestigious music conservatory in Virginia. The fact that he was an Indian from Oklahoma was undoubtedly a factor in his selection. During the time we were seeking out colleges, I sat next to a professor from that school on a train from D.C. to Philadelphia. She advised me that the school was working to diversify its student base and that Damien had a good shot at a full scholarship, so that is where he ended up. When I visited him there, I noted that he was quite a campus celebrity-- this Indian boy from Oklahoma.

He was injured when home for the holidays, and I was working on the phone with the campus nurse to manage his continuing care in Virginia once he returned. She wanted to know the name of the hospital where he was treated. I said St. Francis, which has a facility in both Tulsa and the suburb of Broken Arrow. She pulled St. Francis up on her computer and assumed the care was at the Broken Arrow location because she thought it was an Indian reservation, an indication that Damien being an Indian from Oklahoma was a well-known fact on campus. His heritage is not unusual in Oklahoma, but at the school he attended in Virginia it was unique. He was aware that this was a contributing factor to his scholarship, and when anticipating going off to college he said to me, "I don't know how to be an Indian." I told him: "That's the message. You are really just like everyone else. It is not like you have to wear a head dress or anything."

It was an artsy eastern school and I was concerned about his fitting in there. This proved to not be an issue. He fit in all right, with a bunch of delightful, talented, artistic, free-spirited hippies. They came through Tulsa every summer in Volkswagen vans with smelly tents, wet swim suits, and quarts of Gallo wine on their way to and from some peace and love festival in Colorado, thereby spicing up our mundane empty-nester lives. Most of these semi-vagabonds were vegetarians, and wine is a fruit, I was told.

The girls were sweet. Most had long un-styled hair, perhaps adorned with ribbons or beads. They didn't shave their legs and wore blouses with fringe, thinning jeans with decals, flip flops, and wonderful dangly earrings. The boys wore sandals and clothes comfortable enough to sleep in, and one wore a stocking hat in the summer. They were borderline penniless. I packed sack lunches, slipping in a few dollars and gassing up vehicles to assure the kids got far enough down the road that they didn't come back when their next crisis hit.

One morning we awoke to a very large snow white dog tied to a tree and barking vigorously in our back yard. We were trying to decide who to call about that when Damien, who must have heard the word "police" in our conversation, stuck his head out of his bedroom door and informed us it was just friends passing through. They arrived in the middle of the night and tied their dog to our tree while they slept. It was then that we noticed the Volkswagen van parked in front of the house. We knew the drill and began exploring cupboards for vegetarian sack lunch items and something for the dog. We didn't know if he was a vegetarian, but we were betting not.

One time I put a hundred dollar bill in a sack lunch, leaving it on the counter for wayward travelers who were sleeping in, and went to work. Unknowingly, Damien's dad did the same thing. That evening we had a good laugh visualizing the vagabonds' surprise as they sat in the back of the van foraging through the sack lunch, worrying whether there was enough Gallo to get through the meal, and discovering the two hundred dollars.

Most of his friends were musicians as was Damien. He developed a unique trademark laugh, kind of a dumb a'ha, a'ha,a'ha thing. I was watching his band perform at a club in

Tulsa packed with his friends and groupies. While introducing a song, he laughed. Suddenly the entire club broke out in an imitation. Everyone was going a'ha, a'ha, a'ha while I tried to figure out if I was proud or embarrassed. I quickly came down on the proud side and joined in.

In spite of his goofy laugh, Damien was a smart kid. When he was in college he commented on how stupid he was in high school. He sounded really embarrassed about it. Given some of his college antics, I am not sure his conclusion was sound, but I advised him that anytime you look back and don't feel you were stupid, you have stopped learning and growing. Feeling stupid is a good thing when you are contemplating your past. Get over it.

I was in my fifties at the time I gave that advice. In my sixties now, I am still looking back and feeling stupid. I'm doing so now as I write this book. I hope I am doing that when I'm a hundred, at least I think so. Isn't there something inherently wrong about always feeling you were stupid? At some point in your life shouldn't you be able to be free of the burden of feeling stupid and look back at life without judgment? Of course at that point you may be putting your toothpaste in the refrigerator, the car keys in the sugar bowl, and groceries under lock and key to keep them from the people living in the attic who come out at night to steal your favorite soup spoon and orthopedic shoes, but at least feeling stupid would no longer be on the radar. The burden is lifted. I digress.

Damien coming into my world when he did was a delightful unexpected bonus for me. I had no idea the joy and wonderment he would provide. He has brought richness and variety to my life. Over the years I found myself from time-to-time having conversations with his mother. I felt a huge responsibility to take care of him for her because she could not. When times were tough, I thought of her and hung in there. I did it for her, the mother who could not be there--the one I knew, mother-to-mother, wanted so much for him.

School programs and events were the hardest for me. I always cried and was once embarrassed to realize a video of him in a Christmas program captured my sniffles on the audio. He was so cute. I couldn't help thinking how sad it was that she was not there to see it. As his sorta Mom, I was so proud of him. How proud would she have been?

As Damien began displaying musical talent, oh how I wished she could have seen that. When his dad and I were putting the finishing touches on his tuxedo for the prom, I had to leave the room so he wouldn't see me cry. He was beautiful, and it was just so sad that she was not there to see it. Sometimes I felt guilty that I had the joy of experiencing his life and she did not, and I always felt inadequate--that I could never properly fill her shoes.

Damien formed a band in junior high named *Somewhat Lucky*. I asked him where the name came from, and he said that it was how he felt. He had lost his Mom, so he couldn't really say he was lucky, but life was good. He was *somewhat lucky*. The band has played around Tulsa for years. He writes his own music, and the lyrics are impressive. One of my favorite pleasures is to watch him perform. My girlfriends and I yell along with the groupies: "Damien, we love you." Occasionally we go completely insane and get into the mosh pit.

> Damien's high school buddy and band mate accompanied us on a vacation to Chicago. I asked them to not act normal, but they did. It was like traveling with dumb and dumber. I moved away from them at the airport gate because they were so silly, but they chased me down no matter where I went, like ducklings following a mother duck. They laughed and joked incessantly on the plane. I told the flight attendant I didn't know them and they were bothering me.

> It would have been easier traveling with a baby and a toddler. On the way home I had learned my lesson and sat between them. They had a high old time in Chicago, as evidenced by that fact that I am in possession of a photo of Damien pretending to pee on the sun at The Museum of Science and Industry. It requires an exceptionally creative and comedic mind to come up with the idea to pee on the sun and record that for posterity. They were out of control.

My Damien is now married and a father. A couple of years ago when he and his wife, Erin, were setting up housekeeping, I bought them an exceptional piece of furniture. It happened to be Mother's Day and after dinner that evening, as I was visiting with all three of my kids in a restaurant parking lot, I said, "This is the best Mother's Day I've ever had." Damien, thinking of his new furniture, said, "Me too."

This Mother's Day I happened to be buying him a MacBook computer. As the young technical genius who sold it to us was ringing it up, I told Damien, "Happy Mothers Day," and he says, "This is the best Mother's Day I've ever had." The young *Apple* genius was obviously bewildered. He could probably resolve any technical problem you put in front of him, but figuring that conversation out was a problem beyond his scope of reference.

A few years ago Damien gave me a Mother's Day card that was designed to be from a pet, a dog in fact. It is his nature to do quirky things. I try to keep up. On his next birthday I gave him a get well card. This Mother's Day my card from him was again from a dog--signed with paw prints no less. I have an Easter card in the queue for his next birthday. The beat goes on.

SIBLING DYNAMICS

The dynamics between children are fundamental to their development. Each finds his own place, and how one fits in the scheme of that shapes them forever. Marty, the adventurer; Melanie, the perfect child; and Damien, the creative spirit, each found their spot. Once a spot is taken, no one else can have it. Since Marty had no interest in being perfect, Mel cared about little else, and Damien's adventure gene was missing and being perfect was not on his agenda, there was no serious jostling among the siblings.

Timing has its influences. Among other things, it determines the level of competition. Marty and Mel were born seven years apart. Damien came along when Marty was out of the house and Mel a teenager. Competition was never a significant factor; however, each child experienced different economic and emotional environments. When Marty was growing up, I was struggling financially, and he never had the things his younger sister had. He jokingly referred to her occasionally as a spoiled bitch, but he didn't really resent it. He was happy for her. Damien had the advantage of both his father's and my affluence along with the fact that I had been "broken in" by Marty. He also missed the emotional challenges of the divorce period, although he had his own unique burdens from the loss of his mother.

As Marty moved into his teenage years, it was not unusual for him to be grounded. He was a good kid, but quite the adventurer, which often got him into trouble. The perfect little sister was impressed and wanted so badly to be grounded. I finally invented an occasion to do so, which pretty much made her day. She immediately called her friends, proudly bragging: "I'm grounded."

> Recently my three-year-old grandson eased his way out of his time out corner and his one-year old sister slid into the spot like she really was somebody, and she wasn't moving. She was, by golly, in time out. Her brother didn't know what to do with that. He didn't want to be in time out but he was having trouble with her taking his spot. It was quite the dilemma. Finally, they both sat there, practically on top of each other, jostling for the corner spot.

When Marty got into trouble, The Mel covered for him because she was never in trouble and could take the hit. She took the blame for spaghetti on the ceiling. Anything broken was blamed on the dog. Once children are grown, they tell you the bad things they did. Marty sneaked out of his bedroom window at night. He maintains that every kid does that. I told him that is not true. Melanie and Damien did not do that. We had alarm systems.

Certainly his pack of neighborhood boys had big adventures. One of the dads let them build a lean-to shack in his backyard, so they had a hideout, which was a relief to me because they quit smoking in my attic. Where the construction material came from, I never did figure out, but I could imagine them hauling plywood and boards through the neighborhood at night on bikes. Driving down a street about two miles from home one day, I saw four of the adventurers on bikes pedaling like crazy along the side of the road. I was shocked to see them so far from home and wondered where on earth they were headed, recognizing that the prospect of ever finding that out was slim to none. Mel probably knew, but she was not going to tell.

I can't say enough about Marty's positive influence on her. He was truly a father figure and then some. During her teen and single years, she understood men better than most girls because

178

Marty advised her candidly about how boys think and act. As a result she was nobody's fool.

> Mel was in third grade when I discovered her crying in her room. I finally got out of her what was wrong. A boy she had a crush on in her class had hit her. I took her into Marty's room and asked him, "Marty, when you were in third grade and you liked a girl, what did you do?" Marty, right on cue, said, "I hit her." I looked at Melanie and said, "There you go."

He did pick on her unmercifully, as brothers do. He was known to hold her upside down by her feet and shake her for loose change, but he was incredibly protective and supportive of his little sister. His friends might take advantage of her innocence by asking her if she was an athletic supporter, but you can be sure that is as far as the joke went. Because of his car business and racing, Marty was somewhat of a celebrity in the Tulsa area, and everyone knew you didn't mess with his little sister. He may have shaped her life as much as I did, and she turned out so fine that we can both be proud of what we accomplished.

She admired Marty immensely from the very beginning. When he was a little guy, my brothers took great delight in picking on him. One day his uncles were giving him snuggies in the front yard while little tot Melanie in her ruffly dress, lacy panties, Mary Jane shoes, and Bam Bam pony tail hopped up and down begging them: "Do it to me! Do it to me!" She eventually got a toss in the air, but no snuggies.

Mel and Damien had a close connection from the beginning. She practically adopted the two-year-old little guy when he came into our lives. A teenager at the time, you would have thought she would have resented the intrusion or dismissed him out of lack of interest, but she embraced him like a little brother. She seemed to relish including him in her life, the exception being when he called her "Mommy" at the mall.

Their connection was strong, with Mel often in an advisory role. Damien was a senior in high school when the man who murdered his mother was executed. Most everyone was excited about the prospect, but he wasn't so much. He is a tender-hearted, sensitive soul, and his dad had to ask other family members to tone down the anticipation for his sake. The press was trying to find him so we had the school protecting him and a counselor supporting him.

The evening of the execution was strange. At midnight we were sitting in the living room, the minute came and went, and of course, nothing tangible happened. It was a non-event, but at the same time it was a hugely profound moment. Suddenly, the phone rang. It was Melanie calling from Salt Lake City to chat with her brother. You can always count on The Mel to understand what someone needs.

Marty was out of the house when Damien moved in, and their relationship developed mostly later when they were both adults, although, like Mel, he also served as an advisor. Damien got lots of advice. Marty counseled him when we were battling over his appearance. Alternative music was in vogue and the accompanying buzz haircuts and grunge clothes didn't set well with me. Marty advised Damien that sometimes appeasement is the best policy, and to pick his battles carefully. He also pointed out that Mom is most often right. I was grateful for the support, although I had already given up. If Damien wanted to look like a goober, I was thinking: "Knock yourself out."

> Brother Kelly suggests the practical compromise of letting teens dress however they want when they are with friends, within certain parameters, of course. In return they must dress how you want when they are with you and your friends. This worked well. I could say: "Go ahead and go to the movies with bed head, mis-matched socks, and a hole in your shirt, but tonight we are having company for dinner, and you better have some product on that rooster tail."

Family vacations were critical bonding experiences especially as spouses joined our ranks. These trips were significant experiences for Marty and Damien since they did not have a connection from growing up together.

I experienced very little family travel growing up. We didn't have decent cars and there were just too many of us. We made a trip to the Iowa State Fair and one to Kansas City to the zoo when we were children. That's about it. I don't remember much about either except being piled in the back seat with my brothers, and the highlight of the trips which was Dad taking a wrong turn down a one way street in downtown Kansas City. Panic set in on Mom's part when cars started honking at us, but Dad saw it as an adventure. He laughed about it for some time afterwards and shared the story with everyone once we got back home. I think he saw it as an act of intimidation on his part. Because he always had junker cars, he delighted in challenging drivers in fine cars. With seven people in an old junker car, one child in the rear window, we must have been quite a sight.

His enthusiasm during the Kansas City incident reminded me of him driving down our dusty old country road during a period of severe drought. He was celebrating approaching storm clouds by crazily honking the horn and slapping his hand on the outside of his car door, whooping and hollering--yelling "Rain! Rain! Come on! Come on!" This was incredibly exciting to us small children. Then the rain started and we went nuts. Mom, as usual, was thinking: "Oh, my gosh. What will the neighbors think."

In the seventies I was in graduate school and went on a cruise for spring break. There, for the first time, I was exposed to families vacationing together. Observing teenagers galavanting around the ship with their parents, grandparents, aunts and uncles, siblings, and cousins was a fresh concept--outside the scope of family picnics and raccoons. I knew then that I wanted to do that with my family some day. Fortunately, I've been able to make that happen.

I've arranged family reunions and taken my children and their spouses on trips. We recently celebrated Damien's birthday in Santa Barbara and invited his aunt and cousins on his mother's side to join us as a surprise. His mother's family has included mine in their family events, and both Marty and Melanie are close to them. This enhances Damien's connections all around, and interacting with his family gives me a flavor of what his mother was like, which helps me relate to him. I see her in him.

I not only worked at keeping my children connected to each other, I encouraged connections with the rest of my family. I shipped them off to Iowa in the summers when they were children and insisted on their attendance at significant family events when they were grown. As young adults they lost interest, but I kept after them to participate in family functions, just as my mother did with her children. Now they value those attachments and look forward to opportunities to interact with family. It is easy to not do the work and let family slip away.

Damien was in college when his dad and I broke up after seventeen years together. He and Melanie comforted each other and vowed that no matter what happened with their parents, they would remain brother and sister. He took our breakup harder than I expected. Melanie kept in close contact with him, and I assured him that no matter what happened with his dad and me, he was still My Damien. I was not giving him up, and his

father didn't expect me to. Our bond was strong, and his sensitivity to what I was going through meant a lot to me during that difficult time. My Damien danced with me at his wedding. I thought of his mother and fought hard not to cry.

My children often include me in their travel experiences. After Damien and Erin were married, I went on a cruise with them and her family. I have gone with Mel and Chris to Trinidad to visit his family twice. Marty took me to Auto Zone to get a tire pressure gauge.

The kids are now grown with their own families and are dispersed throughout Oklahoma and California, but they are still connected. Melanie told me she received a phone call from Marty a few days before Christmas asking her if she wanted a 52 inch TV or a new computer, and he needed to know right away-- like right now. Then he told her to look at the picture on her cell phone which was a shot of him appearing to enter the broken window of an electronics store. I think Marty has some of Grandpa Ray in him.

I have friends who have lost children. One Christmas Eve I was having dinner with three girlfriends. Everyone but me had lost a child. Someone brought up how difficult holidays are no matter how much time has passed. Soon we were all trying to find some strength somewhere, somehow to not fall to pieces on a beautiful Christmas Eve with good friends in a nice restaurant in Tulsa, Oklahoma. We were not successful. All was not right with the world, and it never would be.

A friend and I had talked more than once about losing a child being our biggest fear. One day she called me sobbing and said, "It happened," and I knew without her saying another word that a child was gone. A few years later she lost another one. I count my blessings. I think about what it would be like to write a book about your life and to have to include something such as that in it. How do you do that?

If everything is important, then nothing is important. When ranking priorities, family is undoubtedly the most important and many other things seem trivial in comparison. I can be a hard, tough woman. Mom sometimes referred to me teasingly as Hard-Hearted Hanna as she was in awe of the fortitude and ambition so foreign to her. I was occasionally vulnerable but most often strong and resilient. I have applied that toughness to protecting and nurturing my family. I make no apologies for any hardiness or vigor I've displayed. My parents made me strong and sure. My children make me soft, and now my grandchildren make me silly. I'm moving up. Soft and silly. I'll take that.

Before I could be silly with my grandchildren, I had to do the hardest thing I've ever done--face the harsh reality of saving them. There is something inherently wrong with a little person suffering, and saving babies is an experience I would not wish on anyone, but once done, there is nothing like it. Nothing.

7

SAVING BABIES

Stronger Than They Seem

When receiving information from a doctor that translates simply in your mind as *the baby is not okay,* this dark cloud closes in on your world. Everything you thought was important fades away as you focus on this tiny creature, its little chest heaving with every breath as it fights to live. Nothing matters except saving that baby. At least, that is how I felt--twice.

I have two grandchildren born within a year and a half of each other with birth defects requiring multiple surgeries. They are running around today like any other children, and to look at them you would have no sense of their difficult, precarious beginnings. And me, I've taken on a new role in life as Grandma Go Go. All that was done to make that happen is like a dream so fuzzy now that it is hard to believe it really happened. But it did.

SAVING BABY COLE

It was the second day after Cole was born, the day he was to come home. Mel and Chris, my daughter and son-in-law, were at the hospital. I was at their house in California readying things for them to bring the baby home. The phone rang. Mel said someone was coming to pick me up and bring me to the hospital. There was something wrong with the baby. I could tell she was crying. On an early ultrasound something showed up that was concerning, but in subsequent ones it looked as though it had corrected itself. As it turned out, it had not. *The baby was not okay.* Mel couldn't talk anymore. She just wanted me to come.

Years ago when I went to the hospital to deliver Melanie, the doctor announced that she was going to be breech. As labor progressed, I grew more and more afraid. The nurse asked if I wanted to see my husband. I didn't say it, but who I really wanted was my mommy. I knew from Melanie's voice that she wanted her mommy. My crisis when she was born was only a threat. Hers was real.

At the hospital was Mel's friend Vic, who could not have been feeling well because of treatment for breast cancer, and Vic's very cool teenage son Adrian. They stayed with us that day, typical of Vic, unusual for a teenage boy, but he hung with us, a source of unexpected support. To this day I am touched when I see Adrian and Cole together. The little guy has no clue of Adrian's connection to his beginning. Adrian has told me he is in awe of the child every time he sees him. I am as well.

As soon as I arrived, we all headed over to the newborn intensive care unit. Chris was already there. Mel was in a wheelchair pushed by a nurse with Vic, Adrian, and me following behind. Mel was crying. Vic and I, wanting to be strong for her, tried to stifle our tears. We couldn't.

As we urgently marched along, I knew in that moment one thing was certain. Whatever must be done to save this baby, we would do it. I felt a level of determination and resolve I had never experienced before, and I think everyone involved felt the same way. We were up for whatever it took. We were so "in."

Surgery had to happen now. The doctor was on his way. This should have been found and fixed yesterday. It was a life-threatening, intestinal birth defect that can have several serious accompanying problems. Over the next few days, Cole went through a litany of tests, his daddy by his side for every one. We were fortunate none of the related conditions were there.

Although we dodged some bullets, the complication we were left with was bad enough and would require considerable special care and three surgeries over the course of his first year of life.

I have to say, Cole was a lucky little guy. His parents rose to the occasion. I was awed and inspired by them throughout everything that had to be done. They are just the most amazing parents. Their individual aptitudes and skills were a perfect complement to each other. I know, without a doubt, that they got a better outcome for that baby because of their actions. They saved Baby Cole, and I had the honor of being on their team. It is the greatest thing I've ever done.

Chris took the lead in intensive care. I liked my son-in-law a lot before this happened. I loved him when it was done. Melanie did the internet research that paid huge dividends later, and of course, she did the Mom things. Although Cole couldn't eat yet, it was imperative that he have breast milk when he could. We felt as though his life depended on it, and it probably did. My primary job was to keep Mel fed, rested, and on schedule.

Chris learned to read all the monitors and understood the purpose and mechanics of every tube, machine, test, and procedure. He changed diapers and tended to wounds. I was with him in intensive care one day when the nurses became distracted with a crisis in the room. One of them asked Chris to go ahead and perform a procedure on Cole that he had helped with before. It involved numerous steps and sterilized supplies.

I watched him meticulously executing the required care and helped where I could with the crying, kicking baby. When we finished, the baby settled, and I sat down in a chair sweating and drained. Chris stood there, looked around and said, "I need to clean up my station." He began gathering up wrappers, scraps of tape, and other refuse from the procedure, disinfected the countertop and his hands, organized "his station" and looked around for the next thing to do. I just thought to myself: "Wow."

Walking down the hall to intensive care one day, I could see the profile of Chris in the room holding the baby in the palms of his hands, wires and tubes dangling all around. He didn't see me; he was totally focused on the little creature and was talking to him very intently. As I got closer I heard just enough to understand the promises made. Absolutely, guaranteed, no doubt about it, this baby was loved and his daddy was going to take care of him. It was a moment. Later I was in a store and saw a statue of a parent and baby, the parent cradling the baby just as Chris had done. It was in their garden until Cole was big enough to knock it over and break it. I'm okay with that.

When Baby Cole got to go home from the hospital, nurse Debbie and I were watching Mel and Chris strap him into the car seat. She said to me, "I see a lot of babies go out of this hospital, and I worry about many of them and what kind of care they will get at home. I don't worry about Baby Cole." She was right about that.

When we got home from the hospital, Momma Mel kicked in. In addition to caring for the baby, that girl got herself on the internet, and she found a whole slew of mothers who had gone through the same thing. She also did an impressive amount of medical research, reached out to physicians all over the country,

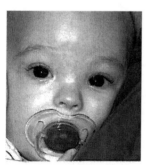

Baby Cole on Morphine after surgery.

and when she determined the proposed treatment plan was not good enough, she sought out leading edge procedures, the best doctors, and the right hospital to fix her baby. She then proceeded to run over her HMO like she was Desert Storm. There was something primal about how she dealt with saving this child. She went after it with a vengeance. She was, by god, going to fix her baby, and no one better get in her way. This included me.

When she started doing this I was disturbed, wondering why she didn't trust her doctor, and I was concerned about her getting too stirred up. I said something to her only once, and she shut me right down. I felt somewhat like her HMO. She was right, though. The original treatment plan would not have resulted in as good an outcome. There was a better way. Often, when I marvel at the little guy today, so incredibly normal, I think about what she did for him.

I recall holding him on my chest as he slept when he was still a newborn and freshly home from the hospital after his first surgery. Happiness is holding a sleeping baby, but something beyond happiness occurred that day. I felt so much love well up inside of me for that little living thing that it brought tears to my eyes. I could feel this intense energy passing from my body to his and wondered how he could sleep so contentedly with this phenomenon passing between us. It felt like little butterflies fluttering from the core of my body to his, and I was totally at peace. Happiness is holding a sleeping baby. Euphoria is holding a vulnerable little soul fighting for his life.

Little Man Cole has completed all three surgeries and is busy just being a three-year-old boy. You would never know by looking at him the history of his beginning. His mother is teaching him manners and his dad takes him camping. He has a tool table, a train set, a fully-equipped kitchen, a little sister, and life is good. He told his Mommy last week his Go Go was missing him, and he needed to fly to Oklahoma. I'm still on the team.

SAVING BABY MAC

Cole was a year and a half old when my youngest son Damien had a baby girl, McCartney Page, who sounded like a little mouse when she cried. We thought it was cute, not realizing it was a symptom of severe heart defects. The next day Damien called me and said, "I'm sorry to put you through this again," and I knew instantly: *The baby is not okay.*

Mac was being rushed to a pediatric cardiac unit at another hospital. The little thing couldn't even cry. She has had two surgeries, and possibly has one more to go. To look at her today at two, gleeful and full of energy, you would never guess that she

189

had such a rough start. Her episode involved many weeks of intensive care and what seemed like a never-ending string of precarious complications.

Again, I was in awe of the parenting. Damien and Erin took care of their baby around the clock, hardly leaving the hospital for weeks at a time. Like Chris, they could read all the monitors and understood the mechanics of the machines, tubes, and wires. They studied every procedure and diagnosis on the internet and were incredibly devoted and hands-on with her care.

McCartney's heart was intentionally stopped for the first surgery and she was put on a heart and lung machine. Imagine doing surgery on a heart the size of a walnut and the tiny veins leading to the respiratory system. We spent long hours in the surgery waiting room receiving periodic phone reports from doctors in the surgery room. Although distracted occasionally and briefly by conversation, somberness pervaded. Not for a second did we lose sight of the profound nature of what was happening in an operating room a hospital wing away where our precious little McCartney Page was fighting for her life in the hands of someone we barely knew.

I will never forget the tone in the room when we got the message they had stopped her heart and she was successfully on the heart and lung machine. It was a relief and a stress all at the same time. Many reports and hours later she was in recovery. Again, it was a conditional relief. We knew we had a grueling recovery, more surgeries, and many challenges ahead. The fragility of life was staring us in the face, and we understood all that it implied, although no one spoke it. Thoughts about that were unbearable, so we buried them deep in our consciousness and focused on the task ahead. I looked at Damien and thought of his Mother and his baby. He deserved both. He must have this one.

Mac was on a respirator. When they took her off, she was in a tent and fighting for every breath, her legs and arms flailing, chest popping--tubes, wires, bandages, and shunts. I had to wonder how this little person could survive it. I watched her struggle, all day, fighting to breathe. The next day she was still fighting. She had fought all night. I thought: "How much can this little thing take? Where does she get the strength?" And I fell in love with her. I mean, she was really something. You go, girl, I thought. You go.

Damage to Mac's diaphragm during the first surgery caused her little chest to pop with each breath. It was hard to watch. She was weak, very weak, too weak to suck on a bottle, so she was being fed through a tube into her stomach. Weeks later Damien tried to get her to take a bottle. She didn't have the strength. Her little head bobbed to the side and she closed her eyes. Damien looked at me and immediately moved on to other care, a distraction from reality, while I fought desperately not to cry. I went home that night very afraid, wanting the world to stand still--not wanting to face tomorrow and what it might bring.

This was just the beginning. Mac had complications and many procedures. It amazed me that a small baby could endure all that. One day I accompanied Erin to a room where they were going to try a special procedure to get a needle in a vein. So many veins had been tapped, we were desperate for one for the IV. Although I was there through all of Cole's surgeries and care, I was not involved much in the medical things--it is not my forte--and I was nervous. Then I thought, if that little baby can do what she is doing just to survive, I can do this, and I hung with Erin, and we got through it. Babies are much stronger than they seem, and so are we.

Damien and Erin took on most of Mac's care during a long hospital stay. I doubt the nurses normally experienced such hands-on parents. Watching them was like *déjà vu* for me. Fresh out of the Cole episode, I felt vulnerable and fragile. The kids stepped up, and their true character and strength came through. I saw Damien for the first time as a man--not a boy. Most amazingly I saw him as a dad, and he was awesome. Erin was a devoted mother, focused and strong, a natural in that setting. I was so proud of both of them. They saved Baby Mac.

Baby Mac gradually improved. A couple of cheery stuffed animals nestled in the corner of her bed. She had compadres, obviously more for the comfort of others than for herself. Eventually she went home with the stomach tube still in place and massive list of special care instructions. Her parents were up for whatever care was required. Erin is from a wonderful, close family. Her dad is a doctor, her mother a nurse, and she had a sister who worked at the hospital. They were all over this crisis from the beginning and all participated in providing continuous support. I was comforted to know they were there.

Mac is somewhat of a poster child for mended little hearts. Her picture showing the scar on her chest has been used in the pediatric cardiac hospital brochures and calendars. Her parents are active in a support group helping other families who have children with heart defects.

As for me, I draw strength and courage from the wonder of this little creature's beginnings, her instinctive fight to "just be." The little gal is an inspiration. Observing her valiant struggle, I know I can handle anything life dishes out, but I wasn't much up for watching any more babies fight for their lives.

BABY BETHANY

A few months later Melanie told me she was expecting again. I acted happy and put on a good front, but honestly, my first thought was, I don't want any more babies. I can't do this again. I was just not feeling it. Then I thought about Cole's and Mac's fight to live, those teeny little things who were so much stronger than they seemed, and I knew I was stronger than I thought. I could handle whatever the future holds, and I could certainly embrace the anticipation of another baby. We had that baby, and this time it was different.

When I got the call the day Bethany Kay was born, I overcame the temptation to ask: "Is the baby okay?" She was. We brought sweet baby Beth home from the hospital, we loved her and took care of her, and that was all there was to it. It was as simple as that, although I looked her over pretty good several times. I spoke to her kicking and squirming little self, asking the question: "Are you okay? Are you sure you are okay? Please be okay. Please, please, please be okay." I don't do that any more. She really is okay.

All of us involved in the beginnings of these babies had already had some remarkable life experiences, but nothing compared to what happened to us during the process of saving them. We participated in something incredibly important and meaningful, something that reverberates into the future. I can't wait to see what these little people bring to the world because of what was done to save them.

It is impossible to imagine what life has in store for them, especially when pondering the degree of change occurring in the last generation. In the case of Cole and Mac it is a marvel that they are even here to experience those changes. It is all such a wonder. I look at their little arms, button noses, hands and feet, their pudgy little thighs, soft baby heads, and budding teeth and never cease to be amazed by it all. Now they are running amuck in backyards and toy stores, creating all kinds of havoc. A generation ago they would not have made it.

These babies are on the threshold of life. I am facing my last thirty years--if I'm lucky. That's a hard thing to admit, but it is true. They and I reflect the cycle of life. I can lean into the end of life experience because these little souls touch me in a way I could never have imagined, because I see the future in them, and because I get to be Grandma Go Go. Through that, I can make a difference in their lives, and they make a difference in mine.

Girlfriends
(Go Go and Bethany Kay--the future)

You expect to influence your children and grandchildren, to offer them support and encouragement, but it is a revelation when you experience these little people giving that to you. I've played many diverse roles during my lifetime, but nothing can touch the pure, unmitigated hope and joy of being Go Go. It is the pinnacle. There is simply, unequivocally nothing else like it.

I don't know why things happen as they do, but what I do know is that for Baby Boy Cole, Miss McCartney, and Baby Bethany all that love could do was done. Oh, and there is more hope and joy to come. Baby number four is on the way.

I once told three-year old Cole that he had the best mommy and daddy in the w-h-o-l-e world. He pondered that for a moment and said, "I'm a lizard."

8

GRANDMA GO GO

Children are dirt that makes noise--
Button-faced little criminals.

As a parent, if you think in your wildest
dreams everything is going well,
you obviously don't have a clue what is going on.

As a grandparent, you must realize you are
about to be kidnapped, and you will hope
and pray that no one pays the ransom.

I had gotten up early to babysit grandkids so their Mom could sleep in. We baked chocolate chip cookies for breakfast. I asked the four year old what he wanted to drink with his cookie, and he said, "Ice cream." So we had ice cream with our cookies.

I raised three children and didn't have a clue while I was doing it. Nevertheless, I can look back now with a fresh perspective and realize I have some insight on how to do it. This wisdom can be applied to raising grandchildren--if I choose to do so. Mostly I don't choose to do so. I am the grandma now, you know, the fun old gal who sits in the tent with a kid with a flashlight, lets him eat cookies and M&M's for breakfast, and convinces Mom he had fruit for dessert when he really had marshmallows.

When my grandson was born, I took on the new identity of Grandma Go Go. I had a trip planned to California to see him when he was a few months old and was telling friends at work that I couldn't wait to chew on his thighs and blow on his tummy. Someone passing by overheard the last part of this conversation and asked, "Nikki, you got a date?" Yes, I did, and I was in love.

Little Man Cole is three now and is my co-conspirator in many intriguing adventures. He is quite the little dude and life is good. He has a Social Security Number, a passport, frequent flyer miles, a bank account, and a gym membership. He has been to Oklahoma, Missouri, Texas, Florida, Trinidad, and all over California. This is in contrast to my generation. Many of us had baptism records for birth certificates, we thought a gym was a place to play basketball, and we had been to Stringtown.

Cole has a gas station, ice cream parlor, race track, train set, a farm, construction company, work bench with tool belt and a complete set of tools, a sand box, tent, hard hat, an assortment of sports equipment, sun glasses, a collection of DVDs, a fire truck, police car, ambulance, two-rider red wagon, stereo, several cameras, too many cell phones to count, a TV remote, a fully equipped kitchen stocked with groceries complete with mixer, blender, microwave, toaster, dishes, pots and pans, table and chairs, and a chef's hat and apron, rolling pin, hot pads, and that is just the tip of the iceberg.

He has Elmo, Dora the Explorer, Handy Manny, Mickey Mouse, a baby doll, a baby sister and a vast assortment of stuffed animals, including a dog that rolls around on the floor barking, and a cat that rolls around on the floor laughing, yes, laughing. (You can't make this stuff up.) He has Spiderman, Batman, Iceman, Robin, and enough dinosaurs to film his own Jurassic Park movie.

He even has electronic equipment and an assortment of musical instruments: a computer, electric guitar, piano, drum set, bongos, harmonica, and microphone. I am thinking he is missing a can opener, amplifier, and chain saw. He has a credit card he swiped from his mother. By the time she discovered he was the swiper, she had replaced it, so he gets to keep it. He has a billfold to put it in. What is going on here? My generation, well, we had "a" doll.

I have been accused of contributing to the madness. This is my response:

It's like this. When you notice a vase is broken and ask your kid what happened, he says, "I didn't do nothing, and I wasn't running." When you discover spaghetti on the ceiling of your living room and ask where it came from, he says, "I don't know, and I wasn't throwing food or anything." Well, that is kind of how it is with my relationship to these toys. "I don't know anything, and I wasn't in any toy stores." That's my story, and I'm sticking to it.

Today, mothers have disposable diapers. (I didn't have disposable diapers, but I disposed of a few.) My daughter also has wipes, a washer and dryer, three strollers, car seats, and bottles you don't have to sterilize. All her children's clothes are fire-retardant. Imagine that. You would think life would be good, but there are two toddlers in her house, and I can't begin to tell you how chaotic that is. The last time I talked to her on the phone our conversation was interrupted with a play crisis when she said, "Cole, don't run the tractor over your baby sister." My Mom had five kids, three of them in three years, so she knew what it is like. Mine were seven years apart. I never knew.

Parenting is a huge responsibility. Grandparenting is an exercise in reckless abandon and a return to immaturity. Both contribute to the shaping of a child. Psychologists say children are blank slates, and adults are writing all over them. I recall a stage Cole went through as a baby when every time you picked him up he would twist and turn to look down at where he had been. He was utterly amazed, like: "Huh, I was there, and now I'm here." He was grasping the concept of here and there and you could tell it was a major revelation to him. Everything is new. Everything a wonder. Every second a learning experience.

Later, he crawled from one room to another checking things out. He was on an exploration expedition. If there was anything new or different, a UPS box, a dog bowl, a pair of shoes, or a laundry basket he looked at it in extreme wonderment. His little voice would utter a high pitched, squeaky "huh" which sounded almost like a hiccup and translated into "very interesting." Things were moving around, coming and going. He was grasping the concept of change, and he was fascinated by it.

Children begin learning physics at a young age. As a small child my little brother spun around and around, getting so dizzy he fell down and hit his nose on the floor. Crying to Mom, he said, "The floor came up and hit me in the nose." Although it was obvious more writing on this slate was needed, you knew at some point he was going to realize what really moved.

You can see the writing on the blank slate as children learn to relate to others. A friend's child, upon spotting Mickey Mouse at Disneyland, ran up to him and exclaimed excitedly, "Mickey, Mickey, it's me, Shawn." One day he will learn the reality of human dynamics and that not everyone knows him already. Another example of human dynamics: When asked her age, a little girl said, "I'm two, my brother is four, and Daddy is king."

A lady spoke to a small child who seemed quite shocked by her doing so. He looked at his mother and said, "She thinks I'm people." I held a door open for a young family and their little girl said, "Thank you, people." Who hasn't heard a young child with new shoes tell you he can run more faster? My son got so excited over his first tricycle that he determined it was "More funner than Cheetos." One little boy went running to his grandma and said, "I am so exciting to see you." You gotta believe it. A child's mind is a blank slate, and it is a huge responsibility to be writing all over it.

I told you guys not to go to Tijuana.

I learned an important lesson when Marty was a child. In a psychology class the instructor made a point of parents not ever calling a child stupid. It occurred to me that I did occasionally call Marty stupid when he did something wrong. Feeling bad about that, I had a conversation with him when I got home and made it clear to him that when I called him that I didn't really mean it. I was quite relieved when he confirmed that he knew that. Then he thought a minute and said, "But I am stupid."

If that doesn't convince you that you are writing all over the slate of a child's mind, I don't know what will. Cole told me one day that he was trouble. I thought that was cute at first, but on second thought realized he was picking up a label that might just stick. Consequently, I told him he wasn't trouble, he was funny. He beamed. He liked being funny. Then he began acting really weird, I guess thinking he was being funny, but it wasn't funny. It was just weird.

CORRALLING LITTLE PEOPLE

Cole is three and a multi-tasker. Wearing his pirate's eye patch, ski cap, swimming goggles, and pajamas, he can work on his ABC's on his "puter" while pestering Go Go in the adjoining chair on her "puter." We are pals, and we "puter" together.

Raising a child is a job, one you can never quit. Although I don't claim to be an expert on childrearing, I know some stuff, and I'm going to share it. You can take it or leave it, but I feel compelled to lay it out there. If you have, or ever will have one of these egocentric, ill-mannered, chaos-inducing noise machines in your world, you are going to need all the help you can get.

A dog trainer I know maintains that he doesn't train dogs, he trains people. He was helping a man whose dog wouldn't play with him or come when he called. I know men in Oklahoma who, if they call a dog and it doesn't come, they shoot it, and I'm not kidding. I always wondered if under the right circumstances they would do that to me. I digress.

The trainer explained why the dog did this. It was simple. The man was b-o-r-i-n-g. The next time the man threw the ball the trainer had him squeal and run in the other direction. The dog retrieved the ball and ran after his owner, jumping with glee like he was saying, "Take the ball. Take the ball. P-l-e-a-s-e, take the ball." The man looked a bit like Pee Wee Herman running about squealing, and I'm betting he never did it again, but he and the dog were finally playing.

Children are like that. Sometimes they simply find us boring. When they are naughty, it is often when we are distracted and not interesting. Kids will play when you are puttering around the house. That is action. Conversely, they will get naughty when you are on the phone or the computer. You are boring. Grandparents are not boring. Consequently, my grandchildren find Go Go intriguing.

If you ask a three-year-old to do something, the response is likely to be a contrary "no," but if you ask him in an excited voice and turn and run in the direction you want him to go while whooping and hollering, he will follow you anywhere--up the stairs, down the stairs, and out the door. He won't follow you back in the door, though. Once a kid gets outside, he is not going to go inside willingly without some form of bribe.

Mac and friend as
Thing 1 and Thing 2

If he won't eat, you can put on his tool belt and feed him with a toy screwdriver, wrench, ruler, and pliers. Did you know that a phillips screwdriver fits perfectly into macaroni? Perhaps it is sad that I know this. Whatever. You can measure green beans with a tape measure and have him eat them in the order of size. A boy will eat goulash out of the bed of a toy dump truck when he won't eat it off a plate, and if you name a meatball after a villain character in a cartoon, he will gobble it up. When you run out of villains, he will eat Tuck the turtle, baby duck Ming Ming, or other miscellaneous pets.

If he lies down on the floor and throws a fit, lie down beside him and throw one of your own. This is a huge distraction he simply cannot ignore, and crying will turn to giggles at which time you can wrestle. You might not want to do this in a public place, though, and I don't recommend doing it in a parking lot. I was tempted once but aside from the potential of getting run over, it could involve tar and that was not going to set well with his mother. Just pick him up and give him your eye glasses to play with. Glasses are interesting.

I often have to get interesting. When a fit was brewing over putting on pajamas, I put the three-year-old's pajama bottoms on myself with considerable hoopla. That was not really an achievable task and in the process I performed an act of which Jerry Lewis would have been proud. Me waddling around the room with size 3 pajama bottoms around my ankles delighted the little package of chaos who determined he couldn't wait to get them on his little self. Being interesting works--sometimes. Nothing works all the time, particularly when trying to get a kid out of a bathtub. I don't have to tell you that.

As a grandparent, I have my limits when it comes to childrearing. I get overwhelmed pretty easily, particularly when there is more than one toddler. You know you have too many whelms when you leave Cheerios from breakfast and peas from lunch on the floor as a later snack for a foraging toddler, when you give up on snapping every other snap on children's clothing and don't snap any at all, when it becomes okay that a child is wearing something backwards or wrong side out, when you have given up plucking your eyebrows and shaving your legs is not even on the radar, when it doesn't occur to you to make your bed even if company is coming, when you are taking morning vitamins at bedtime, if at all, and when it becomes irrelevant that you are wearing clothing backwards or wrong side out. There are just too many whelms.

> While simultaneously playing an alphabet game and trains with my sidekick (we were multi-tasking), I had an out-of-body experience. I was floating around the room observing myself saying: "Come on over here little s, and big R you need to scoot over there." Meanwhile, a train circled on a track around my butt. This event occurred after singing several choruses of a song about sitting in a high chair banging a spoon, running toy cars

through a car wash, hiding in a cardboard box that smelled like, well, like cardboard, and performing a chemistry experiment with Fruit Loops. It was pure, unmitigated craziness, and I loved it, which proved I had lost my mind, therefore, the out-of-body experience.

The revelation was not over yet. My floating-around-the-room self began answering questions from my on-the-carpet-in-the-middle-of-a-train-track self. The question was: "Is this a big W or a big M?" The answer, of course, was: "It can be whichever one you want it to be." Later while pondering letters d and b, my out-of-body self realized I was in a loop while my other self was busy responding to a squeaky voice complaining that my butt was on the track blocking Thomas the Train. I had too many whelms.

That was exclusively a grandma experience. Parents are not allowed to have out-of-body episodes. Someone has to keep it all together, and it ain't going to be grandma.

I don't know what I was thinking when I was raising children, but I don't remember feeling the overwhelming wonderment of their little minds developing that I experience when I'm around my grandchildren. I had no books on childrearing. (After my experience with a book on childbirth, "how to" books were not worthwhile in my mind.) I didn't have access to any parenting magazines or TV shows, and who ever heard of a Mom's Club, child's fitness center, or an internet support group?

By today's standards, I abused my children. I spanked them, bopped them, and I even shook them occasionally. (Time out wasn't invented yet.) We didn't know any better. I recall an incident when my children were fighting in the back seat of the car, and I flailed around hitting them with my right hand while driving with the left. Without seat belts, they were mobile and some serious ducking and dodging was going on, but I did land a couple of hits. Apparently I never did any of these things hard enough to really hurt them, but I wonder if I could have. It is scary what I know now and what I didn't know then.

Kids rode around standing up on the front seat of the car. We mothers were so accustomed to putting our arms out in front of them when we braked that we did it to adults. No adult took offense to a slap to their chest as each of them had done the same thing. That was our representation of a restraining device. A favorite place for kids to hang out was in the back window space, and they bounced around all over the car, crawling from front to back, and window to window. We never heard of car seats and didn't have kid locks on the doors either. I know of instances where children opened a car door and fell out. Imagine that. It is confounding when you contemplate the magnitude of the changes in parenting in just one generation.

MANAGING TEENAGERS
(An Oxymoron)

Here is a news flash for you. Teenagers are obnoxious, scruffy, over-stimulated, hormone raging, reckless, irrational, entertaining, needy, charming, dependent, ungrateful, lovable, smart ass know-it-alls (another George Carlin moment). They are not people. They are teenagers who turn back into people at about age twenty-five.

I was instructing one of my teenagers on the details of defensive driving, all of which he already knew, of course. Having a sense that he wasn't getting it, I advised him that statistically the odds of him having an accident within the first six months of getting his license were extremely high, and that most likely he will have other over-stimulated, hormone-raging, smart ass know-it-all party animals in the car with him at the time. He was doing his usual tune-me-out response: "Yeah, yeah, yeah. I already know everything, and you are bothering me." He had his license only a few months when his passenger says something like: "Hey, man, look at that party." Checking out the party, he rammed the back end of a Cadillac full of blue hairs and did ten thousand dollars worth of damage. Since I was older and had mellowed, I didn't throw a fit or have a conniption as I would have done in earlier years, but I did do the wiser than you, condescending, know it all, arrogant, egotistical, pompous "I told you so" routine.

We often fail to realize what teens don't know, especially since they act as though they know everything. We assume their brains develop at the same rate as their bodies. They don't. In addition to a basic level of ignorance, scientists have discovered that teenagers' brains are not developed enough to anticipate future consequences of their actions. This is why they are such a mess, why they drive recklessly, text like fools while driving, chug-a-lug alcohol, get pregnant, light fire to a bag full of dog poop on a front porch and ring the doorbell, and cease being a person at about age thirteen. The good news is that they turn back into people in their mid-twenties when the capability to anticipate the future consequences of their actions finally kicks in. In the meantime, they should not have access to a credit card nor should they get married.

Ignorance and brain limitations are a lethal combination. I think we should educate them about their being short-changed, thereby increasing the possibility they will listen to someone with a fully developed frontal cerebral cortex. They need to know about their impairment. They won't believe you, but tell them to check it out on the internet, their bottom-line source of authoritative information. Anytime you impart information to anyone over the age of about eight, you need to send them to the internet for research if you want them to really get it. Electronic sources of information trump parental advice. Make sure the net nanny is up and running.

Teenagers will drive you to distraction and, in this case, they have driven me to preaching because I can't help but get on my soap box about managing them. In spite of my rescue tendencies, preaching is not a role I relish. It's too much like nagging. In this case, though, I like to think of it as sharing. Regardless, if there is any time in life when we need all the help we can get, it is when dealing with the precarious times of teens, so here goes. This is what I think I know.

WHAT ALL TEENS NEED TO KNOW
THAT THEY THINK THEY ALREADY KNOW,
BUT THEY DON'T

Teens are not at all intuitive. Things that are fundamental to us have likely never occurred to them. They must be taught basic principles such as not stealing from an employer, the definition of rape, the consequences of alcohol poisoning, always showing respect for law enforcement officers, little things like that. These are not short conversations. They need details. You must give them the language to say no and still be cool. Just saying no in their peer pressure environment is not enough, and they don't instinctively know how to show respect or that trust must be earned. As a parent, we must teach them these things.

When someone proposes something stupid, teens need the language to defuse the situation. I taught mine to say: "Man, you're crazy." They must say it like they mean it, like the other person is really nuts while they are cool. Have them practice saying it. I was in the laundry room when I overheard my teenage son say it forcefully and with great authority while in the garage with friends on a rainy day. What would have happened had he not been trained to say that is a matter of pure speculation. I'm guessing the possibilities were a cigarette burn in the back seat upholstery of my new T-Bird, a fire in the attic, or perhaps something bad was going to happen to the neighbor's cat, who had a perverted fascination with my car and may have sauntered into a teenage nightmare waiting to happen.

Make sure they know what date rape is. They understand rape. They don't understand date rape. It is rampant on college campuses and under reported. I know of a shocking number of women who have had this unfortunate experience their freshman year of college. None of them reported it. Not one. Your daughter is in jeopardy and your son could be in serious trouble because you assumed they knew something they didn't.

Teens need to know that if they are anyplace where someone has a gun, they should go someplace else. If a fight breaks out there is a strong possibility someone will go to their vehicle and return with a gun, particularly in Oklahoma and Texas. They should leave the scene quickly at the first sign of an argument. If friends won't leave, they should tell them: "Man, you're crazy."

Rather than your kid having his friend's back in a contentious situation, teach him to get his friend out of the situation. They need to know how to avoid a fight with dignity when they are challenged--how to walk away strong. The "Man, you're crazy." comment works pretty well, or perhaps "I'm crazy, and I'm afraid I might kill you. I'm out of here." If called a coward or a big old girl they should not respond with "Bite me." Also, they know their momma, or sister, or girlfriend is not a ho, and there is no need to defend her. Just say "whatever" and get the heck out of there. There is no shame in walking away. In fact, it takes more courage to do that than to be stupid.

Introduce them to the fact that nothing good happens after midnight. This may not be a universal truth but it is about as close to one as you are going to get, other than the truth that all men must have a big honkin' stereo and a recliner. When the clock strikes twelve they can still be having fun, but they should be in a safe place and stay there.

Prepare them to act if someone passes out at a party. The person could lie there and die while everyone laughs and takes pictures of them with their cell phones. Someone getting drunk or high and passing out is not funny. They need to load up any comatose teen and get them to an emergency room or home to their parents, and don't deposit them on the front lawn or put them to bed. Make absolutely certain their parents know they are there.

I have a friend who happened to be up in the middle of the night when she heard a car stop in front of her house. A door slammed and the car sped off. Out of curiosity she peeked out the window. Her son's friends had dumped her drunk, passed out son on the front lawn in 26 degree temperature. Had she not been up, he would have certainly frozen to death. How would your kid feel if he was in that car and woke up the next morning to hear on the news that the friend he unceremoniously dumped in a front yard was dead? This proves the point vividly that young people don't foresee the consequences of their actions.

My son saved someone's life while in college by responding to a passed out person when no one else gave it a thought. Rescuing him involved a difficult hike and a boat ride, no less, but at the hospital it became clear that a mother and father would have lost a child by a campfire in the midst of a gang of party animals that night had no one reacted.

Educate teens on when to leave a party. It would be obvious to you and me, but they have no clue. Ask them what they think is going to happen when the parents are not home, there are twenty-some cars parked up and down the street, the music is blaring all over the neighborhood, kids are screaming and throwing people into the pool, and under-age drinkers are chug-a-lugging on the front lawn. They won't know the answer. A teen will hang around until the police arrive, be totally shocked when they show up, and most likely stand there holding a beer in his hand going ta-da-ta-da-ta-da while officers round everyone up or, worse yet, end up with a charge of resisting arrest. Teenagers are not going to get it on their own. You have to give it to them.

When a kid gets his first job, he needs to know not to ever steal from his employer. This includes giving free food, gas, or whatever to his friends. Advise him of hidden cameras, internal controls, and accounting processes that expose such thefts. Then give him the language to resist pressure from friends seeking freebies, such as telling them that his company does lie detector tests, and if he fails he loses his job. "Sorry, man. Can't do it."

Teens have self-esteem issues. Something I said to myself when I felt inadequate was: "I am what I am, and that's all that I am." It was self talk that inspired self acceptance. Young people tend to exaggerate what they see as their inadequacies, and they often compare themselves unfavorably to others. I recall thinking I had a big nose. I have some physical liabilities, but a big nose is not one of them. I also imagined big feet, another unlikely prospect. Once I developed the "I am what I am" mantra, anytime I felt inadequate, I said it to myself. An affirmation of sorts, it reminded me that just being me was enough, that I had value. Sometimes I say it to myself to this day, more and more as I face the harsh realities of aging. Self talk is powerful and can make or break any moment. I can look at an aging body part and think bad things, or I can say: "I am what I am, and that's all that I am," and get busy enjoying life.

As part of child rearing, we should help children and teens with their concept of friendships and how to orchestrate people coming into and out of their lives. They tend to have unrealistic perceptions of friendship. You can save them considerable heartache by helping them understand that not all friendships are forever. Sometimes you have to let people go. If you don't tell them that, they may be too trusting, hold on too long, and feel terrible when the friendship ends. Betrayal can be a shock and overly devastating. People are flawed. Tell them to expect some of that. Also, there are different levels of friendship and sometimes a relationship can be re-defined rather than cast aside. We know these things. They don't.

It is important that teens know how to relate to bullies and controlling people so they are not sucked into that world. This means you must be informed and able to identify verbal abuse and physical abuse, which are rampant among teens. Few parents understand controlling behavior. Shoot, most teachers and many therapists don't understand it. It is insidious. Young people are especially vulnerable to emotional attacks through verbal abuse, which are devastating. On the other hand, your child could be an abuser. There are books on the subject. You and your teen need to read them. I'm still preaching. Flow with me here. Teenagers are a lot of work.

Be certain they understand that when people show them who they really are, they should believe them. Teens tend to build fantasies around friendships and romantic relationships that are not even close to reality. Adults do that, too. I've done it, though not so much anymore. I'm to the point where I quit saying: "Mmmm, I want some more of that." They should not make excuses for bad behavior or a lack of integrity in others. It is not what people say that counts. It is what they do.

Not much good comes out of a kid being snooty, mean or prejudiced. One way to help them appreciate their fellow man is to remind them that every person is some mother's son or daughter. That person they view as weird, ugly, or unworthy has a mom and a dad who love them dearly and want so much for their child. Every person has value, and every person, whoever or whatever they are, is one of us. Each person is *enough* in their own right. We are all part of a common humanity and deserving of love and respect.

My brother Denny's friendship with a neighbor boy growing up inspired me to encourage my children not to be prejudiced or look down on anyone. I told them to seek out the kid in their class or neighborhood who was not in the "in" crowd, and that person will be the best friend they ever had. They took this advice to heart and each one of them proved my point:

> Marty was about eight years old when he befriended Jake, a heavy-set boy in our neighborhood whom the other boys excluded. Marty pulled him into the pack. His mother was so grateful, she thanked me over and over. It changed Jake's life, and it changed Marty's as well. This took some adjustment on the part of the other boys. Fortunately, the Bill Cosby cartoon with a Fat Albert character came out about this time which helped make Jake cool. Still it was a challenge to get the other boys to come around.

I was hauling a bunch of them to the roller skating rink. Jake sat in the front seat because he was so large. One of the boys made a mean negative remark about him, and I turned around, looked the kid in the eye and said firmly, "Not in my car." Jake said, "That's okay, Mrs. Hanna. I'm used to it." How sad is that? I set Jake straight as well, "Not in my car." This set the tone, at least in my car, and Jake's life got better.

In elementary school Melanie informed me there was a new boy in her class. He was African American in an all-white school. I suggested she befriend him, and she did. Years later in high school some tough black girls began picking on her and were working up to a fight. He came to her defense. Who knows what would have happened if he hadn't. He helped me move one time, and I enjoyed the fact that his presence on moving day made the new neighbors uncomfortable. I was tempted to introduce him as my son, just to make them squirm.

Damien was naturally friendly and inclusive. One of his friends had lost limbs in an accident. It meant a lot to his parents when Damien befriended him.

More wisdom. Hold children accountable for their mistakes and lies. Don't make excuses for them. Insist they face the music head on. Reinforce the resulting lessons, but help them realize mistakes are not the end of the world and guide them through the road to recovery and redemption. It is our job to support them through life's journey whatever that turns out to be. Even if they end up in prison, we would go visit them. It's called unconditional love. It kicks in with the first cry of a baby, and it is inherent in being a parent. You are never free of your children, and you never give up on your children. This doesn't mean you defend bad behavior. It means you support them in facing the music and being accountable.

A good kid had gotten into trouble while hanging out with a bunch of boys. They were good boys, but put teenagers together in a pack and things happen. His family was telling him he couldn't make another mistake or his future would be ruined. That was too strong for the circumstances. He *will* make another mistake, and what is he going to think when that happens--that it is the end of the world? We love our children no matter what, but do they know that? Do they know they can rally? Do they know they are *enough*? By virtue of existing they are *enough*. Do they know that?

It is such a rare and exceptional pleasure to encounter a child or teen with manners. Although it is a shock to me on the level of inserting a screwdriver into an electrical outlet to experience a teen doing the mannerly thing, once I've recovered, it is the equivalent of a warm fuzzy. I mean, I just want to adopt them. Well maybe not. I might be better off going to the animal shelter and bring home a pit bull who had attacked a mailman. Manners are important and reflect sensitivity and consideration. Children are never too small to learn manners. Three-year-old Cole's parents are having some success at teaching him manners. When they tell him to go into time out he says, "No, thank you."

Communication is vital to staying connected with children. I discovered a childrearing bonanza in a neighborhood Mexican restaurant. If I thought a kid was having a problem they weren't revealing, I loaded them up and took them out to eat where they would spill it out before the salsa hit the table. If there was more than one kid present, they argued over who got to spill it out first. This is particularly important when managing teenagers who tend to hold back on revealing problems. There is nothing to do in a restaurant but eat and talk. In today's environment you need to insist they put their cell phone away.

I observed a mother and daughter in a restaurant recently, both poking around on cell phones, and neither one of them said anything to each other. I mean nothing, naught, nil, zilch, nada. They were mesmerized by their phones. (You gotta know they do this while driving.) I thought about how unfortunate it was that they ignored each other like that and wondered who could be more important to talk to than each other. What a missed opportunity. Perhaps not all is lost. They may have been texting each other. It could happen, but how sad is that?

KIDNAPPED GRANDPARENTS

Teenagers are tough. Grandchildren are delicious. I don't know how to adequately describe what being a grandparent is like, but let me take a crack at it. Being Go Go is like ice cream, cotton candy, Hershey's milk chocolate nuggets with toffee and almonds, Weezie's homemade pie, and a tilt-a-whirl ride--all squared. Being a grandparent means being adequately impressed when a little guy approaches you while you are eating breakfast and says, "Look at this biggest booger I got out of my nose--all by myself." A grandparent is okay with that and doesn't have a fit when the child generously shares his green treasure by putting it on her plate. She says, "Thank you very much."

Grandparents are important. Children get a good part of their self-esteem from grandparents. You have got to know that when your eyes light up every time you see them, it tells them they are special. It has to make an impression on their little minds, and you are writing on that slate with every smile and welcoming outreach of your arms. You are their window to the world and to their self. It is a huge responsibility.

Grandpa Ray with Marty

As parents and grand parents, we create our children's world. We establish the environment in the home, paint a picture of the outside world, and set the tone of their perceptions of others. Little people don't miss a trick, observing everything we say and do. Their responses are often amusing. My friend loves blues music. When her grandson gets a scolding he takes his harmonica, sits in a corner, and plays the blues. She puts a hat on him. He sobs, wipes his eyes, plays soulfully, and repeats. It is very, very sad to observe a small child with the blues.

Children are really little adorable, button-faced criminals. Each is his very own, individual bundle of chaos and mayhem. If I were a betting person, I would bet on the kid prevailing in most confrontations, if not in the moment, certainly over time. It helps to understand things which will increase your odds of avoiding being a total stooge. Here are some things I know:

> Kids will tell you with conviction that their teacher spanked them for no reason at all, but they will tell you the reason when you pick up the phone to call her.

> They will hide vegetables in a glass of milk.

Boys will fake a bath, but they will still stink.

If you lay out school clothes the night before, boys will go to bed in them so they don't have to get dressed in the morning.

Kids will forge your name on a disciplinary form and tell the teacher you signed it on a bumpy table.

If you agree to let them stay up till ten o'clock on weekends, they may ask permission to go to bed at nine.

When picking out a flower girl's dress or ring bearer's suit, make certain the child understands they are not getting married. This prevents a crisis at the wedding.

Loan your Lincoln Town Car to a teen and he may take it to the drag race track and beat all the cars there. You'll find out about it when a mechanic advises you there is little tread left on your new tires.

When they go off to college, they come home on weekends to mess up their room.

A good way to change behavior is to ask: "How is that working for you? Do you really want some more of that?" (This applies to your behavior as well as theirs.)

It's not all rough going. As a grandparent you get to watch television shows like *Wow, Wow, Wubsey; Phineas and Pherb;* and *Yo Gabba Gabba* which broaden your horizons and neutralize your brain waves. It is better than Bailey's Irish Cream or Grey Goose vodka for putting you into a coma. Once cartoons are over, everything else you might do with a little sugared-up rabble-rousing mischief maker is going to fill you with delight and make you look like an amusing doofus in their eyes and a raving idiot in anyone else's. It is also exhausting. Sometimes Go Go's go go will get up and go. I've stumbled to bed many times after a day with grandchildren wondering what the hell just happened?

At 7:30 the next morning when a little tyke is standing at the top of the stairs hollering "Go Go," I shine and sparkle, ignoring the joint pain as I climb the stairs to get to that pot-bellied little munchkin in his flannel pajamas with feet in them, load him on my back and ignore the joint pain and imminent danger of a series of somersaults as I down the stairs and head to the kitchen in a quest for Cheerios. There I ignore the back pain as he dismounts. Knowing another child is still asleep and that all hell is going to break loose at any moment, I have to wonder how my life came to this.

It was not long ago I was a hard-driving successful businesswoman and at 7:30 in the morning I was nicely finished off--nails manicured, makeup on, hair styled, dressed to kill in high heels and a power suit, carrying a briefcase and driving a nice car to a sophisticated, professional office building where my freshly decorated office, a staff of six hundred, an administrative assistant, mad men, and purposeful work awaited me.

Now I am in a kitchen seeking out Cheerios with a Tasmanian devil at my feet demanding chocolate milk, and although he is willing to say "please" to get it and "thank you" when he does, he doesn't really mean it.

There is a strong possibility I won't get out of my pajamas until afternoon, if at all, and if any teeth get brushed that morning, they are not going to be mine. Yesterday I watched *Willie Wonka and the Chocolate Factory* twice. The sick thing is, I am thinking: "Ain't life grand?" This is just wrong on so many levels, but when you are a grandparent all sense of logic and decorum evaporate as your focus switches to a tiny pug-nosed, wide-eyed kidnapper who has taken you hostage, and even if someone paid the ransom, you would not leave.

Me watching TV

I don't have to tell you that you must be careful what you do in their presence. Cole likes to spank his butt when he dances, something you might think he learned from his Mother and her friend Victoria, who I am embarrassed to say are known to occasionally spank each other on the dance floor. (I'm not making this up.) There is also

213

the possibility that he learned it from Go Go who got carried away one day and spanked her butt while dancing to a children's song done reggae style. Either source of this conduct is probably not good. I am thinking that perhaps a tambourine might legitimize the behavior.

When Cole was born and I first saw him in the hospital, I knew he was smart--you know, above average. I told everyone. This has proven to be true as demonstrated by the fact that if you say "Hey" to him, he will tell you: "Hay is for horses." As bright as he is, though, all the required learning is a bit much for a little guy to absorb, and he does get confused. He called me on my birthday to sing a birthday song and mistakenly wished Chuck E Cheese a happy birthday, which was his two-year-old frame of reference for birthdays. His momma made him start over.

Cole was my first grandchild and my connection with him is tight. I call him my sidekick. We are outlaws with a bad reputation. In an effort to expose him to multiple cultures, I've been working on turning him into a bit of a redneck, much to the chagrin of his trendy west coast Californian father. We must have some Oklahoma influences. From the time he was a baby, when I changed a poopy diaper I yelled, "Whoooo doggies!" As a result, this was one of his first words. When he yelled it for his dad the first time during a diaper change, well, I can only imagine his dad wondering: "What is happening to my child?" I do what I can.

One day his mom got him all excited about where they were going on a family outing. Just as they pulled out of the driveway, the little guy, strapped securely in his car seat, could not contain himself any longer and yelled, "Yeeeee Haw!"

Little boys are dirt that makes noise, and you can count on spending a significant amount of time washing them up and telling them to get their hands out of their pants. This is evident even before a baby is born. If on the ultrasound you can't see if it is a boy or a girl because the baby's hand is in the way, it's a boy.

I have t-shirts made for my sidekick that say things like:

-Babes are checking me out.
-Dude, your girlfriend is tweeting me.
-I live with my parents, but I have my own crib.

-If it happens at pre-school, it stays at pre-school.
-I'm wearing my time out shirt. I wear it often.
-I got grounded for no reason at all.
-Give me chocolate and nothing bad will happen.

Cole's mommy was explaining to him that they were going to fly to Miami. He says, "Your ami? Can I have an ami?" She said, "Miami is a town." "Your ami," he confirms. She explained again, "Nobody's ami. Miami is a town." Cole says, hopefully, "I want an ami, too." Later, Dad said something about going to Miami, and Cole straightened him out saying, "It's not your ami. It's Mommy's ami." I stayed out of it. I remembered the futility of explaining Nowata, Oklahoma, to my kids who worried about getting thirsty there.

Learning is a two-way street. While wiggling restlessly on his little behind, eagerly observing me struggling to assemble a new toy, or shifting on his feet as I'm on a stepstool stretching to reach food coloring for cookie frosting, Cole says, "YOU can do it." This is not so much an expression of confidence as it is one of desperation, but his pleading emphasis on the "you" is motivating. I say that to myself while wandering around a parking lot looking for my car or trying to open a pickle jar, and I think about how cute and smart he is when he says "YOU can do it," beings as he is above average and all.

It is scary to love these little ones so much. They are so precious. I've lost sleep worrying about the possibility that I might not take care of them adequately. After opening a car door and accidentally striking a small child in the head or falling down the stairs with one on my back (an incident I interpreted as an "Oh shit!" moment, while he viewed it as something resembling a carnival ride), I realize the reality of that prospect. Worse yet, I once sat on Zippy, my grandson's imaginary friend. Thinking this was a catastrophe of epic proportions, I apologized profusely. Fortunately, I was immediately forgiven as it was explained to me matter of factly, "It's okay. He's pretend."

Life happens and you want to protect them because in your wisdom you know the world is not always kind. Their complete dependency on those of us who nurture them is what opens our hearts and gives us the fortitude to cope with their antics and unrelenting needs. Doing so is a challenge. The rewards are

215

warm fuzzies galore, sweet snuggles, and a little high-pitched voice that says, "I love you, Go Go."

In addition to being delicious, grandchildren are also all-inclusive home entertainment centers. Until you've had one, nothing prepares you for it. Still, the thing that surprised me most about being a grandparent was the joy of watching my children being parents. This is something I didn't anticipate, and it was absolutely amazing to witness them taking on the role of mommy or daddy and nurturing these incredible babies. It is rather like thinking you have peanut brittle from the Amish bakery and discovering it is cashew brittle instead, you know, more than you ever imagined. Who knew there was such a thing as cashew brittle?

Cashew Brittle

Grandchildren keep you young by bringing the *whoopee factor* into your life. My friend Cookie and I both had two-year-old little guys in our lives. We grandmas were dressed in our ballroom dancing clothes driving to the dance hall when one of us started humming the theme song to a cartoon show. Soon the other one joined in, and we were in full chorus, singing about little animals setting out to save the world.

Then we sang it again and again, louder and louder. We were primed by the time we hit the ballroom--two hot, smokin' grandmas. Watch out, grandpas. Here we come. You are so in over your heads you don't even know. We have game, and we are ready to partee, partee, partee.

216

9

A WONDERFUL NEST

A Home That Rises Up To Greet You

Home is where the family comes together. It is the physical foundation upon which one relies for comfort and peace after ventures into the outside world. Few feelings in life are more heartwarming and comforting than to walk into your home and feel it rise up to greet you.

Having a wonderful nest can make everything else in life richer and softer. It is better than drugs, chocolate, or Bailey's Irish Cream in coffee for relieving stress. It can also be a source of strength and sustenance as well as a joyful form of creative expression. Conversely, it can be a pit that sucks the life out of you. Of course, everyone's vision of what rises up to greet them is different, but whatever it is that floats your boat, it is worthwhile to create that in your environment.

The importance of this came home to me when at a critical time in my life, while plagued with a vague but unrelenting and penetrating emptiness, my counselor included in my treatment plan the task of decorating my house for Christmas, something I hadn't done in years. I was desperate for a solution to my melancholy, so I took her advice, and the sparkly lights and shiny bulbs lifted my spirits, although the aftermath of glitter plagued me for months. It was all over the house, the furniture, my clothes, and me (the last time I saw that much glitter on someone, a cowboy had gotten too close to a stripper). It was worth it, though, as the festive atmosphere elevated my mood.

Having a home that rises up to greet you when you enter has nothing to do with size. I've rambled around in some magnificent houses in which I never felt as secure, complete, and comfortable as I do in the much smaller townhouse I live in now. I didn't need or use most of the space in those places. The eight-foot-wide trailer my husband and I lived in with our new baby in Chicago was a warm and cozy space against harsh winters and roaring jets overhead. Nestling in with Mom in her little senior housing apartment taught me that I could be happy in a place like that--a way of life that is on my radar if I live long enough. I left a huge house once for an interim apartment, which was my healing place, one that wrapped its arms around me and held me snug until I could face the world again. Size doesn't matter. A warm, feel-good environment that lifts you up matters.

Creating an environment for others is something I do as a hobby. The level of obsession in this regard is illustrated by the the fact that I dream of decorating a pirate ship and by the exceptional decor of Coco's condo, the home of the squirrel who lives in a flower pot on my balcony. I am at one with Coco every morning while he eats nuts and I drink my morning coffee--just before my Olympic training begins. Coco has R-30 value insulation and an umbrella to protect his residence from the weather, all color coordinated with the patio furniture.

There is frequently a decorating project on my agenda, even though my sense of style is suspect because of an off the charts affection for black and white--the colors of a pirate ship flag. I often decorate with these non-colors, and I wear black almost exclusively. On the rare occasions when I do wear color, it is such a shock to friends that they label me a piñata and threaten to beat me with a stick. In spite of this attraction to black, opportunities to decorate spaces for others intermittently present themselves. I'm not one to believe that everything happens for a reason, but the assumption that projects are put in my path for some purpose gives me an excuse to take them on. It is not an altruistic thing, though. It is a selfish one. The intermingling of the creative processes of design with a business career has provided a much needed balance to my life. The structured, intense nature of corporate America is draining and constrictive. In contrast, creating wonderful nests is an all-consuming, artful distraction. It can also be an unreasonable neurotic compulsion.

> I was up on a ladder wallpapering my bedroom at two in the morning when a man sat up in bed, rubbed his eyes and asked what I was doing. I said, matter of factly, "Wallpapering. What do you think I'm doing?" I wanted to end that comment with "stupid," but I didn't. You shouldn't call your man stupid.

My son-in-law uses a search and rescue term to describe me when I'm absorbed in a decorating adventure. He calls it *a frenzy with victims*, and that is not far from the truth. Since it is important to me that those I love have places that rises up to greet them when they come home, my enthusiasm for making that happen when the opportunities present themselves has no bounds. Certainly, nothing is going to suck the life out of my loved ones if I have anything to do with it--not with my rescue mentality. They will have wonderful nests.

When my children have a new nest, no matter how preoccupied I am with anything else, I swoop in to create an incredible, expressive place to live. Admittedly, this is done as much for me as for them. I thrill at the process, marvel at the result, and get a pretty good buzz going in the process. The energy level amps up, and the frenzy takes hold. I mean, I could give a hyped-up Yorkie a run for his money.

Before Marty got his first place, he lived like a bear in a cave in an apartment with other young men just out of high school. I went there once and never went back. It was hopeless as far as any prospect of creating a nest. You know this is true when there are no clean dishes, someone is sleeping on sofa cushions on the kitchen floor, someone else on the living room sofa without any cushions, a German Shepherd and several species of bugs live there, and there is no toilet paper.

Soon he acquired his own three-bedroom home and became my first victim. Marty turned it over to Mel and me to fix up, like he had any other option. He was accustomed to me messing with his nest. When he was still living at home his girlfriend was over and noticed a new funky chair in his room. She asked, "Where did that come from?" Marty responded, "I have no idea. Things just appear in my room." That was pretty much how it worked.

For some time after decorating his house, Mel and I went over there to hang out and admire our work. I sat on the sofa saying to myself: "I'm not obsessive, I'm not obsessive, I'm not obsessive." This was Marty's first house, the first nest I designed for one of my children, and I savored the result. It was so delightfully him--cool and hip, classy and edgy. It was about cars and roller skates and included neon lights and funky furniture. It was a guy place--a trendy, jazzy masterpiece. I don't sit around in other victims' houses after decorating them, but I want to.

Melanie has had around a dozen nests. That was fun. Damien has had three so far. All three kids share an inclination toward clean, sleek lines, but over time and with the acquisition of spouses, tastes have changed, providing the opportunity to create something different from my usual contemporary projects. It is important to accommodate different styles as well as snakes, guinea pigs, cats, dogs, babies, and such diverse interests as cars, rock bands, and search and rescue.

Mel's husband, bless his heart, maintains we only pretend to give him a say about the decor, which is not true. He can *say* whatever he wants. We will actually take his advice when we are allowed to select which rope he uses on his next search and rescue mission. I love my son-in-law, but he has more important things to do than select a shower curtain. Although a victim of the frenzy, he need not worry. We won't incorporate anything with flowers, animal prints, polka dots, fur, or feathers on it. Still, having been the victim of my frenzy, he gets nervous. He worries, and I worry that he worries. We're in a loop.

It is especially rewarding to create nests for needy people. Needy is not an appropriate word. We are all needy. Let's start again. It is gratifying to create nests for people who need a break. We all need a break. Let's try another approach. It is fulfilling to create nests for those who are deserving. Of course, we are all deserving. Let's just say it is good to do it for those you run across who have a place they want fixed up. That works. An obsessive decorator must latch on to rescue opportunities wherever she can find them.

The most rewarding part of this is creating a special room for a child whose family is in crisis. Doing so provides a retreat--a soft place to land that cushions their world, and for me it produces a high more exhilarating than nitrous oxide at the dentist's office, which is nothing short of delightful. I mean, really d-e-l-i-g-h-t-f-u-l. It is why I haven't cut back on sugar at bed time. I digress.

Decorating spaces for people with money can be interesting, but it is more fun to do creative things on the cheap for those of modest means who ordinarily would not have the resources for a designer. The affluent tend to be preoccupied with such things as brand names, high cost items, original art by famous artists, and where things come from. (It is grand if it comes from the Dallas market, but not so great if it comes from a north Peoria consignment shop.) There is nothing wrong with that, and I appreciate those perspectives; however, for me it is more enjoyable to do early consignment than Ethan Allen.

Great style and design can be accomplished without real art, brand names, and money. Interesting furniture and accessories are often found in garages, junk rooms, and closets--places that are typically full of treasures just waiting for the right place to land. A desk can be made out of car wheels and a door and coffee tables out of just about anything that is the right height or can be cut to that height. Musical instruments, toys, bicycles, saddle blankets, horseshoes, and tack are perfect candidates for wall hangings. Anything can be painted. I mean anything. Formica is paintable. Fabric is paintable. Shoot, a painting is paintable. Paint over any colors that don't work for the room. If something is the right style, just consider: What color do you want it to be? Then paint it, stain it, or dye it.

Many people are obsessed with perfection and bothered by small imperfections on things--wanting everything to be pristine. It is better to view those imperfections as patina, like the patterns on aging copper. If not too distracting, flaws add character to an item and make it more interesting.

Victims of my decorating frenzies must cope with power shopping. We don't loiter in stores; we swoop in and swoop out. They must also deal cheerfully with public displays of hysteria on my part when an incredible find is discovered. Further, it is important that they have the gumption to not let my enthusiasm overwhelm them if that find does not do it for them. Victims are also required to give up the house keys because things are going to just appear in their rooms. This is asking a lot, but outcomes offset any concerns about trampling on the homestead.

It is a good idea to invest in the effort to educate victims on the concepts behind the design and any requisite actions to maintain it going forward. Otherwise, you can create a wonderful nest only to return a couple of months later to find a bear cave. That said, it is important to note that a person's space is subject to their inclinations, not that of the decorator. I share my preferences herein because of my own passion. Bottom line, though, don't let anyone tell you what to name your children or how to decorate your home. You'll get lots of advice, but the call is yours. You want a stereo system worthy of a recording studio, get it. You want a big honkin' recliner, knock yourself out. You want a bear cave, go for it. If you prefer massive floral arrangements in vases that resemble cremation containers and your home is reminiscent of a funeral home, you go, girl.

Most homes are decorated unconsciously over time. A more thoughtful approach is to define up front how an individual wants their nest to look and, more importantly, how it should feel. Through an understanding of the desired overall look and feel, a vision evolves. Articulating this vision early on in the decorating process assures that the end result is something that speaks to the person. This is amazingly easy to do by getting them to look through magazines and to explore furniture stores. Observe what colors and styles they respond to. Even children have strong preferences.

Next, committing to that vision and making certain everything contributes to it is the key to a cohesive look within each room and throughout the home. Some people don't care whether the look is cohesive. That's okay. Just let it happen. Coordinating spaces is not for everyone, but even eclectic homes benefit from a common thread running through spaces that tie it all together.

While surveying an apartment for one of my son's friends who was fresh out of high school and had acquired his first apartment, I noticed he had what all men have when they get their own place: a leather sofa, a huge TV, and an elaborate stereo set up. Fortunately, the recliner had not happened yet. There was not much of anything else going on, just a coffee table, a mattress on the floor, and a couple of worn towels. He asked for my help and the redemption was fast and furious. In one week the kid had a cool, funky crib.

Shortly thereafter, he called me late at night during his housewarming party. There was considerable racket in the background, and he was slurring his words. "Mrs. Hanna, everyone loves my pad. Thank you. Thank you. Thank you."

Then he lamented that people were spilling beer and food on the carpet around the coffee table. I said, very slowly and deliberately since he was clearly impaired, "Go to the home store tomorrow. After entering you will see rolled up rugs on your left for $20. Buy a plain gray one. Put it in front of the sofa, and don't call me any more at 2:00 in the morning."

"I love you, Mrs. Hanna."

"Yeah. Right. You're a sweet kid and very brave to call me this late. Usually when someone does that I kill them. Good night."

The kid had been trained on "the look," and he had his vision down pat. No doubt his place rose up to greet him when he entered. He eventually got a roommate who put something in the living room that didn't fit "the look and was told to keep it in his own room. This puzzled the new fellow, who had no concept of a wonderful nest and had plans of living like a bear in a cave with a redneck, macho roommate, which his buddy might have been previously but was no more. When it was explained that the item didn't go with the decor, the roommate was totally mystified, but the vision was preserved.

Once a vision is established, the challenge is to make it happen. Edit everything that doesn't fit "the look" or re-make it to be compatible. Collections and family pictures are best grouped together rather than spread all over the house. In general, avoid small knick knacks. Every item needs to be substantial, unique, and interesting in its own right. Avoid things that everyone else has. There are exceptions.

> An occasional misfit piece can be whimsical and add interest. I used a wall mounted singing fish once. These sold at dollar stores across the country and lots of people had them, so it violated the principle of not using popular items that everyone has. (Not everyone had a singing fish, but every fisherman had one.) The fish spoke to me, well actually it sang to me, literally, and mounting it with a wall of trophy fish for a man with grandchildren made it work. A piece such as this requires a name. We named him Maurice. (He had a New Orleans accent.) Maurice had a birthday and was dating. An engagement was pending. (I'll explain later.)

If someone insists on having a recliner, and they usually do, I begrudgingly help pick one out in an attempt to minimize the damage, but I am solidly anti-recliner. Most are outrageously bulky and generally not much to look at, but men in particular love them. I never understood why they are so bulky in areas where you are not going to sit (the recliner, not the men). Whose arms require a foot-wide arm rest? A man told me his huntin' dog's butt was that big, which generated a gross visual. I hoped he didn't put his dinner plate there. I'm betting he did. Recliners also have back fat out the kazoo. Who needs back fat on a chair? Nothing eats up space or dominates a room like a recliner; however, no piece of furniture fascinates the male gender more, and odds are every man is going to have one. If there is a Lazy Boy sale, they may have two. I prefer to avoid them (the recliner, not the men), but I'll work with it.

Unless someone is exceptionally disciplined, it is a good idea to avoid open bookcases. They are a dusting nightmare, if you dust (dusting is gender specific). Further, most people cannot control themselves when it comes to shelves. You can deck a bookcase out nicely and a couple of months later they include a seashell necklace from a trip to Hawaii, a glass bluebird from someone

224

else's trip to Mexico, car keys, an extension cord, catchup and mustard packets, a light bulb, coins, mail, pens, a screwdriver, tape measure, guppies, chargers, mosquito repellant, insole cushions, greeting cards, breath mints, sunscreen, nail clippers, something made out of feathers, flax seed, and dust. These things are there forever with more accumulating in the future. It's a virtual junk drawer. In most cases, it is best to avoid the temptation that open shelving fosters.

As for live plants, they are dusty, messy, inevitably cause water damage to the floor, generate mold, attract bugs, require care when you are gone on vacation, and at some point, are guaranteed to turn ugly. They may become overgrown and take on a looming quality. There are other alternatives, and they can be quite lucrative. Let me explain. Get a pedestal and put a cool statue on it. Give the statue a name and introduce it to guests. Tell them what your statue wants for Christmas and get its birthday on their calendars. Make certain they know he's Irish and likes whiskey on St. Patrick's Day. Acquire another statue, have an engagement party, announce the wedding, register at Target, and suggest wedding gifts. If a kid knocks the statue off while not running, have a wake. The prospects are endless.

What makes a space special is doing something imaginative and fascinating. Before I travelled so much, I decorated with beta fish in brilliant colors matching the accent colors of rooms. I'd put them in wonderful glass vases with coordinating colored rocks or marbles. Each fish had a name. Fred, a brilliant blue beta, set a life span record and occupied a spot on top of the guest bathroom toilet tank for years. I don't have Fred anymore. He's been replaced with a large chrome clock that reflects things and makes them appear larger than they really are.

Most people are preoccupied with their stuff and have too much of it. An acquaintance of mine worried that her kids would fight over some old family antiques after she was gone, so I suggested she pass them on now and referee the process. She felt obligated to keep them until she died because they were family heirlooms, and that was how it was done. Where is that rule written? Look for opportunities to unload things in your home by giving them to someone who values them.

It is not unusual for people to hold on to something they don't like that much because someone gave it to them. No matter how worn, shabby, dated, or out of place an object might be, they keep it. Years of accumulated gifts displayed throughout a house make it look like an overstocked gift shop. Don't display something forever because someone gave it to you. This doesn't necessarily mean you discard it. Just don't display it.

Fortunately, once "a look" is established in a home, people get that, and gifts begin to have some compatibility with what is going on with the decor. Also, with a little imagination, many gifts are adaptable.

> A guest brought me a housewarming gift when I moved into a new home with white-on-white contemporary decor. She entered carrying a rusty brown ceramic rooster with red polkadots on it. As the snowy white decor registered with her it was obvious she believed she had missed the mark. Recognizing the possibilities, though, I accepted it enthusiastically while mauling over in my head: "What color do I want it to be?"

> She followed me into the garage where I stuck a paint stick up the bird's butt and spray painted it white. Next I took it into the kitchen and painted the polkadots metallic silver, glued it on to a silver candlestick for a base, and sat it on a white table in a white dining room with silver accents. It was a sensation--a marvel on the level of Dad's bull shit baler. This chicken is a treasured accessory to this day. His name is Wingman, and he functions as a centerpiece when I serve chicken. He has a birthday, is Italian, and appreciates lemon wine. Wingman is not engaged...yet.

Purging yourself of stuff is a freeing experience. Un-cluttering a home clears the mind. To accomplish this, go through the entire house and get rid of things with this criteria in mind: Is it worth paying someone money to move it and store it? Does it make you feel good when you look at it? Does it express the vision of how you want your home to look? Does it contribute to your home rising up to greet you when you enter? Will your children look at it after you are gone and think: What was she thinking? If it fails any one of these criteria, donate it, trash it, box it up and store it, or consider: What color do you want it to be?

I've created my own special "crib", and it rises up to greet me every time I walk in. Since I travel often, it is particularly sweet to come home to this peaceful place. Done in metro style, it was recently included in a housing tour sponsored by an architectural organization. A reviewer once wrote about it for a magazine describing it as: "A unique, suave, urban style so sophisticated that I didn't know whether to order a martini or get the heck out of there before I broke something." I took that as a compliment.

Often people who see the place for the first time say something like: "I couldn't live here." They are right. White furniture is intimidating. A plumber once said "Wow!" and backed up. I wasn't sure if he was impressed or worried he would get dirt on something. I had a date once (it could happen) who looked around and surprised me with an encouraging, "Good for you." Children are oblivious to the white. If they get chocolate on furniture they think it's cool to drive a fire truck through it. The grown ups are the ones who can't handle it.

Everyone goes through evolutions when it comes to decorating their home, progressing through a number of approaches over a lifetime. In some stages, style may take a back seat to play pens, toys, musical instruments, office paraphernalia, or whatever. When young and unsophisticated, we tend to choose a style that is later viewed with embarrassment. That's a good thing; it reflects progress. There is also a tendency to stick to what you have always known. If your home resembles that of your parents or everyone else you know, you might consider reassessing your vision to be more expressive of your own style. The goal should be a perfect blend of style and function while achieving the feeling that the space rises up to great you when you enter. You will know when you have accomplished that by how you feel when you come home from a long weekend or from a trip to the grocery store and go, "A-a-a-a-h, home."

I can be impeccably detailed when it comes to decor, like the dentist who goes to a party and aspires to fix the teeth of everyone he talks to or the plastic surgeon who wants to fix the noses. When I get into a house, I often yearn to re-arrange things. Sometimes I do, and I don't do it only in homes. More than once I've gotten up from my chair in a business office or conference room and straightened a picture. (A crooked picture is just wrong unless you've experienced an earthquake.) Then I announce to everyone, "I'm not obsessive." I don't think anyone believes me, but I'm not. I just want things to look nice.

10

GENERATION GAPS

*No Matter Your Age,
You Can Never Have Too Much Fun.*

It has been suggested that generation gaps are wider now than they have been since the introduction of rock and roll, which was the primary cultural shift occurring during my teenage years. We thought we were so-o-o-o bad when we embraced rock and roll, which is pretty tame by today's standards. We never saw cleavage, butt cracks, tattoos, pierced body parts, toe rings, or belly buttons. Nail polish was red or pink. When we danced, we were in dance position and nobody hunched anyone--ever. I mean, you would have been arrested if you tried that, and I'm not kidding. We never even heard of drugs. We were pure, but so-o-o-o bad in our own rabble-rousing minds.

The world survived rock and roll, and I suppose we will survive whatever this generation embraces. Older generations judge the next ones harshly, and younger ones are notorious for dismissing those preceding them. Isn't it interesting, the contrast of the *new-life* world of the young and the *end-of-life* world of the old? Isn't it also interesting to contemplate that each of us, in our lifetime, will experience both? We of the older generations see that clearly. I don't think the younger ones have any sense of the reality of that, and maybe they shouldn't. Ignorance is bliss and they have enough to deal with. Growing up, coupling up, and raising children is hard work. We should encourage them to revel in their youth and their cluelessness.

Even so, I would like to see generations value each other more and tap into each other's unique strengths. I could use a nine-year-old mentor as a technical expert, and I could share with young girls how El Niño makes you shop. I would also like to see the generations have more fun together. You can never have too much fun, no matter how old you are.

The pace of change has exacerbated generational gaps. Exposed butt cracks on girls became acceptable in just one generation. I sat in a restaurant noticing five or six pretty young girls sitting in a row of chairs at a nearby table, each with their butt crack peeking out from their low cut jeans, some with ample muffin tops, exposed thongs, and flowers or lightening shooting out of their crack. In my wildest dreams I could not have imagined seeing a girl's butt crack as a common occurrence or that anyone would find it attractive. Even an exposed muffin top is now acceptable. My generation is horrified at that prospect. Apparently we are not trendy, but at least most baby boomers have moved past wearing the same hair style they wore in high school, not that there is anything wrong with that. Each generation has its own interpretation of progress or lack thereof.

Then there is technology. Still reeling from memories of being intimidated by a VCR, I am particularly traumatized by advancements in this area. We can now race dairy cows on a TV game system. Not long ago, we couldn't have imagined the game system, let alone the magnitude of its cultural impact. Talk about cultural impact, I had a young person tell me watches are archaic--everyone uses cell phones to tell time. (I still use my cell phone to send and receive phone calls. It does have a camera with which I accidentally take pictures of my feet among other things.) With this accelerating rate of change, it is going to get pretty crazy. Although it is difficult to imagine what it will be like for the next generation (colleges may have to introduce courses on eye contact), I wouldn't mind hanging around long enough to see it. It's gonna be a show.

AGE IS THE FROSTING

Every generation has its issues. There are people in my age group who don't like being referred to as seniors and may even give up senior discounts rather than admit they are one. I'm not one of those people. I am what I am, and I'll tell anyone what that is. I am actually proud of my age. After all, I'm still here, I'm rocking it, and I've still got it going on. Actually, I have no idea what "it" is, but whatever it is, I've got a gut feeling I've still got it, and my plan is to keep it, whatever it is. That said, let's get real. I'm not sure what the heck is going on, especially when I'm on the computer, phone, GPS, or DVR, and I've given up on understanding befuddling televisions commercials, most of which leave me wondering: "What are they selling?"

Lumping people in their sixties into a senior category with those from four previous decades is a bit like lumping a kindergartener in with those in their forties going through a mid-life crisis. Regardless, being called a senior is okay with me. I am pleased to be lumped into the same category as Gene Hackman, the ruggedly handsome type I admire. One of my friends asked me, "Have you seen him lately? He's looking old." My response was, "He is old. Shoot, I'm old. Have you seen my back fat lately?"

Fortunately for those in their sixties now who are bothered by the senior connotation, the label "boomers" is catching on. It is derived from the fact that we were born during the World War II baby boom, which distinguishes us from those who, as children, experienced the The Great Depression of the 1930's and leave restaurants with a purse full of Sweet'n Low, not that there is anything wrong with that.

Life is a process of making memories, and once retired you have time to reflect on them. That is where my generation is right now. We revere the past, the source of our wisdom. I have many years of wonderful memories, and I take Ginkgo Biloba every day to keep that memory sharp. I only take half a dose, though, because I don't want to remember everything.

When people ask me what I do now that I'm no longer working, I often lie. Simply being retired has a boring ring to it, so I say I'm training for the Olympics. Someone recently asked me what not working was like, after they made it clear they did not believe the Olympics scenario. I tried. I describe retirement this way. Time is gentle. When you are working, time is your enemy. You are always fighting the clock. Once retired, time is your friend. You can do things like let people in front of you in line at the grocery store. The real blessing of retirement, though, is that time is space in which to create.

Coping with aging is all about frame of reference. There are many positives. A 104-year-old lady said that one of the advantages of being that old is that there is no peer pressure. Another old fellow pointed out two positives: "My memory is not as good as it once was. Also, my memory is not as good as it once was." In spite of these positive possibilities, it is best to manage expectations and think in terms of *some*.

You don't have to go all out anymore. I work out some and eat healthy sometimes. I take some vitamins, some minerals, and some other supplements sometimes that I don't really understand what they do, but I'm hopeful that someday they will pay off somehow.

Sometimes I get a flu shot. I even got some kind of shot for shingles to protect against some virus and another for some nasty strains of pneumonia. I pursued a shot for something called yellow fever so I don't turn yellow in case I go somewhere exotic sometime, such as somewhere south of Texas. However, someone, somewhere decided they don't care if someone over sixty gets yellow fever. Some nurse said I could have some yellow fever vaccine only if I contacted someone for some kind of appeal, and if I was going someplace like Guatemala or Tobago. I would only do all this if I was determined to live some more, which sometimes I am and sometimes I'm not. (Sometimes I have a really, really bad day.)

I work some crossword puzzles to keep my mind sharp, and I do some yoga to keep some body parts somewhat flexible. I say somewhat because some days I can touch my toes and some days I can't. Someday I am going to make friends with my tummy and some other less obvious body parts, although there are some parts that are so far gone it would take some kind of major miracle beyond the realm of possibility to view them as friendly under any circumstance. There is some down side to all this effort, and I worry some about it. I worry that the outcome will be some extra years somewhere in some nursing home at the end of my life wondering if there is some reason why I'm still here.

We seniors are a diverse group for sure, spanning a forty or fifty year time span. Some of us are slowing down and taking the back roads while others are still driving in freeway fast lanes and are more vigorous than ever; however, we recognize that could change at any moment. We face the reality that you are only as strong as your weakest part, and our parts are moving around, freezing in place, or completely giving up. One of my girlfriends decided her *hoo ha* was her weakest part. I'm not a doctor, but I told her I never heard of anyone dying because of their *hoo ha*, and she ought to pick another part to worry about.

Some boomers have pacemakers that under the right circumstances will open a garage door while others are running marathons and swimming laps. Some have enough mechanical implants to qualify as a robot, and others rarely see a doctor. With this diversity among us, it is challenging to associate with a generational identity. We don't have a clear sense of who we are. We do know that we are not young. Fortunately, this does not mean we cannot be immature. Ain't life grand?

Aging has, in a sense, inspired me. It makes me want to have too much fun, to live every moment to its fullest, to live day by day in a state of gratefulness, to not die with my books still in me, and to relish all the joys I can muster up. I want to drink frozen margaritas until my toothpaste won't foam the next morning, break some rules, move my birthday from December to January, and eat the frosting off the cake. I'm going to play hard and drive fast. You won't find me driving slow in the fast lane. You won't find me texting while I drive either. I'm not an idiot.

Which brings me back to the younger generation and the pace of change. I watched my two-year-old granddaughter proficiently and intently navigating a multitude of apps on an iPhone in a restaurant and realized the toys stashed in my purse held little interest for her. The most amazing thing, though, is that it is clear I'll never catch up to where she is today, and she is two! Clearly, in spite of the fact that anything electronic makes me feel like a cat scratching on linoleum, I must enter the world of technology, and I do so kicking and screaming, with grave trepidation, and a peculiar sense of adventure.

LOVE ME SOME TECHNOLOGY

I've learned not to compare myself to my younger self or to younger people--a losing proposition for certain. This doesn't mean I don't engage the young folks. My favorite place to do that is at the *Apple* store. I embrace technology because I have to, not because I want to, and I will take whatever medication is

233

required to make that happen. In the process of doing so, I have discovered that the younger generation is the road to my own personal technological revolution. This is possible because *Apple* is, well, I don't know how to describe it. *Apple* is *Apple* and there is nothing else like it. Technology ruined my life until I bought an *Apple* MacBook laptop. Now I can do stuff.

When we older folks bring our Macintosh computers into the *Apple* store because, well, because we don't know what the hell is going on, the little geniuses in their royal blue t-shirts greet us cheerfully. They ask me, "What's up?" I say, "I don't know what the hell is going on." Whenever I remind them that I am a technical idiot, they refuse to endorse that concept. In fact, they actually take issue with it and suggest that I am a remarkable budding technological expert. It is the most delightful and amazing thing.

Not all their input is appropriate, though. A young man on a help desk asked me if my cookies were activated. I was insulted, and I made certain he knew it. Still, most interactions are wonderful generational bonding experiences. I even helped a young man with his business class homework. We got an A.

I have to go to the *Apple* store often because my computer has me in a perpetual state of surprise. Many times when I touch it something happens that I don't expect. I spend a considerable amount of time wondering what the hell just happened and talking to myself: "Whoa....." "Wow!" "Whoooh." "What?" "Eeeeeek!" "Really?" "SUPPLIES!" "OMG" and "Holy shit!" This is intensely frustrating, but it has an up side. I get to seek help from the *Apple* children. It is uplifting, you know, to go into a happy place like the *Apple* store and have the youth find you remarkable. You know the truth, though. You are an ignorant technological idiot who has to refer to your notes to know whether you are downloading or uploading whatever it is you are trying to get "in to" or "out of" your laptop.

At the *Apple* store some young technical genius was demonstrating features on my new laptop and asked me to think of a song to download from iTunes. I couldn't think of any (a senior moment), so he suggested Simon and Garfunkel. I told him I was way cooler than that and requested a Snoop Dog number. I really don't know much about Snoop Dog, except that he must be hip since he goes around with his pants on the ground and that we have a common interest in gardening. I know this because he raps about garden tools, you know, hoes, and he has a fascination with grass. I also considered Bon Jovi's *Slippery When Wet* but thought better of it. Anyway, I made my point. We settled on Jimmy Buffet.

The younger generation is redeeming itself in my eyes in the realm of *Apple* technology, and you, too, can experience this hopeful trend in any *Apple* store in malls throughout America where you can commune with the children. It is a refreshing, technological, generational sea of frigging hope and inspiration.

Determined and hell-bent, I installed an *Apple* computer, a wireless thingy, and a printer all by myself with only nine help desk calls. I was a high-tech momma, let me tell you. One of the calls to the help desk was to report missing cords. The young fellow was very nice. After a long and pregnant pause, he said, "IT IS WIRELESS." I said, "Okay, thank you."

Here's a feature for you. The MacBook has a little dot at the top of the screen which is a camera. I did not know this, so it was quite a shock at one point in the installation process to suddenly see myself pop up on the screen, large as life, in my jammies, hair askew and no makeup. The angle was not good. It showed my neck, for god's sake, made my nose look big, and the lighting was horrible. Worst of all, there was cleavage, which generated severe panic, the kind that sets off the fight or flight response. I was on the world-wide web with cleavage and looking like crap. Undiscriminating men all over the world will be wanting me. I was panic stricken. (You can't make this stuff up.) So I rushed back to the bathroom to fix up in order to appeal to the more discriminating males.

After regrouping, I adjusted the screen for a better angle, softened the lighting, and reported the problem to a help desk child who assured me no one saw it but me. "But I'm all fixed up now," I said. Anyway, I now have tape over the little dot which is a camera. I just don't trust it. My computer is in the kitchen, and someone might see me loading the dishwasher naked.

I have too much fun at the Apple store. There are older people like me there, but the younger ones have a special appeal because nowhere else do young people engage my generation unless they need a co-signer or a low-mileage car. Although young people are generally a challenge to captivate, it is important that we maintain a connection with them. They may not realize it, but they need us for our wisdom, and we need them to put Rod Stewart ringtones on our phones and Grand Canyon screen savers on our computers. When I accidentally take a picture of my feet with my iPhone, they can show me how to get it on Facebook.

ENGAGING THE YOUNG

By virtue of our senior status, we are always leading. In fact, we can never *not* lead. We can't eliminate generation gaps, but we can build bridges. The challenge is to get the attention of the younger folks, and nothing is more engaging than a good time. Every generation has this one thing in common: You can never have too much fun. Here are some ideas on how to have fun.

When teens are coming for a visit, surprise them by pulling your pants down to a level comparable to theirs. This might create a hell of a muffin top, but hey, your objective is to relate. Many young people have muffin tops that will rival the one you had for breakfast, and they think nothing of it. If you can locate one of those temporary tattoos, you can have a lightning bolt or rose bush shooting out of your butt crack.

I would not be so optimistic as to conclude that this would produce any profound revelations in young minds of the revolting nature of where they wear their pants or what pictures they imprint on their asses, but you can bet it will distract them briefly from their cell phones. On second thought, probably not. Most likely they will whip one out, take pictures of you with their phone, and your skanky, tattooed ass will be floating around in some cloud in cyberspace FOREVER. People will be viewing it on their cell phones while lounging on boats in the Bay of Fundy.

You might sprinkle your emails with acronyms. Start with a few BFFs (Best Farting Friends) and OMGs (Oh, My Gracious), or LOL (It's funny).

-OMG oxy tank malfunctond UUUUUUUUUAAAAHHH
-OMG podiatrist died no LOL hamer tow oweeeee
-OMG calcium pill stuk in throat AH-AH-AH-AHCH

-BFF Hazel dating retired bull rider OMG

Then throw in some text with no punctuation, misspelled words and acronyms you made up yourself.

> eye halve 2 sa I wr rite bout ^^^^^ U be plsd 2 no
> I snd u $$ u git @ CHZQER enjoey hv fn no thx
> necesari I hart u ~~~~~ :)*&^%$broccoli#@!+-=

It's hard to believe there is a message in there somewhere, but there is, and the dollar signs will get their attention.

Here's an idea. Leave them two voice messages a few minutes apart, both saying the same thing. Then have someone send them one that says they are worried about you. Don't expect young folks to actually do anything, though. After all, they got the text and have money on the way. Life is good and the electronics store is still open. Here are more ideas:

> When young people are perplexed because your earrings don't match, or your bra is on the outside of your blouse, simply tell them, "That's how I roll."

> When they get manic on the keyboard (and they will) ask them if they've taken their medication today. Then ask them to give you some.

> Ask to borrow their car. Return it with empty Ensure cans and a pair of undies in the back seat.

> Ask for a toe ring for your birthday.

> Wear a tie with no shirt. Tell them sometimes you drink and dress.

> Share with them that Effie is going commando.

> Order a dessert with powdered sugar on it and put some on your nose.

To positively influence the lives of young people you really need to step into their world. You could have them load auto dial numbers on your cell phone, making certain they understand that *Old Biker Women Gone Crazy* is one of your most frequently called numbers. Ask them if you were to get a tattoo, where would you put it and speculate on what it would look like when you are one hundred. Perhaps you should ask them to help set you up on a social network or a dating site. Make it so hilarious they will want to show their friends, but realize that these things are visible to people in New Zealand or Tanzania. The younger generation is global as is their technology. You could end up with a new honey in a hut somewhere.

You might want to show some interest in texting or tweeting, but I don't recommend actually going through with any of this activity. These things are addictive and distracting, unless you are interested in minute-by-minute accounts of meaningless events in the lives of countless people and if it doesn't bother you if someone you are communicating with crosses a yellow line and ends up plastered across the front of a Mack truck.

An excellent way to engage young people is to dance. They just want to have fun. Music is fun, well, not all music is fun. Some of it can make a person crazy enough to want to kill somebody's cat, but dancing is always fun, and every kid has a source of music on his phone. Funky is out. You must move on to bump and grind so you can really bust some moves, which to this generation means hunching in various acrobatic positions. If you happen to get down so low that your weak knees won't let you back up, just use a stripper move. Send your butt up first and the rest will follow. Don't be afraid to spank your butt, or someone else's. Work out moves you can do on one leg, while always being conscious of the propensity to list to the dominant side. One-legged bumping and grinding helps improve the sense of balance and demonstrates that you can multi-task. Young folks are into multi-tasking. It is why they cannot spell.

Bump and grind music is a valuable tool for cementing generational bonds, and you can do yoga to it which is infinitely better than a CD of tweeting birds and running brooks. I can attest to this personally. You do need to realize, though, that bump and grind yoga activity will be a topic of reflection at your funeral. This could be a good thing or a bad thing, depending on what the rest of your life was like. Worse yet, there is a strong possibility people will be tweeting about it in Bali.

Because the young are sometimes dismissive of older people, it is important that we never speak of health issues in their presence.

They really don't care if we are at risk for deep vein thrombosis. Regardless of this fact, we should not underestimate the impact we can have on them. They may not be particularly interested in what is going on in our world, but they do like it when we are interested in theirs. We just have to figure out what that is. I hesitate to discredit the entire generation by suggesting it is probably not the news, national debt, or international relations, but it is most likely true that many of them are more interested in racing cows or angry birds.

Most young people don't pay much attention to anyone outside their arena. (We were the same way when we were that age.) Make no mistake, you are by nature outside their arena. To engage them, you must be interesting. Although it is a long shot, there is some prospect that if you are intriguing beyond any normal state, you will get an opportunity to impart wisdom--you know, something about work ethic, the importance of education, the value of saving money, how phones were once used to talk to people, and that when you were a child you had "a" toy.

Here is a true story that illustrates the value of education. A man finished his basic training and was off to the war in Korea. All the men in his unit had an assignment except for him and another fellow who had been overlooked somehow. Consequently, they were allowed to pick the unit to which they would be assigned. Looking over the list, the man chose the mortar pool thinking he was selecting the motor pool. Needless to say, no one wants to drag a Howitzer M198 around in the mountains along the front lines of North Korea, but he did so and survived. Education is important. So are family connections.

Another way to engage the young is to create family bonding experiences in which all ages can participate. Here's a thought:

> Establish a family anthem--a song everyone in the family knows and can sing together at family gatherings. In addition to the bonding potential, it will give them something to do at your funeral. I got this idea from a friend whose family may have toked a bit too often and eaten too many Twinkies in the sixties. I say this because every Christmas this family "clucked" (yes, clucked, like a chicken) a Christmas song around the dinner table. I didn't ask why anyone would do that, but you have got to wonder.

Anyway, one Christmas Aunt Pearl was not able to attend the family holiday dinner and they decided to give her a call to include her in the clucking of the Christmas song. At the end of the song there was a long silence at the other end of the line, and then some man with a voice much too low to be Aunt Pearl's said, "Who the hell is this?" The phone bill later revealed he was in Ohio, which is important because Aunt Pearl was in Arizona. It is probably a good thing to have a family anthem. It's probably not a good idea to cluck it like chickens to strangers on the phone.

Music is a communal agent, but when it comes to bonding with the younger generation, it will most likely be up to you to do the outreach. Young people have so many distractions, they are not going to do it. Be a distraction. The world may not be waiting to listen, but share your wisdom anyway. Put it out there.

Don't you just want to smooth the road for the young and make it all better when they hit those bumps? Our well-seasoned generation anticipates ahead of time those events that make a person feel like someone re-shuffled the deck. Young people don't see them coming. This is called bliss. I envy them that. A lot of that bliss is generated from fun stuff we have the good sense not to do anymore. Perhaps we should not deprive them of their bliss with too much counsel. We want them to have fun, and we want to be part of that fun. This can be a huge distraction from the fact that you can die at any time. That is the big difference between us and the young. We know we are going to die. I just hope I don't die doing dishes.

I think of Grandpa and Grandma Bray and how they were fun to be around even in their old age, how they made me feel when I was facing the challenges of life, how they had such high expectations which made me want to measure up, and how I felt their unconditional love when I didn't. Behind the fits and conniptions was love. Behind Shuppie's fun-loving spirit and Weezie's comforting homemade goodies, there was love. Dad's quirky fun and Mom's staunch dependability reflected love. My brothers had my back out of love. I want to pass that forward. It is all about investing in the young and relishing the return. That is fun, and you can never have too much fun.

11

THE IOWA INFLUENCE -- STILL

The Next Thirty Years
The Future is Frosting

Time and geography have put an expanse of history and distance between the world I experienced in those early Iowa years and my life as it is today. Still, those beginnings shaped me, and their influences continue sixty-some years later.

I still have that driving ambition.
I still get a buzz from hard physical labor.
I still reel from the futile attraction to country boys.
I still swear, and I still feel bad about it.
I still rescue every chance I get.

DRIVING AMBITION -- STILL

When I retired three years ago, I was told that those who have dedicated most of their life and passion to work often feel lost when they don't have that anymore. People tend to link their identities to their work, and when that is gone they don't know who they are. To a corporate executive who suddenly becomes just another retired person, the sense of loss can be extreme. In my case, I had invested so much of myself into my career that I was burnt out when I retired. My last three years were spent merging companies and installing important programs. This was crucial, purposeful work and a grand way to cap off a career, but it had taken its toll. I was ready to be *just a girl*. Consequently, I floated rather blissfully into retirement, or so I thought.

I was also told that you should retire *to* something not *from* something. That was my plan. I was going to write, an old passion of mine since my journalism days in college that had been tabled for an all-consuming career. I had books, magazine articles, speaking tours, and an adjunct professorship in mind. Then life happened. Actually, to put it mildly, *all hell broke loose,* which thrust me solidly into the rescue mode and dampened any prospects of realizing those dreams. (I'll share more about that later under the heading of rescue.) After managing through these crises, I found myself in a general state of melancholy. Apparently, in spite of all the wonderful benefits of not having to go to work every day, I was not going to coast blissfully into retirement after all.

Life was not working for me anymore. I began reading my AARP magazine and stopped throwing away the Aerosole shoe catalogue. I was living in fear--a constant dread of the prospect of a serious health crisis, or worse. I felt disconnected, disappointed, and out of step with everything around me. Technology was keeping me from my dream of writing. I was bitter about the loss of love and the recognition that I'd never have that again. That was my choice, but it was still a loss. I couldn't figure out where I fit in anymore. I didn't know how much quality time I had left, so I thought, "Why bother? Why do anything?" It was resignation; I was coasting. That was against my nature, and it generated severe internal conflicts.

My therapist set me straight. As I talked about my feeling of worthlessness, she suggested that I live as though I have thirty more years left--one third of a lifetime. Otherwise, I could be sitting in a nursing home at ninety regretting the wasted life, thinking of all the things I could have done and didn't--thirty years worth of participation in life lost, thrown away. That is the worst-case scenario, worse than dying. She suggested that just because you are older doesn't mean you don't matter and that I should shed my preconceived notions about what the end-of-life years are like. "Define them for yourself," she said. "Be a role model for what that can exemplify." I got it, and I labeled my next thirty years "the encore years," an additional performance even better than the original show, and I now see the possibilities of realizing that.

I'm now living life full out. I don't have a bucket list. I'm too busy living to fool with one. I've found a sense of purpose in writing and have discovered so many connections that I can hardly keep up with them all. Until someone tells me definitively that my time is limited, I am going to assume that I have thirty more years left, one third of a lifetime, and I plan to make the most of them. There will be no coasting here. Although I have mellowed from earlier years, the driving ambition of that Iowa farm girl who had something to prove prevails.

More importantly, I think about the message I am sending to the next generation of what being sixty, seventy, and eighty is like. I don't want my daughter to think: "Poor Mom. She's old and things are bad." Instead, I want her telling her friends how cool her Mom is and all the things she is doing so she can look forward to her own encore years some day.

I formed a publishing company. Several books are in the works. I'm in an intense learning mode, taking seminars and classes on writing, reading books on the topic, drawing on my journalism education, and learning everything I can about the publishing business. It is said, though, that the way to learn to write is to write, so I've focused on that. I'm certain that as I learn and grow I will later look back on this biography, my first writing effort, with some embarrassment, but I write.

Writing is more challenging than I expected. I've had to become technically literate in ways I could never have imagined, and just about every aspect of producing a journalistic effort has changed since I studied it in college. A good example is in the areas of punctuation, grammar, and spelling. The rules have evolved and in some cases there aren't any. In fact, there is considerable controversy today over these subjects which left me wondering how to do them right. Years ago when I was a secretary, there were hard and fast rules. This is no longer the case.

In an act of desperation I sought the advice of young, hip intellectuals who suggested this: "Punctuate any way you want. Just don't do commas stupid." Another suggested eliminating commas altogether, and one proposed using smiley faces instead. As for spelling, the advice was, "Not to worry. Nobody can spell anymore." Someone said, "Like never use whom. Like it always sounds like freakish and like all hoity-toity like." As they chuckled over a crude innuendo about a dangling participle, I said, "Enough." There was no point in getting into split infinitives, and it is unlikely they have any idea what a dangling participle really is. They were no good to me at all. How nice it must be to have the mental freedom to do things any way you want. As for me, I'm a bit more proper, but their perspectives do make me feel better when I start a sentence with a conjunction or end it with a preposition, which I like to do.

Because of a burning desire to get things out of my head and on to paper, my first book is this memoir. It is freeing to get your personal story documented, and it is a comfort to know that you won't die with that story still in you. However, this is only a partial account of my life. Not only is there more to live, there is a lot in the past that I won't write about until, as I said earlier, some old boyfriends and a couple of cowboys die or start putting their saddles on backwards.

Nevertheless, other books are in the works, a couple of them business related. I was a player in interesting transitional times, participating in pioneering influences that have changed the business community, this country, and even the world. Those experiences are unique to that time and will never occur again. They are the foundation of today's reality. More importantly, they are rich in teachable moments. Someday I will write about them. Then there was disco. I loved disco. Maybe I will write about disco. There was also the era of The Urban Cowboy and the honky tonk. Perhaps I will write about that. Even more interesting was an interlude with law enforcement. I loved going on patrol and to this day when I hear a police car running hot, I want to hop in. I should write about that. The possibilities are endless. I could go on and on.

Older people don't always appreciate the significance of their experiences to those who follow. Additionally, younger people are so distracted with the challenges of their early lives that they are not focused on the contributions of their predecessors. This is exactly why the autobiographical process is so valuable. Younger generations may not realize it, but they need to know what we know, and we have an obligation to capture our wisdom and pass it down. Just as my enlightenment over the Bette Davis autobiography gave me the courage to face my personal crisis in the seventies, at some point, with some person, everyone's story has the potential to make a difference, probably beyond the writer's wildest dreams.

Ambition and passion go hand in hand, and I've developed a passion for memorializing life. As a result of the rewarding nature of my personal experience with writing this book, I'm sharing with others the value of doing so by teaching courses and speaking to groups about biographical writing. A book on why and how to do that is underway. My goal is to inspire others to record their lives for posterity. When I can't do that anymore, I can see myself in a nursing home with my computer, or whatever gadget is fashionable at that time, collaborating with compadres there to capture and publish their stories and lessons learned as gifts to their families--the end stage of my thirty-year plan.

I spent many hours interviewing my mother before she died. By then I had the good sense to question her and other older people about their early histories, and I found their stories incredibly interesting. I recall vividly sitting on the floor at the foot of Uncle Bob's recliner asking him questions about how he met and fell in love with Aunt June, a delightful love story, and what it was like fighting in three major battles in the Pacific in World War II. It was a "wow" experience to hear his stories firsthand.

Uncle Bob made a profound statement. He said that he and Dad believed the same things about religion, although they never talked about it. Interesting. I have many regrets about not exploring the minds of others who are now gone. If only I had pursued with Dad some of the conversations I had with Mom. I have a feeling we believed a lot of the same things, although we never talked about them.

And so, I have retired *to* something. I am a writer. Whether I have one year or thirty left, I will be writing. I don't know if we were born to do certain things, but I do know that when you stumble across something that lights your fire, you have found the key to passion, purpose, and a source of energy. The ambition flares again, and so I write.

HARD LABOR -- STILL

That wonderful feeling of going to bed bone tired rarely happens these days. Exercise and exhaustion from gardening is now restricted by my urban townhouse front yard, which is about the size of my bathroom. Hard labor is limited pretty much to workouts at a fitness center. I have historically kept fit most of my life, although I went through a phase in my fifties when for exercise I would sit. Then the necessity of fitness was driven home by a single, profound incident, you know, one of those defining moments.

> I happened to have a boyfriend at that time. (It could happen.) He was helping me squeeze into a bustier-type bra designed for an evening gown. The bustier came down to kind of a v-shape in the stomach area. He hooked the back for me. When I turned around he was staring with shock and awe at a massive and strangely out of place v-shaped roll of fat on my belly pooching out below the bustier. When he rallied enough to speak he said, "That's gonna show."

> Desperate, I quickly located a panty girdle and slipped that on over it eliminating the belly roll but causing a significant roll of fat to materialize at the top of my thigh. It was obvious that was going to show, so I traded it for a long-line girdle which produced a disturbing monumental roll of fat just above the knees.

> At this point my boyfriend insisted that I stop, suggesting that if I go any further I will have fat ankles and, as he said, "There ain't no way to cover that up."

My gaining these unnecessary pounds resulted in my daughter giving me a set of weights and a fitness manual for women over fifty for Mother's Day. I was hoping for chocolates. Her encouragement got me going again though. I was pumping iron.

At one point I even had personal trainers, Levi and Danny, who tried to kill me. Although I might have unintentionally encouraged them when I entered the workout center and asked them to "beat me, hurt me, make me write bad checks," it was still wrong for them to abuse me the way they did. I stuck with it, though, mostly because Levi and Danny were cute. When they demonstrated exercises, sometimes I asked them to repeat. I needed to study the movement thoroughly to get the technique just right, and sometimes I do things I shouldn't.

My second most favorite workout involves yoga, my first being disco. Yoga is much harder work than most people think. If you don't say "Oh my god!" after holding a position, you are not doing it right. Most men make light of it, and I can attest to the fact that you will never get a cowboy or a railroad man to do it. I shamed Levi and Danny into doing it once and they turned into girly men before it was over, although they were cute in the process, and I was glad I asked.

Physical activities were enticing to me while growing up and still are. I may be in better shape now than I have ever been in my life, especially with my training for the Olympics and all.

LOVE ME SOME COUNTRY BOYS -- STILL

You gotta love them, those country boys, but I don't act on it anymore. It doesn't end well, at least for me, and often for people around me. For example:

> My man left, and I was devastated. At my regular nail appointment I shared what happened with my manicurist. I cried and she cried. Soon the other manicurists around us and their customers became intrigued by the emotional turmoil and got in on the story and the misery, and they cried. I mean, it was a sad, sad, sorrowful situation.

> Hairdressers became curious about all the drama and teary emotion, and they and their customers were soon swept into the doom and gloom. Every woman in there knew in her soul it could happen to her, and a dark, angry cloud came down and swallowed us all up as though the life force was being sucked out of us.

> As we sank deeper and deeper into the abyss, our only defense was bashing the interloper, disparaging the unfaithful, and spewing considerable man-hating dialogue, all of which further ravaged the anguished group. The cloud darkened, the gloom deepened, and happy salon chatter turned into melancholy whispers and awkward silence. It was grim.

> Later, sitting in my car as I was leaving, I looked back inside the shop. A lady had just entered and was looking around like, "What happened?" It was blatantly clear that in spite of all the pretty hair and fingernails, I had

single handedly brought this normally cheerful, chatty, upbeat place down, down, down into the depths of despair. I mean, Dante could not have done it better.

Given the nature of the betrayal, I should have been thinking, "You aren't leaving, thank god, are you?" Instead, I was feeling like the victim of a drive-by shooting, and I shared that with everybody. I should have brought champagne and cake, but I brought Dante. Realizing this was a defining moment, and it changed everything. Going forward, I still wrestled with the in-your-face demons of the loss, but I determined then and there that I was going to save myself from the doom and gloom.

I couldn't do it, though. In spite of that resolve, I could not pull it off. The wound was too deep, the pain too intense, and that was the end of love as I knew it. The hurt of heartbreak owns me-- still. I don't do love anymore. I perceive it as annoying. Yet, a country boy catches my eye occasionally. It is a sickness.

A girlfriend and I were in Macy's passing through the men's department and two guys in Wrangler jeans, boots and feed store caps were looking at shirts. One of them had picked up a pink shirt and was staring at it in dismay and said, "That's just WRONG." Knowing my propensity to be lured by the good-old-boy persona, my friend dragged me away, but OMG, he was s-o-o-o cute standing there, looking at that pink shirt and saying what he said. I mean, really, he was.

This attraction to country boys is undoubtedly the result of Iowa influences. My dad and brothers were country boys, and I admired them immensely. And then there was farm hand Dale, winking as he chewed on that chicken leg. I didn't have a chance.

One thing about country boys I never understood was their fascination with hunting. I cooked rabbit, squirrel, deer, frog legs, pheasant, quail, duck, mystery meat, and testicles, and I never liked any of it. Nevertheless, if some old country boy shot it, I picked the buckshot out of it and cooked it--except coyote. I never cooked coyote, although I've had their carcasses in my trunk and on my front porch. And, I never cooked rattlesnake.

I was visiting family in Iowa, and we had all just filled our plates with Christmas dinner when one of the men looking out the picture window spotted a coyote in the pasture across the way.

To say that all hell broke loose at that moment is an understatement. Within minutes the whole neighborhood was alerted and men with walkie talkies, rifles, hunting dogs, and four-wheel drive pickup trucks were converging on the coyote from all directions. We women folk watched out the picture window as we ate our dinner along with Dad and Grandpa Bray. Dad didn't participate because he thought it was unfair that the coyote didn't get to have a walkie talkie. At least that is what he said. I think he was holding court with his common sense and some of Weezie's cherry pie.

In spite of the fact that there is a fine line between hunting and looking stupid, I was thinking how cute the guys looked running around the field in their hunting gear, their weapons locked and loaded, exuding that "I hunts it, I kills it, I eats it" mentality. My attraction to country boys is a sickness--still--but I'm weary of wondering: "What the hell just happened?" So I avoid them.

I used to be attracted to gloomy men, who I mistakenly thought were mysterious. Each ultimately turned into an omnipresence. Once I learned that lesson, I shifted to the opposite end of the spectrum--cowboys with shiny, sparkly eyes and fun-loving, wild and reckless natures. That was fun, but I couldn't keep up. Also, cowboys get into your car with manure on their boots and think nothing of it. Worse yet, no matter how fine he is, some cowgirl somewhere, is sick of his shit, and odds are she is psycho and into mud wrestling. I tested out a few fellows in between the gloomy and the reckless, but by then I had so many issues that I needed suitcases in which to carry them. Although I wouldn't have missed any of these romantic dalliances for the world, I'm done here. I'm not bitter. I gave as good as I got. I'm just not interested in dancing around any more sad, sad old sorry situations and getting tattoos on my heart. I give up.

At the age of three, I was the flower girl at a wedding. While on the stage, I looked out at the crowd and became so embarrassed that I lifted up my skirt and hid behind it. That's how I am with men these days. I may flirt a bit, but I'm gonna hide--or perhaps run like someone left the gate open.

We had a dog when we were growing up on the farm in Iowa who was frightened of Dad and ran to the closet every time he said anything to her. Dad bragged to people about how smart the dog was. Then he'd give her a command to go to the closet. Of course, the dog was going to go to the closet no matter what he said, but people were impressed. I'm rather like that with men. They say something to me, it doesn't matter what it is, I'm going to my safe place. The last time a girlfriend set me up with somebody, I ate all the food in my house the day before, trying to calm the anxiety. It was not pretty. I'm sticking to my safe place, except for a few coffee buddies with whom I contemplate the world situation. I have them trained up. They know not to pee on my leg and tell me it's raining.

I SWEAR -- STILL

Let me frame this up. It is embarrassing. What can I say? I am improving, but I still swear occasionally and always at the worst times. My last words, if I get any, won't be "Oh Darn." It is in my nature in some insidious, uncontrollable way. I feel bad about it, but I've given up on completely licking it. I decided some time ago that if a guy I dated was offended by my swearing, he needed to get another god damn girlfriend.

It is hard to imagine that I learned this behavior in Iowa, the virtual center of propriety, but I did. I've sworn as far back as I can remember. Swearing adds a cadence and emphasis to dialogue that is overwhelmingly expressive. At certain levels of communication it kicks in, and I am powerless to resist it, as if I'm on some kind of auto-pilot. It's an addiction, you know, similar to gambling and crack. I need a treatment plan.

I've made some progress, learning to say "Really?" instead of "You've got to be shitting me"; and "That's interesting," rather than "What the hell?"; but I still think "holy shit" is the most expressive phrase around. I am working on substituting "heck," "darn," and "cow" for certain bad words, but I am not loving them, especially "cow," which doesn't have any smack to it at all.

I do consider swearing a vice; however, I don't have any other vices. I don't gamble except for the few trips Mom and I made to the casino because too many coins accumulated in my change jar. I drink only occasionally and moderately. I never smoked although I toked a couple of times when I was young and stupid, after which I ate something like a whole box of Kellogg's Sugar Smacks and the best carrot sticks in the universe.

250

I have always been devoted to my men, probably to a fault, and I have never checked out any of those nasty internet sites or phone chat lines, although I did pay for a magazine once just to see Bert Reynolds naked. (That was a historical event, and I am not apologizing for it.) I'm no longer looking for "the next man to blame," so I don't date anymore in the interest of not making another man feel inadequate and driving him to rebel and grow a beard. I'd rather fall into chocolate or caramel than fall in love, although I must confess my mind does wander into the steamy arena occasionally, particularly when it comes to pirates. (I'm not dead yet, and I don't think pirates care if you swear.)

I've been known to run amuck with girlfriends occasionally, but only in the harmless territory. I've never been arrested. All in all, I am a pretty good old gal. People are flawed, and I have issues, but except for a few occasions involving children, Aunt Weezie, and four pastors, I'm not asking for any do overs on swearing. I swear. (Pun intended.)

The problem is children. I have grandchildren. Fortunately I do pretty well in their presence, and I can tell you unequivocally that if a little guy says "Dame it, woman!" (sp intended), it was not me who taught him that. Someone has been watching too much television.

Perhaps it is wrong that it is a comfort to me when small children swear and I had nothing to do with it. It makes me feel that perhaps there is some natural tendency to do so, which suggests an excuse for my bad behavior. For example, when a tiny, sweet little girl was learning to speak, her mother encouraged her to say "drink." She said, "Shit." Mommy said, "No, it's drink." She said, "Shit." "Drink." "Shit." Finally, Mommy said, "Never mind." The girl said, "Nebermine," reached for her drink and said, "Shit." I'm sorry, but that is a girl after my own heart.

RESCUE -- STILL

One of the values of writing your autobiography is identifying a prevailing theme for your life. This is enlightening, introspective information that creates an awareness of what drives behavior. My main theme is clearly rescue. I see a problem and I'm all over it, usually with considerable fortitude, determination, courage, and enthusiasm. I mean, don't get in my way.

I've learned to pull back a bit and have developed an appreciation for boundaries, but it doesn't take much to get me into the *frenzy with victims* mode, the colorful way my son-in-law describes me in certain situations, and it is reasonably close to reality. I'll take it.

As a rescuer, when things are calm, living is a bit like waiting around for the next shoe to drop, the next crisis to happen. You are always looking for the next rescue, like an addict chasing a high. On the other hand, when crises come in waves and they involve babies and loved ones, what can be managed or absorbed is limited and a craving for detox sets in. At that point, I would trade that rescue rush for a soft recliner with back fat.

My retirement years began with a coincidental rash of mandated rescue situations: Baby Cole's birth and the subsequent surgeries and special care, Marty's frightening widow-maker heart attack, Miss McCartney's birth and the ensuing surgeries, my mother's declining health, the 2008 financial fiasco which disintegrated my equity portfolio, love lost, computer viruses, and dreams trampled. I dug in and did what needed to be done in all these instances, but they took their toll.

Once things settled down, I again experienced another theme of my life which is wondering, *What the hell just happened?* It took a while to digest all that, and I experienced a time of vast emptiness where nothingness and wanting collided. I could not go back, could not move forward, and could not tolerate where I was. I asked myself: "Has my life come down to this?"

It was time to rescue myself. I reclaimed my power through writing this book. It required that I immerse myself in my past-- in my life lived. In doing so, I fell in love with myself as a child. I felt her pain, reveled in her glee, and cherished her resilience and grit. I also fell in love with the woman I became. In doing so, I acknowledged with certainty the pure, unmitigated bliss of a life fully lived and a future eagerly anticipated. I do matter. I am enough. Just by being, I am enough. My life has come to this, and it is good. The future is frosting. With newfound strength and resilience, I am now able to focus on the encore dreams, although that could change at any moment. I stand ready for the next rescue--still. It is what I do.

FULL CIRCLE

In the introduction I suggested that we view life as just trying to matter and that just because we exist we are deserving of love and compassion. I also proposed that we are always leading, that everything we do all day every day makes an impression on someone. You can never *not* lead.

Some believe that all things happen for a reason and that people cross your path for a purpose--that there are no accidents. I'm not sure about that, but if you live from that perspective, you are naturally generous and kind and life is rich and rewarding.

It requires diligence and focus to operate under that premise, though, and to do so we must be vigilant, monitor our behavior, and constantly remind ourselves of that perspective. I know this because when I forget I feel bad. When I am "in the zone," I feel good. Living under this premise is not as simple as it first appears. Sometimes I feel good and bad at the same time like when a woman attempted to steal my man, and I got revenge by letting her have him. Being "in the zone," I was generous and kind and didn't put up a fight, although I had a vague feeling that I was doing a bad thing. However, sometimes you just have to save yourself. The other players were no doubt doing the same. In the end, it was the best outcome for everyone.

I have come full circle. While growing up in Iowa, I was just a girl. Then life happened, and I became a lot of things beyond that simple, basic persona. The complicated manifestations of my adult life showed up. They changed me and continue to be very much evident in my identity today, but they are fading-- falling away like ice tumbling from an iceberg. Those that remain are taking on simpler, less intense characteristics.

As I settle into the encore years, an emerging tranquility is setting in. I no longer lament over regrets, wear jeans so tight I have to lay on my back on the bed to zip them, or care if I die washing dishes. I know now that it is how I live in the moment that counts.

My life has come to a place of gratitude. I'm thankful every day for being a part of life happening and for considerable accumulated wisdom that gives me peace.

I've learned that bad days are always followed by good ones, and I accept the fact that if you eat a cinnamon roll the size of a small dog, you will gain weight. I know that when I swear the stock market goes down or I have a low tire. Well, maybe not. I tell myself that to muster up needed discipline. Sometimes it works. Some is progress.

I have also learned that occasionally the people living in my attic eat my last PayDay candy bar and that my lifestyle is not conducive to having a pet. My solution is to consume all candy bars in one setting and to get a cowhide rug for a pet and name him Rufus. I harbor no guilt over the candy bar inspired sugar buzz, and I don't have to feel bad about neglecting my pet rug.

I am a master of women's issues and was successful at convincing my two-year-old granddaughter that she shouldn't sit and sympathize with her brother while he is in time out for hitting her. I have come to understand that when a man invites me to a gun show, I should invite him to a Mary Kay party. I also know that when someone insists I'm going to like some guy, it is going to take a lot of mushrooms to make that happen.

I accept that technology is not always my friend. When a help desk child tells me to upload files to 32-bit mode, I know to say, "Okay, sure, like that is going to happen." When someone I love moves the icons around on the computer, I know he is messing with me. Further, when a friend on Facebook asks me to water corn on his virtual farm because he is going on vacation, I know to de-friend him. Anyone who farms on a computer can water his own damn corn.

I've learned to face reality head on. Bliss is crazy wonderful, but it is not sustainable. To appreciate the peaks, you must embrace the valleys. How this is done is a measure of character. When your highly educated child says, "I spelt that completely wrong," it's okay. He's going with the trend. You can't spend time contemplating the world situation and have a good day, but that doesn't mean you don't pay attention. Worse things than politics can happen. Sometimes you face the perfect storm, like when you wake up from a nap and NASCAR is on TV.

I find freedom by shrugging off convention when it suits me. Freedom is going out for coffee in residual make-up and pajamas with a savage hairdo and not being embarrassed when friends infer you are taking "the walk of shame." Freedom is never ever having to chase a tan again, recognizing that a sandy beach means sand in the butt, that camping means tics and mosquito bites, and that you are not a candy-ass wimp when refusing to get on a motor cycle or ski slope. Freedom is changing the definition of success when you fail, using commas any way you want, making peace with your tummy, and accepting the fact that it is possible to have cellulite on your shoulders.

I've learned to cast off regrets. I no longer regret mom jeans, big hair, attending the wrong funeral, or driving off in the wrong car at the valet stand. I'm so over the fact that I ate mystery meat in Russia that might have been Yorkie. I am no longer remorseful that I didn't have any anesthesia while birthing my first child causing me to have so much with the second that I don't remember a thing. I don't regret dating Scooter or calling a man with one front tooth a can opener and imagining how handy he would be on a camping trip. (Fortunately, I don't go camping.) I've forgiven myself for not rescuing bait, and I don't lament my youthful failure to realize that when people show you who they really are, you should believe them.

If someone labels a person, I'm going to do research before worrying about him running for political office or making me soup. I know that labels in our fear-based society are often distortions, if not outright lies, that are designed to manipulate. A man once labeled me staid because I was looking for a man who would not scare small children and because I was not into showing cleavage to God and everybody. Staid? Come on now. I was once a disco queen, and I wear leopard print heels. I had perfect timing for turning on the twinkling feature of the Christmas lights on my bed. Not everyone can say that. I am just crazy enough to surprise someone with a salad for their birthday, and I microwave my bubblegum. I relate to the person who said that trans-vaginal ultrasound probe is a good name for a rock band or an airline and, at one time, I could beat just about anyone at Pac Man. Not everyone can say that either. Staid? I don't think so.

Finally, I don't apologize for the nonsensical fun of *Monty Python* and *The Rocky Horror Picture Show* or any outrageous costumes, props, paraphernalia, or behavior surrounding these activities. Embracing novel recreation does not mean I've sustained some sort of "dain bramage" but, instead, that I have learned that you can never have too much fun.

I know all this now, but most importantly, I know that I'm so happy I could marry myself. Through writing this book I found that Iowa girl again and fell in love with the child and the woman. Enriched by new life experiences but grounded in earlier ones, that girl, the one who came *Out of Iowa*, is here-- still. Although flawed, scarred, and forever vulnerable, she is strong, feisty, engaged, and just trying to matter, proving that:

> You can take the girl out of Iowa, but
> You can't take the Iowa out of the girl.

12

LESSONS LEARNED

You are what you are and that is enough.
Just by being, you are enough.

The most awesome thing in the world is new life. Every newborn is a unique little person from the very beginning. It is not like you had a baby. It is more like you had a person--an incredible, tiny, distinct product of two other incredibly distinct people who are the product of two other...well, you get the idea. It is fascinating--the beginning of a person.

One-year-old Bethany has had an "air" about her from the day she was born. You can see it in her earliest photos. It is reflected in the curious, matter-of-fact way she observes people, how she confidently responds to situations, and how she calmly but assertively interacts with others, the exception being when she met up with Santa Claus. With her actions, her posture, her way of being in the world she says: "I am here. I belong. Here I am. I am safe. *I am in my place.*" Can you imagine being in the world with the perspective of *I am in my place?* I mean, how cool is that? It captivates me, and it tickles me to no end. There is just no one else like her, never has been, never will be, and she is certainly, without a doubt, in her place.

I don't believe she was necessarily born with all this sense of self. I've observed the intense parental nurturing she experienced from day one. Realizing the impact of that, it makes me wonder what poor parenting does to babies that start out like Bethany but don't get the subsequent nurturing required to blossom. You gotta know that how they are treated from day one leaves a mark so impactful that it can change who they are.

Not only are we each born different, everyone's reality is unique to their own experiences. Furthermore, their interpretations of these experiences are derived from how they innately view the world, and everyone views it differently. All this contributes to the tapestry of life.

When I was managing operations and forming teams, I often thought about the significance of that. People's differences are a team's strengths. By shutting out those who think differently than we do, we miss out. Their fresh views and insights are our enlightenment, even if we don't agree with them. Additionally, their views are real to them, and they are entitled to them just as much as we are to ours. No one has all the answers.

I have learned many lessons in my sixty-five years of living, some of them hard-earned and all valid in my mind. They may not be true for everyone, and they may not even be valid for me in the future. Perspectives are fluid and learning never ends, but these lessons exude a level of wisdom that can only be attained through the burden of experience. They are relevant because they have the potential to inspire critical thinking.

And so, here they are, my lessons learned. I hope some of them are new and meaningful, although I expect that many simply articulate what the reader already knows. Others are so specific to me that they may not fit with the reader's reality. So be it. They are representations of a robust lifetime of teachable moments--my lessons learned. Take them for what they are worth. There are a lot of them. I am old and well seasoned and, as is my nature, I'm not holding back.

- If you find yourself apologizing to people frequently, consider talking and acting in a way that doesn't cause you to be sorry for your behavior in the first place.

- You can't retrieve a word, once it is said. You can say you are sorry, but it is still out there. It's going to leave a mark. It is a wound that may heal, but there will be a scar. Be diligent in editing what you say and how you say it.

- **Don't pack vibrating children's toys in luggage when you are flying.**

- Maintain modest expectations in relation to fairness. It is elusive since fairness is defined differently by each person.

- Truth is elusive. Each person having the same experience or observing the same thing will interpret it from their own unique frame of reference, building their own story around the facts. One person's truth is not necessarily another's truth.

- **You or anyone else believing something doesn't make it a fact. It's a thought.**

- It is a good plan to qualify any statement of universal truths. Even scientific laws are often later proven to be untrue.

- If it doesn't make sense, it's probably not true. Re-evaluate.

- Forgive your parents for poor parenting. You will be a parent one day, and trust me, you will not execute that role perfectly. Parents generally do the best they can with what they have and what they know. You may never know the demons with which they wrestled. Give them a break.

- Don't use incidents of poor parenting as an excuse for your own screw ups. Hangups are a choice. Choose to hold yourself, not your parents, accountable for your actions and outcomes.

- **If the baby's hand is in the way during an ultra-sound, it's a boy.**

- Be discriminating about telling stories about children when they are present. Some of the things you think are cute or funny are embarrassing to them.

- Children are not spoiled by your generosity unless they become ungrateful and take it for granted. As long as they say thank you and mean it--share.

- **If you swear in front of children, don't follow up with an "Oh shit!"**

- It is not always true that anything worth doing is worth doing well. Sometimes it is better to get something done half ass than to not do it at all because you cannot do it perfectly.

- People who have had a positive influence on your life have invested in you. You owe them a return on their investment.

- Live your life full out so when you look back on it in your twilight years, you have no regrets.

- Don't loan a friend money. Give it to him. Consider it gone. If he is a worthy friend, he will pay you back. If not, don't give him any more. Interestingly, people who don't settle debts usually come back for more.

- Never co-sign on anything for anyone, not even your children. Ever. Otherwise, you may not be able to buy your next home or car because they owe money, and one late payment can lower your credit score. There are other solutions to financial problems. Co-signing is the worst option.

- **When taking food to someone's house for dinner, make sure you have the right address *before* you hand over the food.**

- If you don't feel you were stupid when you look back at your life, you are not learning and growing.

- Your children will view the world differently from you. This is a channel for enlightenment. Embrace your child's world. Don't make him wrong because he is not like you.

- Avoid relationships with people who put you down. If they care about you, they will champion and validate you. If you can't avoid them, ignore it when they say demeaning things. Have compassion. They are most likely hurt children.

- **If you enjoy riding in the golf cart with your brother, don't say "that sucked" when he doesn't do well.**

- Forgiving does not require that you forget. It means you've moved on. Sometimes you think you've moved on, then something reminds you that you haven't. Bummer.

- Define success yourself. Don't let others, or the world, do that for you. It only matters what you think. It's your success or failure, not theirs. You get to decide.

- When trying to change the behavior of children, change their attitude and the behavior will follow. For example, if a teenage girl is slumping because she thinks she is too tall, nagging her to stop will accomplish nothing. Convincing her that being tall gives her the advantage of presence will bring better results. Point out a wonderful tall woman as a role model. (Most tall women want to be petite, and most petite women want to be tall. Most women want to be pretty, pretty women want to be smart, dumb women want big boobs.)

- Everyone leads regardless of their station in life. **You cannot not lead.** Consider the messages you are sending by how you live your life daily.

- Your actions should match your words. Look for occasions when what you say is inconsistent with what you actually do. These are integrity gaps. We all have them. I had one in 1977. Get rid of them. Quit saying it or start doing it.

- You are lying to yourself and others by presenting yourself differently than you really are. If you are weak, or bad, or wrong, admit it. There is nothing wrong with being vulnerable. You can work to overcome and improve. Inner strength and confidence come from being real.

- **Nothing is accomplished by putting groceries in lay-away, but you can make soup out of catchup.**

- An early indication of toxic people is that they are ultra sensitive to being disrespected and are constantly offended. Their history would most likely reveal that they were hurt as a child. This is not an excuse for their meanness, but it helps explain it. You need to know that the damage runs deep.

- When someone does you wrong, don't hold on to the fantasy that they will get theirs. They probably won't. Karma is a myth. Things just happen. Get on with your life.

- Living well is not the best revenge. There is no best revenge. Get on with your life.

- People who try to control you often treat you really nice most of the time. They are masters of manipulation. Displays of intense caring cloud reality. Isolated incidents of meanness should not be ignored. Meanness is a red flag, and it will escalate. They need to get serious help, or you need to get out.

261

- Don't listen to what people say. Watch what they do. This is huge. It can save you a lot of heartache.

- Because someone is not conservative does not mean he is a liberal. Because someone is not liberal does not mean he is a conservative. If you are dying for a label, call him an American.

- There is a lot of lying happening on the internet.

- **If a man is quiet, it does not necessarily mean he is mysterious. He may just be stupid.**

- People change so much in their teens and early twenties that you cannot be sure how they are going to turn out. No one should get married until they have a sense of how they and their potential partner are going to turn out.

- When you fall in love, don't get married. If you feel compelled to act on love, get engaged, but put some time on it before getting married.

- Play the cards you are dealt. Don't waste time and energy on the *what if's* and *why me's*. Screw them. Work the deal.

- **Don't ask an older person how they feel unless you really want to know.**

- Tell children all the wonderful things they can do. Don't assume they have any sense of their potential.

- Children need validation of their feelings. Don't dismiss them because you don't think they are real. They are real to them.

- Do not praise children for being smart. Praise them for what they do. Being smart is not something they accomplished, and it is not the key to achievement. Aspiration and effort are.

- Don't ever call a child stupid or any other bad word. You may not mean it, but he will believe it. You are writing on the chalkboard of his mind when you say it.

- Children should do work around the house and be praised for their efforts. This creates work ethic, builds character, and teaches them the joy of contributing to a team.

- **Roadkill is a viable topic for a children's song.**

- Children will turn out okay if their father sings them songs about being drunk, a monkey being drunk, or a dead skunk.

- You may lock up your guns and teach your children gun safety, but parents of your children's friends may not. Give your child instructions on what to say and do when a friend talks about a gun or whips one out. Be specific and role play. The answer to "Do you want to see a gun?" is: "No, and I have to go home now." Then they must tell mom and dad about the gun.

- You may have a net nanny on your computer, but your children's friends may not. We live in a world where small children have direct access to porn and violence. I have a feeling if they see it they are not going to say: "I have to go home now." (Toddler Bethany was caught banging away on her momma's computer. Interestingly, a message on the screen said: "You do not have sufficient permission to do that.")

- If you have to go into the water to rescue someone, take something that floats with you.

- **If you have a baby boy, one of your parenting requirements is issuing a frequent ultimatum: Get your hand out of your pants.**

- Everyone thinks his beliefs are right; therefore, everyone else's are wrong. This means that everyone who believes something different than you believes that you are wrong as well. Further, this means that in someone's eyes everyone is wrong. What kind of world is that? How is that working for us?

- Believe what you want, but don't assume everyone else is wrong because they believe something else. People who believe some very strange things are quick to judge others who believe some very strange things. How strange.

- Be cognizant of who you follow if they are mandating what you believe. What makes anyone so special that they get to know things the rest of us don't? Maybe they don't really know. Just because they think it and say it, doesn't make it true.

- No single source has all the answers. Radical people distort facts big time to support their beliefs. Don't be used and manipulated. If you believe everything a single source says, you are not thinking. The answer will not be in your best interest. It will be in theirs. Embrace logic and think for yourself. Draw conclusions issue by issue. You can figure it out.

- If you agree with everything a group proposes, you are in a state of *group think*. This makes you a prime target for manipulation by people seeking power and influence who most likely do not have your best interest at heart. They are running their own agenda, often through distortion and exploitation. Think for yourself. Consider each issue independently of a group. Pursue valid details and protect your own best interests.

- Don't let people lead you into the victim mentality. It is an effective and brilliant mode of manipulation. You are being had. Making people feel like victims is a selfish leader's way of manipulating them for their own personal gain, and it is very effective. It works well--for the leader.

- **When running around in a hail storm with a bucket on your head, you are at risk for being struck by lightening.**

- Your life will have its crisis points. They will pass. Don't over-react. Consider whether it will matter in five years. Ride it out.

- Although you might feel as if it is the end of the world in times of crisis, most are minor blips in the whole scheme of life. Later you may see them as inconsequential or positive life-changing, defining moments. They are often progress squared.

- When times are hard, if you can identify the worst-case scenario and develop a plan to deal with it, the other options are suddenly less intimidating. In the worst of times, know that it has got to get better. There is no place to go but up.

- Often, in times of crisis, a good coping mechanism is to say to yourself: "This too shall pass." Hang in. Time is your friend.

- It's okay to feel depressed for a day. Flow with it. Get down into the muck. Tomorrow is a whole new day.

- We tend to judge ourselves more harshly than anyone else. If you ever feel inadequate say to yourself: "I am what I am and that's all that I am." That is enough. What you *are* is enough.

- At times of your worst embarrassments, no one really cares that much about them except you. Make fun of yourself, if you can. We are all goofballs and noggin heads at some point. Get over yourself, and go on down the road.

- **Stay away from people with guns who are looking for their anti-depressants.**

- Some people advise you to never say anything bad about yourself. Words are powerful, so there is some validity to this, but it can cause you to be out of touch with reality and not take accountability for your actions. Be real and face your flaws and mistakes head on. Admit it, fix it, or accept it, but don't deny it.

- Do the work to be a person of substance. Sometimes a *fake it till you make it* approach to coping can give you needed confidence in a challenging situation, but when you do this often and start buying the fake part of it, you become a blowhard or a politician.

- If you want to be informed, you must get information from multiple sources. If you only look for information that confirms what you already believe, you are going to live in an artificial reality. Others will manipulate you.

- Learn to distinguish between news reporting and commentary. There is a lot of commentary these days. It may be food for thought, but it is not fact--often far from it.

- Don't let people label you. Twice I had a man tell me I'm crazy. They tell me that because they want to make me feel bad (because they love me so much). The second time I said, "You ain't seen crazy yet."

- **Watermelon stealing is a noble pastime.**

- Don't let anyone tell you that you cannot go to college.

- College is not for everyone. You don't have to go to college to be successful.

- You don't have to be successful in terms of a career in order to be successful at life.

- If you suspect your teenagers are having problems they are not telling you about, take them out to eat. Children will spill their guts over chips and salsa.

- Befriend someone who has few friends, and you will have the best friend you ever had.

- **You can't grow corn successfully in Oklahoma, or peonies either.**

- Remind your grandchildren how lucky they are to have the wonderful parents they have.

- With children you take what you get. When they drive you to the brink, remember they are your job.

- You are never, ever free of your children.

- If someone is taking care of your aging parents, don't interfere. Just say thank you.

- The worst thing that can happen to a family is that they fight. It is better to give in on an issue even when you are sure you are right than to have a big brouhaha over it.

- **Children will turn out okay if their father sings them songs about prison, especially if the songs are about getting out of prison. It's about freedom.**

- Having a small acreage is not all it is cracked up to be. You have to mow it. There is not enough land to do anything with but too much to take care of.

- When things really get bad and you hit rock bottom, it will get better. There is no place to go but up. Keep the faith.

- It is okay to just lean into things. You don't have to give everything all you've got. Sometimes we just try too hard.

266

- Wine might help you get to sleep but you will wake up at two in the morning with a nasty headache.

- **Nothing good happens after midnight.**

- Teens should be taught that when they do something bad they must tell you about it right away so you are not "mortified" by hearing it from someone else.

- Do the right thing, even when you don't feel like it. Do it anyway. Do it, and then some.

- **Just because a guy's name is Purdy Hapy does not guarantee he's happy.**

- It is a good thing we are not all just alike. People have different strengths and weaknesses. It takes all kinds of people with diverse qualities to make a strong team. If all team members are just alike and think alike, the team is weak. Value and respect differences. Engage people different from yourself.

- Wear sunscreen. Don't use baby oil with iodine for tanning purposes. It stains the skin and the swimsuit.

- **When in a foreign country, you are the foreigner.**

- If someone you love requires medical care, don't do what the doctors say without question. Be involved, get informed, and take control. Some medical professionals are motivated more by their income and professional comfort level than the patient's best interest. It is nothing for them to drill a hole in a head for brain surgery. They do it all day every day, and they get paid for doing it. To you and your loved one it is a huge deal. Doctors don't deal with the consequences. You do.

- Don't assume doctors are up-to-date on the best treatments with the most optimal outcomes. They often do what they have always done and what is familiar. It is unlikely they are going to send you and your money off to someone else who does it better. You want the better, you have to seek it out.

- Make certain doctors know you are paying attention. Insist on understanding the logic behind every medical decision. When the results of a test don't change the treatment, perhaps you don't want to take the test, especially if it is invasive.

- Accept that the medical profession cannot fix everything.

- **Bailey's Irish Cream will make you want to take a nap, even if it is in coffee.**

- It is okay to work on weaknesses, but by putting effort into developing strengths, you get the biggest bang for your buck, and you are happier focusing on your positive attributes.

- Don't defend people, particularly your children, when they do something wrong. This doesn't mean you don't support them and help them overcome the incident, but you are not doing them a favor by defending them no matter what. It is exceedingly important that people accept accountability for what they do. Help them face the music so they learn they can rally from mistakes and come out on the other side.

- Children lie. Parents who maintain their child does not lie are doing that child a huge disservice. Integrity is not innate. You much teach it to them.

- Sometimes small children lie because they don't want to upset you, not because they are trying to protect themselves.

- **Teenagers lie because their mouths are moving.**

- When children misbehave, they are most likely bored.

- If you have friends who have lost children, you need to know that holidays will never, ever be the same--not just Christmas and Thanksgiving--all of them. Mothers Day is brutal.

- Your home can be a place of respite that feeds your soul or it can be a place that clutters the mind. Make it a place that rises up to greet you when you enter. For most people this requires organizing, editing, and letting go of things. It's just stuff.

- **March Madness is not a sale at Macy's.**

- Cultures where women have little or no influence are full of festering violence. Maternal influence is not possible if women are not respected by their male counterparts. Little boys grow up to lack sensitivity and are mean.

- There is evil in the world, people who would do your children harm. They often look like everyone else and are cunning and manipulative. Be vigilant. Protect all children. Rely on your intuition. Trust must be earned and continuously proven.

- **Because a boy was run over by a car as a child and survived does not mean it is okay to nickname him speed bump**.

- Don't let anyone isolate you from family and friends. People who truly love you will want to share you with others. They will not make those close to you out to be villains.

- Be cautious about saying bad things about another's family. They can say them. You shouldn't do so without serious cause.

- Be aware that setting security as a goal is limiting.

- Don't think it is the end of the world if you get fired. I got fired once for being a terrible waitress. I was a terrible waitress. (I was told not to let the door hit me in the butt on the way out.)

- **When your last child leaves home you will anticipate doing naughty things in the kitchen, but you won't.**

- Expectations are the root of most relationship problems. Communicate your expectations clearly and don't assume people know what they are unless you tell them.

- Manage expectations--yours and others'. If you examine disappointments, you will notice they often come from having unrealistic expectations. Don't build fantasies around others.

- Don't make excuses for people's bad behavior. When people show you who they really are, believe them.

- Don't let other people name your children.

- Don't let others decorate your home with gifts. Years of accumulated gifts make it look like an overstocked gift shop.

- **There are four quarters in a football game.**

- Sometimes the best way to relieve stress is to take a break, and sometimes the best way to relieve stress is to not take a break and get some things off your "To Do List."

- **Sometimes the best way to relieve stress is to eat a Snickers.**

- When asked if you've lived in Iowa all your life, say: "Not Yet."

- A little bit of Irish is okay, but if a guy is really, really Irish (or anything else), he can go be Irish someplace else. You want someone who is just who he is--real.

- A guy who wears black socks with shorts and sandals is going to wear float trip clothes to Thanksgiving dinner.

- How smart a person is has to do with where he is. The smartest man I know parked a Volkswagen Beetle on a California beach only to discover it bobbing in the ocean after the tide came in. No surfer dude would do that.

- **Don't take a full dose of any memory inducing medication unless you want to remember everything.**

- Be generous with your successes.

- Make new memories with old friends. Don't just get together. Do something fun.

- It is possible for a parent to make every child feel as if they are the favorite.

- What is most important in a relationship is how you make each other feel.

- Love is a gift.

- Be nice.

- **Be proud of where you come from. I'm from Iowa.**

INDEX

What The Hell Just Happened?

ABOUT THE AUTHOR

Nikki Hanna was raised on a farm outside a small Iowa town. After high school she attended business college in Omaha, Nebraska, then married and moved to Chicago where she and her husband worked for the airlines. In 1966 they moved to rural Oklahoma and eventually divorced after eleven years of marriage. Nikki raised her two children, as well as a beloved third child who entered her life at the age of two.

In 1976 Nikki settled in Tulsa, Oklahoma where she began a career which eventually led to a senior executive position in a large corporation. She has a B.S. degree in business education and journalism, a Master's Degree in Business Administration, and is a retired Certified Public Accountant and Toastmaster.

Nikki is now in her sixties and claims to be training for the Olympics (which may be evidence of a serious integrity gap). She lectures at colleges, universities, and graduate programs on leadership, management, and biographical writing. Nikki also offers speaking and entertainment programs for seniors and for professional, charity, and women's organizations.

www.nikkihanna.com

TO ORDER

Available on Amazon, Kindle, or www.nikkihanna.com

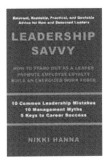 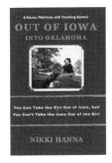 

NAME_____

ADDRESS_____

CITY_____STATE_____ZIP_____

PHONE_____EMAIL_____

        Quantity_____ *Leadership Savvy* - $19.95
        Quantity_____ *Out of Iowa* - $19.95
        Quantity_____ *Capture Life* - $14.99

To Order by Mail: Send check to:
Patina Publishing
727 S. Norfolk Avenue
Tulsa, Oklahoma 74120

To Order by Phone: 918-587-2451
To Order by Email: neqhanna@sbcglobal.net
To Order from Website: www.nikkihanna.com

Details on educational programs, entertaining speeches, and book readings on biographical writing, leadership, aging and retirement, and women's issues are available. Discounts are provided for volume purchases of books. Comments on this book are welcome at the above contact points.

Made in the USA
Charleston, SC
12 September 2012